OFFICIALLY
DISCARDED

EASTERN EUROPE 1968 – 1984

EASTERN EUROPE 1968~1984

OLGA A. NARKIEWICZ

BARNES & NOBLE BOOKS
Totowa, New Jersey

DJK
50
.N36
1986

©1986 Olga Narkiewicz
First published in the USA in 1986 by
Barnes and Noble Books
81 Adams Drive
Totowa, New Jersey, 07512

Narkiewicz, Olga A.
    Eastern Europe 1956–1982.
    1. Europe, Eastern—history—1945—
I. Title.
DJK50.N36   1986   947   85-22985
ISBN 0-389-20607-5

Printed and bound in Great Britain

JUN 2 5 1986

EASTERN EUROPE, 1968 - 1984

THE ROAD TO THE UNKNOWN.

Chapter V:

Leadership and Party Under Stress.

Chapter VI:

The CMEA's Economy and World Recession.

Chapter VII:

The Aftermath of the Recession.

Chapter VIII:

Intra-Bloc and International Relations.

Chapter IX:

The Road to the Unknown.

PREFACE

This book has been written in response to renewed interest in Eastern European events in the last two decades. The difficulty of assessing these in a rapidly changing political and economic global climate is well documented. This task is even more complicated by the rise of new ideological trends which seem to indicate that the problems encountered by the Socialist Bloc are the result of conflicts between institutionally monolithic structures and the reality of pluralism built into the system.

Such conflicts are not new. Writing in April, 1917, Lenin expressed doubts about the viability of separating bourgeois government from the dictator-ship of revolutionary workers and peasantry. He put the view that 'Marxist tactics cannot be based on the unknown ...'. Some sixty years later, a similar view was expressed by a Eurocommunist party, which stated that the failures of the system highlighted the 'contradictions between a political system, a model of a bureaucratized state that controls and decides everything over society's heads and the interest and desires of society, of the workers, for participation, for decision-making, power and Socialist self-management.

In writing this work, the author concentrated on changes in the system in the post-Stalinist period, which were intended to reduce the political, economic and social contradictions within Eastern Europe, but have often accentuated them instead. From 1960s onward, governments in the Bloc have been more prone to experimentation and pragmatism in order to ease tensions and improve economic performance. However, many of the measures owed more to monetarist theories than to perceived socialist ideology. An analysis of the events in the six Eastern European countries which belong to the CMEA and the Warsaw Pact, their bilateral relations, their relations with the USSR and with the non-Socialist world, as well as of their administrative and economic difficulties, demonstrates that the conflicts do not arise solely out of inherent tensions, but also because of sudden changes of course.

The road which the Eastern European governments have undertaken has had its successes and failures, but their tactics were not mapped out in accordance with ideological desiderata. One must conclude that their tactics were based on the unknown, though it cannot be inferred from this that failures arose out of lack of strategic planning. The ideological framework of Marxism has not, till the advent of Eurocommunism, allowed for rapidly changed circumstances. Eastern European states were subject to more radical changes than almost any other states in the world, and they were not prepared, either ideologically or practically, to meet such changes. In the event, their task may have been impossibly difficult, regardless of ideology. Conclusions, if any can be drawn, are left to the reader.

Most of the book was written while on study leave at the University of California, Los Angeles. My thanks go to Professor Andrzej Korbonski, Director of the Center for Russian and East European Studies at UCLA, whose help and hospitality have made much of my research possible, as well as to the bibliographers at the University Research Library, whose extensive knowledge of sources has enabled me to concentrate on my work.

In many ways, the work is a personal tribute to Leonard Schapiro, for many years Professor of Political Science at the London School of Economics, who died tragically in late 1983. While he did not always agree with my views, he was a true friend and a strict critic of standards. I hope that some of the values he taught me have been passed on in it.

Olga A. Narkiewicz
London, 1984

Chapter One

THE BALANCE OF POWER

---

1. Introduction

Stalin's death, de-Stalinisation, the change of
leaderships in Moscow and in most Warsaw Pact
countries, brought about radical changes in the
social, economic and political order in all the
Eastern European countries. This change was
expressed in the Hungarian Revolution and the
Polish coup of 1956; but though these events had
an immense bearing on the leaderships, they changed
little in the balance of power in each country.
Leaderships were shuffled, sometimes radically
changed: concessions were made to the popular
discontent in that the consumer industries were
developed; secret police powers were curtailed and
a measure of local democracy was introduced in some
countries.
    Nevertheless, the essential order remained the
same: the parties led; the bureaucrats had the last
say, the police were empowered to intervene as a
last resort; and the final word on external (and
often internal) policies remained with the men in
the Kremlin. Throughout the period of Khrushchev's
government, such order was maintained less through
terror (despite the intervention in Hungary), more
by persuasion from Moscow and a fear of the
consequences of total de-coupling; should indeed
such de-coupling become possible. Eastern European
leaders and part of the population were persuaded
that while some change was necessary, a complete
reversal of the existing order would be very
dangerous indeed.
    However, Khrushchev's personality and his own
particular brand of personal politics had much to
do with the acquiescence of Eastern European
countries to this state of affairs. Once

1

Khrushchev was removed from leadership, to be followed by the much less charismatic Brezhnev, the position became less easy to assess. Brezhnev was a more remote leader, with none of the easy personal relationships which Khrushchev struck up apparently so freely. The new men in Warsaw, Budapest, Bucharest; and the old men in Prague, Berlin and Sofia were less in touch with this party bureaucrat than they had been with the gregarious, outgoing Ukrainian. It was not certain how far he would want to follow Khrushchev's relaxation both in political and economic fields; or whether, indeed, he would press for a reversal of the reforms which had been carried out in the late Fifties and early Sixties.

These considerations played a large part in the policies of Eastern European governments and parties in the late 1960s; and made them very cautious about taking radical decisions. What had been done in the name of de-Stalinisation, was allowed to stand. The small relaxation of government policy was irreversible. But the future could not be envisaged, and the immediate reaction was to sit tight and do as little as possible in order not to rock the boat. The uncertainty was not confined to the Eastern Europeans. Western politicians were equally uncertain about Soviet policy in the Sixties. As one famous French writer put it: the Soviet leadership

> were ready to modify the relations between the USSR and the East European countries, but were not ready to accept the Hungarian revolution, multiple parties, or declarations of neutralism. The suppression of the Hungarian revolution, however, did not halt the evolution towards autonomy in East Europe. At this point, several questions arise. Has this greater autonomy brought with it greater diversity in their internal regimes? Or greater diversity in their foreign policy?

And answering his own rhetorical question, he stated that

> There is no visible correlation between the degree of internal liberalisation and the degree of external diplomatic independence.

Rumania, the only East European state to hint at territorial claims against the Soviet Union, the one which has opposed Comecon plans with greater determination than any other country, was much the slowest of the popular democracies in introducing liberalisation at home.[1]

Writing in the mid-1960s, this writer, a well-known opponent of the USSR, came to the following conclusions:

a. that the economic-political regimes in East European countries still belong to the same species, and that the differences in the institutions inseparable from the regime do not yet affect the core;

b. that the national identities have not been destroyed by temporary domination exercised by the Soviet Union;

c. that the Soviet Union had experienced radical failure in East Europe. 'It has not russified the area. It has not converted the peoples to Marxism-Leninism. It has not convinced them of the merits of the institutions built up in Russia since 1917'.[2]

It is hardly surprising that Raymond Aron should assume that the USSR's aims are of that order. But if this were so, why not russify the non-Russian areas of the Soviet Union first? Yet the Russians have never attempted either an overt or a covert effort at russification of the Uzbeks, Turkmens or the Tatars. Far from it, they have actually undone the harm of the Tsarist regime, which russified forcibly for several centuries. The 'radical failure in East Europe' to convert the peoples to Marxism-Leninism may be an illusory hope.

East Europeans may be far from delighted with one-party rule, state ownership of the means of production and distribution and the chronic shortages of consumer goods and hard currency for foreign travel. On the other hand, ninety per cent of the population are glad to have free access to educational facilities, health services

3

and cheap holidays. Nor are they unaware of the fact that all Eastern European populations have a higher standard of living than the Soviet people themselves - whether this is the index of better management or of 'fraternal' help from the USSR is problematic; the fact is that this is so; even during hard times.

The economic-political regimes in Eastern Europe still remain of the same species, and will do so as long as the USSR remains a great power, and wishes to exercise its right to obtain two benefits: on the one hand - to have a Cordon Sanitaire against aggression from Western Europe; on the other - to have model socialist states on a smaller scale than the Soviet Union. This last is an important point in proving to the Third World countries that a smaller scale socialist country has a raison d'etre, and that a socialist economy can be sustained without an enormous input of capital and labour.

It is difficult enough for the Western observer to realise what the Soviet policy is vis-a-vis Eastern European countries; it is much more difficult for those inside the goldfish bowl to know which way to turn. However, they are all (and that includes dissident Romania and de-coupled Yugoslavia) aware that a major upheaval would bring Soviet troops inside their countries; but minor changes can be tolerated. As a strategic analyst put it succinctly after the invasion of Czechoslovakia in 1968: Soviet policy has suffered from a form of dualism:

> on the one hand, the Soviets sought a policy of "decompression" in Eastern Europe, or more properly, a policy of managed change in the Stalinoid political and social process in the former satellites; on the other hand, they continued to insist that such change must be evolutionary, rather than revolutionary, and that changes must take place within the framework of the unity of the socialist camp under Soviet domination. Since 1960 the Warsaw Pact has become the main mechanism of such managed change in Eastern Europe. The events culminating in the occupation of Czechoslovakia are indicative of this dualism in Soviet policy. The leitmotif in Soviet policy was a search for a peaceful solution to the mounting crisis, paralleled by a concerted

effort to be prepared for a military solution in the event of the former policy failing'.[3]

2. Post-1968 Developments

The Czechoslovak crisis arose out of a combination of several important factors; the most weighty among them were the fact that the Czech government did not de-Stalinise at the time that the Poles and the Hungarians did, and that the Czech economy, partly as a result of the immobilisme of the past, and partly because it had run out of momentum when other Eastern European economies were growing (i.e. the East German economy) was unable to catch up on modernisation in the 1960s – the upshot was dissatisfaction caused by the gap in popular expectation and attainments. This dangerous state of affairs was compounded by the inept and brutal way in which the current President, Antonin Novotny tried to quell the growing dissatisfaction.

It must be stressed that in Czechoslovakia, the discontent was felt by every stratum in the country, and by each national component as well. Thus, the Slovaks became openly hostile to the ruling Czechs, with the Moravians coming closely behind, rebelling against the Bohemian hegemony. The party was torn between the differing aims of the liberals and the Stalinists, as well as between the national wings. The intellectuals in the media, the universities and the economic organisations were dissatisfied with almost every aspect of the government's policies. The working classes and farmers were concerned about their falling standard of living.

But there was a special factor to Czech discontent; unlike the Poles and the Hungarians, who put the blame fair and square on Soviet intervention in their domestic affairs, the Czechs were well disposed towards the Russians (owing to old Slavophile ties), and felt no hatred of the Soviet Union. They tended to blame their own government for the problems of the country, including the particularly bloody purges and executions during the Stalinist period. Thus, when Novotny called in the Russians to help, in the person of the then First Secretary, Leonid Brezhnev himself, in December of 1967, one of the

Slovak dissenters in the Central Committee:

> Dubcek, who had been educated in the Soviet
> Union and spoke perfect Russian, was able to
> persuade Brezhnev that he was neither a Slovak
> "nationalist" nor a "deviationist" and also
> obtained from him a promise that the Czechs
> and the Slovaks would sort out their problems
> without Soviet interference.[4]

As the pressure for Novotny's dismissal grew,
he himself announced his resignation as First
Secretary at a plenary Central Committee meeting
on 5 January, 1968. But he retained his post of
President of the Republic, and attempted to
manoeuvre his close associate, Lennart, as his
successor for the secretaryship. This was
defeated, but not in favour of the Czech economic
liberals (those in the running were Kolder and
Cernik). The person who got elected was - perhaps
rather expectedly, as he got on splendidly with
Brezhnev - the Slovak 'nationalist' Dubcek.
However, it was a hollow victory, for on
becoming First Secretary, Dubcek found that most
of the apparatus in the most important areas, such
as Prague, was controlled by Novotny's proteges
and faithful henchmen. Hence, as one source
stated, Dubcek was forced to appeal to the public
opinion at large to help him in purging the
Stalinist apparatus.

> When late in January 1968 the journalists of
> the capital came to him for the customary
> guidance and instructions he told them that
> they would no longer be guided, but left free
> to voice their own opinions and
> interpretations.[5]

In this way, the Prague Spring arose amid
general discontent, but was fostered by the new
leadership for its own ends. It must be said that
a more experienced or a more resourceful person
might have hesitated to put such a bold experiment
into practice. Even Khrushchev did not denounce
Stalin to the media; he made his 1956 speech to a
select body of top party officials. And even
then, the results, both in the country and abroad,
dramatically overtook the original aim, which was
simply to strengthen and legitimise Khrushchev's
own succession.

An extraordinary stroke of fortune served Dubcek better than his own actions could have done: a senior official in the Czech secret police, a ruthless purger and close friend of Novotny, escaped abroad and sought asylum in the USA. This defection made Novotny dispensable to the USSR; Dubcek was allowed to get on with his 'New Course' from April 1968 onwards. However, the delicate balancing act which he had to perform: on the one hand, trying to stifle attempts by the Stalinists to oust him; and on the other - trying to hold back the radical reformists, did not bode well for the Czechoslovak experiment. In fact, while Brezhnev may have been happy to see Dubcek in the saddle, the government which was most unhappy about the Czech developments was the one which had the most to lose by any real liberalisation within the Bloc, particularly in a developed socialist country: the East German government. It may have been symbolic that on 23 March 1968, Dubcek was called to Dresden to give an account of his activities to the Warsaw Pact countries meeting there. He told the Warsaw Pact that everything was under control, even though simultaneously, purges of Stalinists were going on, an avowed reformer, Josef Smrkovsky, was elected the Speaker of the National Assembly, and the Central Committee began expelling Novotny's supporters from its body. Almost immediately, plans were made to convoke a new Party congress in September 1968, in order to eliminate the defeated faction, and the 2000 Words manifesto was published calling for more rapid purges of Stalinists.

Pressed by the Soviet leadership, Dubcek repudiated the manifesto, but also refused to attend the Warsaw Pact meeting called in Warsaw on 14 July 1968. This may have been done in order to demonstrate his independence (as one source claims); but it may have been a measure of his fear of some unpleasant consequences of attending.

The mechanisms of the Warsaw Pact take-over in Czechoslovakia are described by Bradley in some detail - according to his account it was not an invasion, but an orderly infiltration of Czechoslovakia by Warsaw Pact troops accomplished with the agreement of the Czech government;[6] the invasion executed on 21 August 1968, was simply a final intervention. As Bradley states: 'The question now was who within the Czechoslovak

Communist Party would hold power on Soviet terms'.[7] The scheduled congress (held in August 1968, after the Warsaw Pact invasion) packed the presidium with reformers, but was declared invalid, and a compromise presidium which contained both reformists and hardliners was installed. It was not until April, 1969, that most of the reformers were eliminated, and Dubcek resigned.

This picture is hardly consistent with the image of a brutal Soviet intervention in internal Czech affairs. True, there was intervention and - true- it was opposed by a large number of Czechoslovaks, both Communists and non-Communists. But a number of Czechoslovaks desired this intervention just as ardently as it was opposed by the reformists.[8] Dubcek's successor was another Slovak, Gustav Husak, who, despite having come into the Central Committee as a reformer, proceeded to purge the party and government apparatus of all the new men. It was not till November, 1969, that most of the laws passed during the 'Spring' had been repealed and the presidium was packed again with hardliners, most of whom had served in the Novotny apparatus. Of all the reforms, only the new Federation Act, conferring an equal status on Slovakia, remained but it was so complicated that it was not implemented till 1971.

The Central Committee's manifesto issued in November, 1969, reiterated that Czechoslovakia was a Socialist democracy, based on democratic centralism, collective ownership of the means of production, and the leading role of the Communist Party. Thus, with the exception of the progressive measure to equalise the status of Slovakia, all the other measures were regressive. Most Western scholars call the 'normalisation' of Czechoslovakia a form of neo-Stalinism. This is surely incorrect. The measures which the reformers passed or wanted to pass included many which would be incompatible with Czechoslovakia remaining within the Socialist Bloc - such as a proposal for a pluralist system and the leading role of the intellectuals, and not the party, as well as various liberal economic ideas suggested by Ota Sik. Given this, it would be unreasonable to expect the Soviet government to acquiesce in the experimentation, particularly when it was so strongly opposed by the East German government.

The Czech reforms had to go; unsurprisingly the Czechs refused to put up an armed struggle to maintain them. This was partly a traditional Czech response but may have also been an index of realisation that there was a limit beyond which the Russians and their allies could not be pushed - unless there was Western intervention on Czech behalf; an intervention which would clearly involve a war between the two great powers. In some ways, therefore, there was a degree of acquiescence and a degree of co-operation. Otherwise, a former reformer, like Husak, could hardly have become the new purger of the reformers. (There is a slight analogy with Janos Kadar in 1956 in Hungary, but it is tenuous because the Hungarian revolution was a completely different phenomenon from the Czech Spring). Other factors have also to be taken into consideration: how many Czech troops were actually co-operating with the invading armies? How many officials and Party functionaries were glad to see the allies invade to save their jobs? How apathetic were the non-politicised masses? None of these questions have yet been answered satisfactorily for obvious reasons - an objective assessment is impossible in the circumstances.

However, there is another side to this story. Because the Czech opposition to the take-over was non-violent (excepting the anti-Soviet riot after the ice hockey match in early 1969) and maybe not even very convincing, the measures taken against the reformers were not Stalinist and did not match anything on the scale of the Hungarian purges after 1956. Also, possibly the memories of the purges in the early 1950s (and the retribution exacted on the guilty in 1968) held the hand of those who would have been very harsh. At any rate, at the start of the counter-reform period, people lost their jobs, there were some prison sentences, there was a lot of petty harrassment - but no executions, show trials or other Stalinist phenomena.

It was not till a later stage, when a new reformist movement, based on rather different premises appeared (particularly the Charter 77 movement) that larger scale repressions were resorted to. But even these, unpleasant though they were, had little in common with Stalinism. Hence, however oppressive 'normalisation' may have been, it did not take the form of bloody purges or even large-scale hounding of the elite.

But there was one factor which made the reform period more difficult to forget. The reforms were sparked off by the dual pressures of an autocratic system and a slow-down in the economy. The autocratic system was phased out, and the post-reformist government did not revert to the abuses practised by the Gottwald and Novotny regimes. Unfortunately the slow-down in the economy was not helped either by the reforms themselves (which may have worked had they been implemented on a long-term basis) nor by the 'normalisation'. While Husak gradually managed to improve the standard of living (a car and a weekend cottage being the aim of every family) the Czech economy did not return to its earlier buoyancy. This was due partly to the government's caution - too many bright people in management could produce a new reformist movement - and partly to the Socialist Bloc's decision to make East Germany into an economic showpiece of Eastern Europe. At any rate, by the time the 'normalisation' was on the way, the Bloc had other worries, many of them centering on a new aspect of an old problem: Polish opposition to Communism.

3. Old Grievances, New Struggles

Prague was not the only Eastern European city which experienced a surge of unrest in the Spring of 1968. In Warsaw the student revolt started in the early months of the year, sparked off by the production of a play by Mickiewicz, which could be construed as anti-Soviet, and which was banned by the authorities. On 8 March, thousands of students demonstrated against disciplinary measures imposed by university authorities against two students, Adam Michnik and Henryk Szlajfer, who had been involved in an earlier protest. A large contingent of militia was called in and when the students refused to disperse, they were charged with batons, with many casualties. As a result, there followed three days of riots in Warsaw and protests in every university town in Poland. The protests which included sit-in strikes on university premises lasted till 23 March and were branded as 'intellectual', 'cosmopolitan' and possibly inspired by either

Zionism or American money.

We have no way of knowing whether any American money was involved in the initial protests. However, with or without encouragement, the population, and most particularly, the young intellectuals had plenty of grievances to complain about. The experiment of popular democracy and non-Sovietised socialism which Gomulka had promised an enthusiastic nation in October 1956, had long since been overtaken by _immobilisme,_ corruption and abuse of power by those who had proclaimed themselves the nation's saviours in 1956. Yet the social revolution and increased expectations of the educated part of the population (and thanks to the excellent educational facilities this was growing all the time) were thwarted. 'Taken at face value, the criticisms of the Gomulka system - the accusations of bureaucratic ineptitude, blocked careers, and political and economic stagnation - were essentially sound and could be supported by Poles of widely differing political persuasions', said one analyst, who attributed the unrest in Poland to the actions of the 'Partisans' led by Mieczyslaw Moczar. However, these grievances were taken up by the 'Partisans' with a special aim in view

> ... all these articles paid tribute to the achievements of "October", while rejecting its spirit: not once did they raise issues endemic to the 1956 upheaval, such as the role of the party or the preservation and broadening of intellectual freedom. In short, the Partisans were making a demagogic effort to extend their support beyond their institutional bases in the security forces and mass media, an effort which partially succeeded - for a time. Even young people rose to the bait. However primitive and lacking in ideas they found the "old soldiers", many ambitious young Poles whose careers had been blocked by bureaucratic dead weight, and who wanted to see Poland "moving again", aligned with the Partisans.[9]

For reasons which appear to be well-documented, political analysts describe the 1968 events in terms of a power struggle between the established leader - Gomulka; and the 'Partisan'

11

leader - Mieczyslaw Moczar. Just why Moczar, not a great statesman and a man of empty words rather than of action; moreover, not a very young man either, would have decided to make this bid for power, has never been very clear. The fact is that at this stage, power in the Socialist Bloc was passing into the hands of liberals, or potential liberals. Dubcek had power thrust upon him (almost despite himself) for this very reason. In the circumstances, one must suspect that Moczar's bid - never very convincing, despite its rather unpleasant features - was being made on behalf of some third party.

One would have wished that the third party were the young Poles, disappointed in their expectations of good jobs and a higher standard of living, and that Moczar represented the quest for the promotion of 'ethnics' because of the undoubted former imbalance in the number of non-ethnic, possibly even Russified, senior officials. But this does not seem very likely; Moczar, apparently a pleasant personality in private, was not known as a particularly benevolent politician. The only other explanation could be that Moscow was worried by the growing unrest both in Czechoslovakia and Poland (soon to be followed by further restiveness in other countries of the Bloc) and that it was hedging its bets on hardliners with a nationalistic cast of mind, as a way of diverting discontent into a well-controlled channel.

This may explain why, despite many years of perfectly liberal policies towards 'non-ethnics', Gomulka suddenly got in on the act, with his speech to the party <u>actif</u> on 9 March 1968, classifying Jews as those who were faithful to Poland and those who were not. His close associate, Andrzej Werblan, head of the Central Committee's Education Department, also contributed an article in June, 1968, discussing the non-socialist leanings of various Poles of Jewish origin, including those who had been Communists all their lives.[10]

According to Johnson, what saved Gomulka was the nationalist course pursued by the Czech and Slovak Communists. Under the circumstances, Moscow would obviously prefer the well-tried formula of an obedient, liberally-minded leadership, rather than the uncharted waters of a nationalist hardline leadership. There also was

the problem of foreign Communists getting upset by
what appeared to be an anti-Semitic campaign in
socialist Poland. Gomulka was saved, but harm had
been done both to the Polish government and the
people, and to the country's intellectuals. Many
Poles of Jewish origin, most of them able and
highly qualified economists, sociologists, medical
specialists, decided to emigrate under the dual
pressure of accusations and fear of losing their
jobs. Nor did Gomulka save his job for long.

The disturbances of 1968 had further effects.
Moczar failed to win a full Politbureau seat at
the Fifth Congress in November, 1968. The party
apparatus concentrated on purging the media (both
the writers and the by-now influential film
directors); the universities (over 100 academics
lost their jobs at Warsaw University; many
students were imprisoned, an educational reform
was implemented, intended to limit politicisation
of students to a great extent); and all those
considered to be 'revisionists'. Gomulka appeared
to be the winner, but he was being pressed by the
younger meritocracy into making reforms in the
economic sphere. These men advocated economic
reforms on the Hungarian model and a nationalist
trend approaching the Romanian policy. A more
conciliatory policy towards the Catholic Church
was also advocated.[11] The author of this
assessment concluded that 'The emergence of a new
leadership stratum raises at least the possibility
that the "Gomulka era" may have come to an end,
and that a new era dominated by a rationalizing,
modernizing "national Communist" elite ... may be
in the offing'.[12]

Perhaps it is rather ironic that Gomulka lost
his post finally not because he opposed the
reforms of the meritocratic elite, but because he
began to support them in 1969. It was the
economic and political shake-up begun in 1969 that
led to the violent riots in the Gdansk, Gdynia,
Szczecin and Sopot areas, when the government
suddenly increased food prices drastically a few
days before Christmas of 1970. This was not the
disciplined crowd of Czechs, who would not be
provoked into violence. Nor was it the
intellectual revolt in 1968. This riot was
different both in intensity and in style, and did
not bear much resemblance to the riots which
brought Gomulka to power in 1956.

It was the riot of peasant-workers, lured to

13

work in the shipyards with promises of high rewards, being suddenly thwarted by a government which had only yesterday supported their higher expectations. This is an important factor to remember, because it has a bearing both on the bitterness of the riots and on their subsequent transformation in the late 1970s and early 1980s. Perhaps an eyewitness account best serves to illustrate this point:

The price rises were published on the evening of Saturday, 12th December. On the following Monday, in front of the Directorate of the Gdansk shipyard, a crowd gathered. ... The workers were coming from all sides, in overalls and helmets. Several thousand people gathered in the square ... They demanded the withdrawal of the price rises and talks with the authorities. No one came. The crowd left the shipyard and went to the building of the Regional Committee of the (party). Later the procession, many thousands strong, marched ... summoning people to join the strike.

However, the first big clash did not occur till Tuesday:

Early that morning a procession formed in the shipyard and marched on the city. This time it was not to the Regional Committee building, but to the city police headquarters ... About 8.00 a.m. part of the ground floor of that building was occupied. That was probably when the first shots were heard and the first victims killed. The authorities brought tanks into action. The only possibility of defending the occupied positions was to attack the forces of the militia by driving vehicles at them at high speed. An escalation of tension followed, the work-force decided to burn the Regional Committee building. By about 10.00 a.m. it was on fire ...13

The rest of the story is well known by now: the Soviet government disturbed by Gomulka's mismanagement of the matter and by bitter fighting in the most strategic region of Poland, helped Edward Gierek (who had not been in the running for leadership in Gomulka's scheme of things), an able and popular party boss in Silesia, to isolate

14

Gomulka. On 20 December 1970, at a Plenum of the Central Committee at Natolin, Gomulka and all his associates were voted out of the Politbureau. The new leadership repealed the price rises and began discussions with the workers.[14]

As can be seen from the above, while the Polish riots had some resemblance to the Czech Spring in that they were primarily caused by a worsening political crisis and a bad economic situation, their content and passage were completely different from that of the Czech take-over. Also, it is notable that the 1970 riots were (so far as we know) spontaneous, and that the workers were isolated just as the intellectuals had been isolated in 1968. It was not till later on in that decade that the two strata would co-operate. But this episode will be discussed after the crisis caused in 1973 by the oil embargo, has been analysed.

4. Developing A Model System

While events which reduced Poland to a social and economic standstill and which broke Czechoslovakia up into ever-more-hostile factions were happening, other countries in the Socialist Bloc could not complain too much about either dissent or the breakup of social and economic forces. Several of these countries experienced a so-called 'economic miracle', either as a result of increased foreign aid, as in Hungary and Romania, or because of internal reform, as in East Germany. None of these countries were devoid of either dissenters or of reforms; it is merely that dissenters were either stifled or placated, and reforms were carried out quietly and with consultation with Moscow, to avoid the devastating results which occurred in Czechoslovakia. Hungary and Romania will be considered in a different context; that of economic experiments, and international relations.

East Germany must be considered in this chapter, for here the aims were not dissimilar to those of the Czechs and the Poles (though perhaps not so far-reaching), and here also some real attainments were made. East Germany had had a bad start in the Socialist Bloc: undergoing a traumatic invasion by Soviet troops and a huge

exodus of population immediately after 1945 and
throughout the next two decades. It had to deal
with the problem of a divided Berlin and a divided
country. It had to adjust to the fact that the
wealthy, industrialised and mining areas in the
West as well as the coal deposits in the
South-East were no longer in her possession. Nor
was the territory of East Germany an
agriculturally rich area. The Saxon and Prussian
lands were good enough for growing potatoes and
rye; very little else would grow in the sandy,
eroded soil.

Yet despite all these drawbacks and despite
political and geographical problems, the East
Germans had hardly any difficulties with
dissenters. True, there was an abortive and
short-lived workers' uprising in 1953, but this
was sparked off by economic rather than political
grievances. Instead of dissent, there was an
orderly and well-considered attempt at reform from
within (rather than from above or below) the
system. This is said to have started in 1956
under the impact of Polish and Hungarian events.
The reform movement was confined to intellectuals
well-entrenched in the system, which may explain
why the proposals did not alarm the leadership.

Marxist theoreticians formulated demands for
humanistic socialism; scientists wanted to free
scientific research from party control; economists
argued for an autonomous administration of workers
(or workers' self-management); and educators
wished to end the system of political selection in
educational institutions. The Institute of
Sociology in East Berlin and the Walter Ulbricht
Academy of Political and Legal Science in
Babelsberg became the centres of reform-communist
ideas. The movement used the word 'reform' rather
than 'revisionism' partly out of caution and
partly because it expressed its views better.

The formulation of a far-reaching reform
programme was put forward by a group of SED
functionaries who: 'intended no break with
Marxism-Leninism but ... wanted to free it from
Stalinism and dogmatism and to lead it back to its
humanistic and undogmatic intellectual
basis'.[15] Those who advocated the reform were
searching for a 'specific German road to
socialism' and made a point that disobedience to
the party had a long history; quoting Karl
Liebknecht who broke party discipline during the

First World War in order to save the party.

As summed up by Lippmann, the programme was very far-reaching, considering that it came from the top echelons of the party. It called for democratisation within the party; for the restoration of a form of multi-party system; for the restoration of a free parliament; for an independent foreign policy, without affecting relations with the Socialist Bloc; for the restoration of freedom of the churches; for university autonomy; and the abolition of the secret service and secret trials. In other areas, it called for the introduction of workers' councils, end of forced collectivisation, and development of small private enterprise both in industry and agriculture. Though Lippmann compares the programme with the 1968 programme of the Czechoslovak Communist party, it could more aptly be compared to the Kardelj programme unfolded in Yugoslavia after the break with the Bloc.

The author of the actual programme, the editor of a Marxist journal and lecturer at the Humboldt University was arrested and sentenced to ten years of hard labour, of which he apparently served seven.[16] But the severity of this treatment (which was to be repeated by the East German government during the Czech reforms) while it slowed down the reform movement, did not end it. Professor Robert Havemann delivered a series of lectures at the Humboldt University in 1963-64, claiming that the division between the party and the scientific establishment must be restored. He was dismissed from his chair; expelled from the Academy of Sciences and deprived of his party membership. Nevertheless, he remained free and in 1968 gave an interview to an Italian newspaper condemning the invasion of Czechoslovakia.

It would appear that despite such rough treatment of dissenting intellectuals, the regime had learning capacities. This was shown in the significant economic and administrative reforms carried out in the 1960s: reorientation of the economy to new electronic technology, use of cost-accounting, up-grading of party cadres and rejuvenation of the party apparatus, partial decentralisation of the economic and administrative activities, a university reform; all these tending to shift the centre of decision-making from the party apparatus to a new

class, which has been called the 'institutional-
ized counterelite'. This class works within the
system and does not challenge it, but applies
scientific principles to problems, which brings
about a gradual liberation from party dogma. As
one top official remarked:

> The SED is faced with a dilemma. In order to
> give credibility to its slogan of achieving
> international standards, it must make maximum
> use of modern science. But in so doing, it
> must free the analysis of important social
> processes from the bonds of its direct
> influence. For if data biased by the party
> perspective are fed into the computer, the
> results obtained are ultimately worthless and
> do not accomplish their purpose.[17]

Such reforms may appear very insignificant by
Polish, Czech or even Hungarian standards; however
they have one great advantage: they have
strengthened the East German government not only
vis-a-vis its great protector, the USSR, but also
improved its relations with West Germany and
allowed it to carry out a relatively independent
economic policy outside and within the Bloc. The
spin-off of this policy is the fact that the East
German economic situation improved dramatically in
the mid-1960s, and the resultant improvement in
the social situation could only work for the
benefit of the regime. It may be that the East
Germans are timid or over-disciplined; Lippmann
explains it by the fact that the present
generation brought up under Nazi and later
Communist regimes, has no experience of democracy
and no wish to experiment with it; conversely, it
could also be true that the population (including
many intellectuals) are satisfied with the modest
increase in their standard of living; with being
sheltered from homelessness and unemployment, and
even with not having to deal with the problem of
'guest workers', like their Western brethren. In
a country which can watch the West German
television in most of its territory, such
considerations cannot be excluded.
    The decision to liberalise (usually dated
about 1963) the economic system without touching
the political system, obviously proved difficult
to implement. In the event, the economic system
had to become much more efficient, owing to

external events (i.e. the collapse of the Czech economy in 1968 made it imperative that East Germany produces much more industrial output of the kind which Czechoslovakia used to produce), and due to generational change: new experts were better educated and more eager to experiment than the old ones. But the political change could not be held back for the same reasons. In 1970, Walter Ulbricht was 77. It was clear that the party would have to find new leadership fairly soon.

The top party apparatus has been classified into three wings and analysed on the basis of their apparent tendencies by one writer;[18] the first consists of the technocrats, willing to change the system, well-educated, and co-opted because of their expertise; the second of the dogmatists, older, less well-educated, faithful party hacks, and hence unable and unwilling to change or innovate; and the third of the 'middlemen' who aim at a position somewhere between the two extreme factions.

Events, however, prove how dangerous it is to cast Communist leaders into roles. One of the dogmatists, Erich Honecker, was said to fit the 'stereotype of the colourless, disciplined and cautious party bureaucrat who has little understanding of the "new economics" ... It is clear from his public statements that he has been strongly opposed to the idea of a rapprochement between East Germany and West Germany'.[19] Yet this leader, whose appointment was supposed to bring about repressive anti-Western attitudes later turned out to be the most outgoing one both in economic and political matters; the one leader who was able to bring about new prosperity and good relations with West Germany. It is not the purpose of this chapter to find out why Honecker changed his attitudes on coming to power; it is merely intended to point out that preconceived ideas about Communist leadership can be self-defeating. The course East Germany took under Honecker's leadership will be discussed later on in this work, in connection with economic and international relations problems. At this stage, it is important to look at Eastern Europe as a whole, to find out its exact priorities in each area.

5. International Relations and Mutual Suspicions

In many ways, 1970 was a watershed year both for
Europe and for the world. On the global scene,
the US had a new president, committed to ending
the war in Vietnam. The Middle East had just
recovered from the effects of the Six-Day War. In
West Germany a Social-Democratic government,
headed by a genuine anti-Nazi, Willy Brandt, had
been elected in late 1969. And the Eastern Bloc
was slowly getting over the trauma of the Prague
Spring. Iran and all Arab states were selling oil
cheaply, in order to rearm the anti-Israeli states
for a future, decisive victory. The developed
world enjoyed a high standard of living, based on
cheap oil, and the underdeveloped world was hoping
to join soon in the bonanza. Coexistence was
being phased out to give way to detente. While
there were many trouble spots and even more
hiccups, the world was keeping its fingers crossed
that the worst crisis may be over.

On 3 January 1970, the Warsaw Polityka ran a
front page, leading feature on the new political
climate in West Germany. The article was signed
by Mieczyslaw Rakowski, who had been a spokesman
for the Polish government on liberalisation for
some time. Rakowski quoted a West German
acquaintance of his as saying that at last many
Germans in his country felt happy because the new
government was genuinely anti-fascist. The
foreign minister was quoted as saying that
'politicians must now begin to eliminate mutual
suspicions', adding: 'they don't only exist in
Eastern Europe'.

The article was significant both because of
its timing and its content. It is clear that the
peoples of Europe, and some governments, were
hoping to make a fresh start: to end the
state-of-war between the two blocs, and to begin
genuine co-operation. The reasons were plain to
see: apart from a new course stemming from
Washington, anxious to end the Vietnam War without
loss of face; and a somewhat similar attitude in
the Kremlin, which heartily wished that everybody
would forget Czechoslovakia in 1968, there was a
looming realisation that the constant nervous
tension within Europe and between the two
super-powers had only led to localised wars and a
reduction in the standard of living. Since the

mid-1960s it became easier to gauge how much better off everybody would be employed on peaceful pursuits, instead of toting guns without an end in sight. It needed some ten years since de-Stalinisation and the arrival of an American president with genuine anti-Communist antecedents for such a situation to arise, but arise it did. On reflection, it is perhaps strange that this had not happened earlier, but maybe the appearance of a new post-war generation in middle-management (in the broadest sense) changed the scene. This also showed, for the first time, how desperately everyone in Europe was looking for peace and a degree of stability, and how tired everybody was of 'Cold War' attitudes.

There were, obviously, several aspects related to the quest for peace. The USSR had its own reasons for wishing to stabilise the European system further after the summer of 1968. Some authorities claim that Soviet aims may have been either to remove US influence from Western Europe, or to preserve the status quo in Europe in order to stop the disintegration of the Socialist Bloc.[20] Either of the two motives, or a host of allied ones may have contributed to the Soviet stance. However, it must not be overlooked that the Eastern European governments also had some views on the matter, and that these views were not necessarily parallel to those of the Soviet Union. The main worry of Socialist governments at this stage must have been the economic situation and the resultant social upheavals, as witnessed in Poland and Czechoslovakia. The relative prosperity of East Germany since it began its economic co-operation with West Germany did not escape other governments' perceptions; nor did the fact that East Germany (almost alone out of all Eastern European countries) did not experience the convulsions which affected other countries.

The problem was not so much whether to build up relations outside the Bloc, but how to do it. The Eastern European Bloc lacked a mechanism for joint action in the political sphere. Unlike the EEC which in addition to its economic tasks, also had a political arm, the CMEA was a purely economic organisation without powers in the political sphere, and limited even within its economic sphere by various long-established clauses.[21] Hence, the only joint body which could begin the new campaign was, ironically enough, one which had been set up for military purposes: the Warsaw Pact organisation.

The attempts by the Warsaw Pact countries to make peace overtures to the West dated back some years. One of the most important and comprehensive ones was the Bucharest Declaration after the July 1966 meeting of the Warsaw Pact Political Consultative Committee.[22] A series of further statements were made, leading eventually to the setting up of the Security Conference in Helsinki in the early 1970s. In the meantime, lacking any concerted response from either the EEC or NATO, both still locked into semi-Cold War postures, individual countries of the Bloc began to make bilateral arrangements with Western European countries.

Each country was driven by its own specific needs, but there was a pattern to the moves which was indubitable. It seems clear that a policy decision was made to concentrate on opening up relations with West Germany. On the face of it, this was a sensible decision. West Germany was the strongest economic power in Western Europe and the one most prepared to grant cheap credits to the Eastern Bloc. On the other hand, it could be argued that Germany's economic strength only showed its feet of clay. It was a country divided - the loss of East Germany and East Berlin could never be forgotten, even if the loss of the land east of the Oder-Neisse line could be pushed into the background; secondly, it was a country politically subject to NATO, even if some of NATO's commanders-in-chief were Germans; thirdly, it was a country which, under CDU governments for some twenty years, had never strayed from its line of implicit loyalty to the USA, with which it had a special relationship: a relationship of client to patron, to put it at its mildest and least offensive interpretation.

USSR had long ago accepted that West Germany was an important link in the European chain and started up diplomatic relations with it in 1955. The next country to do so was Romania, which started diplomatic relations with the FDR in 1967 much against the opposition of the Ulbricht government in East Germany. While this has been interpreted by most Western analysts as a move to assert Romania's independence of Soviet foreign policy, and to demonstrate to the rest of the Bloc that Romania's interests are, or could be, linked to the West rather than the East, this is too simplistic an explanation in view of the fact that not only had Romania consistently retained the Bloc's main policies, but also in view of the fact that other countries followed Romania's path.

However the situation is interpreted; the main outcome was that when the Warsaw Pact leaders met in Moscow in December, 1969, to discuss the change of governments in West Germany, all Eastern Bloc countries were encouraged to begin bilateral relations (economic and political) with West Germany, despite apparently strong East German objections.[23] The result was the beginning of bilateral talks between Poland and West Germany and USSR and West Germany, as well as a strong rapprochement between Hungary and the 'Danubian Basin' countries, most cogently, Austria and Yugoslavia. This outcome left the East Germans no choice, but to accede to the joint decision of the Bloc. On 19 March 1970, the heads of state of West and East Germany met in Erfurt for the first time since the two states had been created.

This brings us back to the article in Polityka which appeared so fortuitously at the beginning of 1970. It is quite true that Poland was desperate for Western credits and that West Germany provided her with very generous ones. It is also quite true that the Americans were eager to open up the East European markets, in view of the fact that the war in Vietnam would come to a close (though in fact it still dragged on for a few years) and American industries would need to readjust to peacetime markets. It is also true that the European co-operation had been desired by some members of the EEC for some time and the Helsinki Security Conference was in the offing. Nevertheless, the cohesiveness and decisiveness of this new peace offensive, coupled with a bid at a large degree of economic co-operation needs some explaining.

There are, of course, those (on both sides of the divide) who see in this policy a new independent line designed to set the Eastern European governments free from the Moscow line. Kleiber (from a Western point of view) belongs to this school:

> Our examination of the policy lines followed by Romania, Hungary, Poland and East Germany in promoting the joint Warsaw Pact effort to

23

organize an all-European security conference
has revealed telling differences in their
respective approaches to the problem of
security; and it has pointed up as well the
gap between their several positions and that
of the Soviet Union. At bottom, these
differences stem from the nation's various
perceptions of the nature of the threat to
their security, which in turn are determined
by the evaluation of three fundamental factors
in their political environment: first, each
country's perceived vulnerability to Bonn's
outstanding claims upon its territory ...;
second, the degree of legitimacy enjoyed by
the regime ...; and third, the degree of their
economic and political dependence on the
Soviet Union.[24]

If Kleiber is to be believed, Romania has
decided to work for a loosely connected European
security system which would allow her to become
completely independent of the USSR, and would
enable her to forestall Soviet intervention in her
internal affairs. This may be quite true, on the
other hand, it is also true that Romania cannot
undertake any military action on her own, being
within the Bloc in the most literal sense, and
that (as of writing this in the middle of 1984)
Romania has acted as a link-man in various
East-West crises, always showing an 'independent'
line, and yet apparently never swerving from the
main objectives of the Bloc: the objectives
being, on the face of it, the de-coupling of
Western Europe from the USA; greater independence
for Western and Eastern Europe to make decisions
for Europe as a whole, and better markets for
Eastern European goods in Western European
countries, as well as better and bigger credits.
    There seems nothing anti-Soviet in these
undertakings. On the contrary, they are directly
connected to the Soviet policy of making all
Socialist countries technologically advanced,
economically sound and socially acquiescent. The
burden of maintaining Hungary after 1956 and
Czechoslovakia after 1968 has produced this new
course. Such course may have been maintained till
the present day (1984), had it not been for
unexpected (or perhaps surprising) developments in
the early 1970s. They will be discussed in the
next chapter.

CHAPTER ONE : FOOTNOTES

1. Raymond Aron: On Polycentrism, Survey no. 58, January, 1966, p.11.
2. Aron: On Polycentrism, p. 12-13.
3. Roman Kolkowicz: The Warsaw Pact: Entangling Alliance; Survey, No. 70-71, Winter-Spring Issue, 1969, p. 86-87.
4. J.F.N. Bradley: Politics in Czechoslovakia 1945-1971 p. 184; quoting Dr. Lubos Kohout: Dokumenty z Barnabitek; Kulturni Tvorba, 1968, no.15, p.3.
5. Bradley, Politics, p. 186.
6. See Bradley: Politics, p. 192-194.
7. Bradley, Politics, p. 193.
8. There is a vast number of works concerning both the period of reforms - or the 'Prague Spring' as it became known - and the Warsaw Pact intervention in Czechoslovakia. The key works dealing with these events are as follows: G. Golan: The Czechoslovak Reform Movement Cambridge, 1971, O. Sik: Czechoslovakia. The Bureaucratic Economy New York, 1972; and H. Gordon Skilling: Czechoslovakia's Interrupted Revolution, Princeton, 1976.
9. A Ross Johnson: Poland: End of an Era?; Problems of Communism, January-February, 1970, p.32.
10. Johnson: Poland, p. 32-35.
11. Johnson: Poland, p. 37-39.
12. Johnson: Poland, p. 40.
13. Edmund Szczesniak: Notes on Biography; in: The Book of Lech Walesa, p. 30-31. It is interesting to note that Walesa, who first smelled gunpowder in the 1970 riots, was the son of a smallholder, trained as an agricultural mechanic and was a member of the ZMW - Union of Rural Youth, the youth section of the official Populist Party. His first six years at work were spent in an agricultural machinery station. He did not join the Gdansk shipyard till 1967. See: Szczesniak: Notes, p. 27-29.
14. For a brief treatment of the situation, see: O.A. Narkiewicz: Marxism and the Reality of Power, p. 182-183. There is a vast literature on the subject, but it is encapsulated in an article written soon after Gierek's

take-over: A.   Ross   Johnson: _Polish Perspectives, Past and Present_; _Problems of Communism_, July-August, 1971, p. 59-72.

15. Quoted by Heinz Lippmann: _The Limits of Reform Communism_; _Problems of Communism_ May-June, 1970, p. 16.
16. See: Lippmann: _The Limits,_ p. 17.
17. Quoted by Lippmann: _The Limits,_ p. 19.
18. See: Peter C. Ludz: _The SED Leadership in Transition_; _Problems of Communism,_ May-June, 1970, p. 23-31.
19. Ludz: _The SED,_ p. 27.
20. See: Wolfgang Kleiber: _Security Priorities in Eastern Europe_; _Problems of Communism,_ May-June, 1970, p. 32.
21. For the functioning of the CMEA and the limitations on the Council's powers, see: _Wspolnota Socjalistyczna RWPG, Osiagniecia i Perspektywy,_ Warsaw, 1975; a compendium by authors from all the CMEA countries; translation from the original Russian book, published in Moscow by Politizdat in 1973. CMEA's powers and statutes are analysed in Chapter 1, particularly p. 7-23.
22. This and other moves up to 1970 are described in detail by Kleiber: _Security Priorities_, p. 32-44. Also see: Richard Lowenthal: _Trends in Soviet Foreign Policy,_ in John W. Strong (ed): _The Soviet Union under Brezhnev and Kosygin,_ p. 235-248.
23. See: Kleiber: _Security Priorities,_ p. 42. For an Eastern European point of view see: J. Kokot: _Od Poczdamu do Helsinek._
24. Kleiber: _Security Priorities,_ p. 43.

EASTERN EUROPE'S NEW ECONOMICS

---

1. Crisis of Confidence

> Dissatisfaction with economic and social
> policy, with the way the affairs of the party
> and state were being managed, has been growing
> and spreading for a considerable time. This
> dissatisfaction became a crisis of confidence
> in the leadership of the party and government
> ... we must state that unfortunately somewhere
> in the mid-1960s ... the crisis in the
> leadership of the party and state became more
> and more apparent.[1]

Napoleon said that an army marches on its
stomach. The same could be said of nations;
particularly nations which had been deprived of
many basic comforts throughout the Second World
War and the Stalinist period. While the late
1950s and early 1960s brought a measure of social
and economic relaxation to the countries of
Eastern Europe, none of them, despite the
installation of new leaderships, and despite
Soviet pressure, were capable of improving the
standard of living dramatically. More
importantly, it was impossible to treat the basic
problems of the economy without a drastic revision
of the system. That, of course, was the main
difficulty. The economic catastrophes of the
Stalinist period, imposed on economies already
devastated by the war, coupled with the
persecution of able experts up to 1953, have laid
waste what used to be a fertile and often
prosperous - though by and large underdeveloped -
region.
One can go on discussing for years whether a
capitalist or mixed-economy formula would have

been a better recipe for success than a socialist economy formula for any, or all, of these states. The fact is, that by definition, this formula was forbidden. Nor was it possible to change the basic form: the state had to own all the means of production and distribution; there had to be centralised planning and control. In any case, it is doubtful if any single prescription would have sufficed for countries as diversified in their resources and economy as Eastern Europe. After Stalin's death, the Soviet leadership recognised two important factors: a) that the economies of these countries were not adaptable to Stalinist, Soviet solutions; and, b) that unless prosperity increased, the early troubles in Eastern Europe would become unmanageable. This lay behind the decision to allow each leadership to make 'small decisions', like partial decentralisation or partial de-statification; while the 'big decisions' - like the form of the system - would remain in Soviet hands.

The problem with this approach was that it met two mutually opposing forces: on the one hand, the new leaderships were not installed for their economic or social expertise, but because they were loyal to the USSR, while managing to maintain a modicum of independence and popularity at home; on the other - the shortages and mismanagement of twenty years or more (if one also counts the pre-war years) could not be put right immediately, even with the maximum of resources and able management. Resources and able management were lacking everywhere and had to be fought for on a day-to-day basis; the leaderships, insecure and uncertain of their position, were unwilling to effect more than the most minute changes, in order not to jeopardise their standing.

In the event, it says a lot for the ingenuity and persistence of the technocrats that a great deal of progress was made in several countries; and that this progress in some instances gave the population at least the basics of a developed economy. In several countries progress was made in a piecemeal, often hesitant, manner, but it was sufficient to maintain a modicum of concensus. The fact that this was not the case in Poland and Czechoslovakia brought about the Prague Spring and the 1970 change-over in leadership in Poland.

The crisis of confidence, about which Gierek spoke in 1971, did not disappear in the 1970s.

One of the main reasons lay in the oil crisis in 1973, which all but stopped the most ambitious development plans in countries intent on rapid industrialisation and the development of high technology. However, this does not explain why the crisis did not affect all countries to the same extent. It could be that in the countries where the governments were either accepted (as in East Germany) or tolerated (as in Hungary) or never questioned (as in Bulgaria), it was easier to introduce reforms and sustain them despite an external crisis. On the other hand in countries such as Poland, which relied heavily on foreign investment, or Czechoslovakia, which had to reconstruct its economy with a government imposed on it against its will, it was virtually impossible to proceed, once the international oil crisis penetrated to Eastern Europe.

2.   The Politics of Economic Success

We will first look at countries which managed to have a relatively successful decade (from 1968-78) despite the problems of the oil crisis and international debt. These countries' population, traditions and economy differ widely, and they all adopted slightly different approaches. Thus a model of successful management is not really possible; though a comparative approach may provide some enlightenment on how success was achieved. The countries which can be counted as successful are: East Germany, Hungary, Romania and Bulgaria.

Naturally, there is no objective measure of success even in a field which can be quantified like economics. The interpretation of success depends on the base from which it started; on the aims intended to achieve or achieved; on the way in which both the experts and the population experiencing the measures react to them, and on the attitudes of the ruling elite towards the objectives. To take two extreme examples of what is meant, one can look at the Stalinist measures in the period of the earlier Five Year Plans, which were intended to expand and maximise the heavy industrial base on the one hand; and at the monetarist experiment in Britain in the period 1979-83 on the other. The former was undoubtedly a success in terms of expanding coal, steel and electricity production, but it was achieved at an enormous social cost, as well as at the expense of other industries (chemicals, agricultural tools, consumer goods). The latter was intended to stop inflation, and in that it was apparently very successful. However, the disinflationary measures produced large unemployment, a slow-down in industrial production, and an influx of foreign manufactured goods, which - like raw materials - would have to be eventually paid for in currency which had first become grossly overvalued and subsequently very undervalued. This seems to be one of the main arguments between economists and social and political historians: quantifiable economic success does not necessarily square-up with social or political success.

There is an even greater problem with measuring the success or lack of success in Eastern European states: the political divide between the proponents and the opponents of the socialist system makes it almost impossible to assess the <u>real</u> rate of success in Eastern European states: there are too many reasons why the actual state of the economy should be distorted. Again, to take one example: in 1980-82 the main topic of conversation among Western economists was the Eastern European debt to the West; it was said to be the largest ever, and it was admitted freely that Eastern European countries (most notably Poland which was counted among the biggest debtors) would be unable to pay if off, or even to service it. Possibilities of various kinds of sanctions were being discussed, and the Eastern European governments were blamed for incurring such large debts and not using the money in an appropriate way. Again, the socialist system rather than the oil crisis of 1973 were blamed and bankers were accused of lending large amounts of money to totalitarian governments, who were unable to run a free market system. By 1982 it slowly transpired that the Eastern European debt was minute; (at its peak, in 1981, the aggregate net debt of CMEA countries to all the creditors is said to have stood at 67 billion US dollars) compared to that which had been contracted by Latin and Central American countries. Here the markets were free - none freer in the world - and yet for very similar (though not exactly the same) reasons, Argentina,

Brazil, Mexico and others were and are unable to even service the debt; which amounts to some 800 billion US dollars, or some twelve times the Eastern European debt.

Moreoever, within the Bloc, there are palpable differences: Czechoslovakia, which had borrowed very little and had used the money to good purpose, has been in an economic crisis for nearly two decades; Romania which had immense credits is also in serious trouble, which would have been much more serious, had she not been given generous help with more capital. East Germany which has special financing arrangements with West Germany and which appears to benefit from Common Market subsidies <u>sub rosa</u>, has had the best economic performance of all Eastern European states. Thus, neither the type of the economy, nor the amount of debt, nor the particular system of government, seem to make much difference. What appears to have made a difference to <u>all</u> economies on a global scale, was the quadrupling of the price of oil, bringing about inflation, bringing about, in turn, high interest rates, bringing about stagnation, and bringing about an inability to repay debts, or to continue development. These factors have affected all countries, and there is no proof that they affected Eastern Europe any more than other countries.

Hence, anything that one can say about those economies has to be hedged with careful conditions. Moreover, in the face of ideological commitment to full employment and of hidden subsidies from the USSR - and to some extent from Western bankers - the Eastern European economies have become distorted, though unfortunately it is impossible to compare this particular distortion with the distortion which occurred in market economies, as it is of quite a different kind. As a result, one gets assessments which vary from extremely optimistic ones to very pessimistic ones, both being based on the same numerical data, but on a different political attitude. Which means, in the final analysis, that neither the economists, nor the historians are able to draw a true picture of the Eastern European economies.

However, certain facts are constant. These are that in all Eastern European countries economic reforms started in the mid-1960s, that in some of them they have gone on till the 1980s without interruption; that in others they have been interrupted and taken up again, often in the same form, and that all of them have been undermined by the large rise in oil prices in 1973-4, coupled with the burden of hard-currency debt. This applied to countries which did not contract such a large debt as well as to those which did, because under the prevailing system, they were expected to make good the shortcomings of the heavy debtors.

Possibly the biggest problem which the economists and historians have to deal with is that the reforms were started by Marxists, on the basis of unquestioning acceptance of certain communist preconceptions, such as the expropriation of private property and the rejection of capitalist methods. One need only look at the way Ota Sik's reforms are treated by a Western economist, to understand the big gap:

> Ota Sik ... formerly Director of the Institute of Economics at the Academy of Sciences,... was made a Deputy Prime Minister in the short-lived government formed in April 1968, after the fall of Novotny ... Sik has, of course, spoken as a communist who, while criticizing the methodological errors of the Stalin school, based his own economic concept on "the necessity for socialist market relationships", which were to replace the "over-simplified, mainly quantitative approach to planning" ... What he was after was greater efficiency of the existing system and not its abolition ... He was the master-mind behind the five-year plan of 1964 and of the New System of Economic Planning and Management of 1967, in which he tried to match the need for central indicative planning with the desirability of decentralized management based on business productivity and individual initiative.[2]

But, concludes the author: 'Goodwill and intelligence proved no match for the inner contradictions inherent in the communist economic system, which thrives on "democratic centralism" and fears nothing more than the rise of genuine democratic forces.'[3]

In fact, the 'democratic centralist' system is no more afraid of innovation than the bureaucratic market system, it is simply more difficult to introduce innovation because of the much more powerful immobilisme in a centralised system; and it is only at a later stage that demands for more political freedom are made. Indeed, this is the main problem of introducing reforms in the systems, perhaps most dramatically illustrated by the case-study of Solidarity in Poland, but quite obvious in all other countries which maintain the socialist system.

This is denied by the same author later on in his article:

The industrial parts of Eastern Europe, where the process of manufacturing and trading had reached a high degree of division of labour before the last war, proved least suitable for Stalin's type of planning and management. When the ravages of the war had been repaired and the political controls emanating from Moscow had been relaxed, open debate started. Practical reforms became possible when major economic predicaments defied the crude remedies of normative planning and administrative intervention. Whilst credit is due to the economists, they were able to make themselves heard only when, and as long as, political relaxations coincided with economic difficulties.[4]

The actual fact is that economic difficulties make the government demand reform and innovation; it is in the wake of such reform that political relaxation occurs.

What, then, were the reforms which it was deemed essential to introduce to make the system more efficient and responsive to needs? Their list is very long, but the main demands were to replace the bureaucratic methods of planning controls by non-bureaucratic methods; to limit central authorities to major decisions on planning and investment; to delegate more authority to executive bodies, such as industrial trusts and trade associations; to strengthen the authority of factory managers, to increase incentives for managers and work-force, to make profitability a chief measure of plan fulfillment; to bring prices in line with shortages and preferences; and to be able to trade in foreign markets without state interference. All or some of these were either introduced or attempted in all Eastern European countries, all or some of them are said to have either had a measure of success, or to have been dismal failures; or indeed to have caused further trouble - as in Czechoslovakia and Poland. It is the analysis of this rate of success or failure which is most difficult, because it depends on the interpretation of data and not on the data itself.

We must return again to Klatt, who maintains that most of the reforms pointed in the right direction. The curbing of central administrative power, delegation of authority to managers and industrial trusts, cost-accounting, and the changes in price mechanisms (most difficult of all to implement), all helped to improve the economies, but they did not go far enough. Other reforms were of a highly technical nature and needed a period of time before they could be pronounced a success. Though the reforms are said to have begun in Yugoslavia and were taken up by Czech economists, it is perhaps too easily forgotten that they were all very akin to (or indeed based on) 'Libermanism' which had become highly respectable in the USSR since Khrushchev began to support it. Secondly, the value of judgements of some economists on the whole question hardly bear examination. As Klatt maintains:

> The invasion of Czechoslovakia marked an important setback for the cause of economic reform, not only in this country, but also in the USSR and Eastern Europe in general. With the subjugation of Czechoslovakia to Soviet rule, the hopes of economic and political liberalizers were dashed ... no ready return can be expected in the foreseeable future to the political self-expression that was tolerated in Czechoslovakia before the country was invaded.[5]

In fact there is no doubt that the invasion of Czechoslovakia both slowed down and limited the economic reforms; on the other hand, it did not stop them. On the contrary, in some instances, as in East Germany, they were introduced on a large scale because of the need to re-industrialise the Bloc. Thirdly, while it is not questioned that economic reforms are difficult to introduce without political liberalisation, this need not be a sine qua non for economic reform. It is only some economists who insist that the political and the economic system is so interconnected that the one is impossible without the other. In fact, in centrally planned systems, it is easier to introduce economic reforms without touching the political framework; and in market systems nobody would dream of joining political liberalism and economic liberalism unless there was a desire to do so (consider the example of Pinochet's Chile, for instance).

Having discussed the difficulties of assessment, let us now turn to the question of what - if anything - was accomplished in those countries which were considered successful, even by non-socialist observers.

3. Hungary: Success and Failure

The philosophical trend of 'humanist socialism', expounded by the Polish intellectuals (primarily Adam Schaff and Leszek Kolakowski), which had been taken up by the Hungarians and Czechs[6] in the 1950s and 1960s, was first intended as a social document. However, it was clear that in some contexts, such as state socialism, it had to have an economic application. Indeed, part of the Yugoslav experiment with decentralisation and workers' councils, however imperfect, was based on the understanding that in a socialist state economics had to be related to social relations.

Humanist socialism became the venue of non-philosophers in a round-about fashion: since the economists were looking for an ideological rationale for reforms, which was not tainted with capitalist ideology, they found this a perfect base for the new theories. While the process was slow and often almost surreptitious, it nevertheless gained ground throughout the Bloc. The Poles began economic reforms after 1956, only to find them ineffectual in 1968; on the other hand, the Hungarians, whose revolution was much more violent than the Polish October, were forced to make their reforms work, simply because the country was devastated after 1956.

Writing in the early 1960s, one economic historian maintained that there was no danger to the socio-political system from outward violence: 'The real danger can only be evoked by the lack of

35

courage to face the intricate problems which are partly inherited from the past and partly of our own making.' And further:

> Rationality in the analysis of the problems, active humanism in outlining the objectives, noble pathos in the effort to convince the reader - these are the properties that lend these economic papers the character of a genuine essay ... The author fully understands, experiences and approves of the great economic and social changes which determine progress in our present age. His socialist humanism, on the other hand, makes him confident that mankind will ... ultimately come to identify itself with the requirements arising from the new socio-economic realities of the day.[7]

Vajda's thesis is simple, yet important: because the Hungarian economy was paralysed after the 1956 Revolution, when production was at a standstill, and by January, 1957, industry only produced 28 per cent of previous year's production, the danger of inflation, unemployment and complete exhaustion of stocks, forced the Hungarian economists to rethink the whole basis of economic activity. By 1960, Hungary had achieved a great deal, both in augmenting production and in cultural and social respects.

> The volume of products of the nationalized industries had increased enormously, unemployment had disappeared, and the health and educational standards of our people had improved considerably. Development had, however, not been even. Power production had lagged behind the overall development of industry, improvements in technical standards behind increases in quantities produced, and productivity behind the numbers of workers newly employed. The pursuit of quantitative results had led to the exaggerated exploitation and exhaustion of some of our raw material resources and, as a result of the neglect of agricultural production, we had been forced to import large quantities of foodstuffs whose cost considerably decreased, though it did not completely swallow, the foreign currency income from agricultural

exports ... Year by year the number and volume of unfinished constructions had increased and the rate of housing construction had lagged behind requirements. All this had been reflected in a temporary decrease in the standard of living.[8]

Radical steps had to be taken to improve the economy after 1956; this was done with the aim of increasing production by applying new machinery and decreasing production costs. The command structure was decentralised and plant managers were given independence and were encouraged to operate profitably, and to draw up realistic plans which could be achieved. One of the most successful experiments was the introduction of profit sharing, which amounted to from six to eight per cent of incomes. Real wages rose by 27 per cent between 1957 and 1959, while the index of consumer prices rose only by two per cent. But the system had its drawbacks: factories aimed at the biggest profits and preferred to produce goods which would bring these about, neglecting production which would not bring in immediate profits. Neither did the system encourage research into new techniques and new products; there was also the problem of price distortion, which inhibited co-operation between factories and industries. New methods were being tried out to regulate the industries in such a way that they would be synchronised, and to stop large increases in price rises, as the efforts to obtain larger profits could lead to distortions which would not help the economy as a whole.

The problems of Hungarian agriculture were much more difficult to solve; the main reason being the low productivity of small farmers and the fact that prices were fixed by the state and all products were bought up; thus the small farmer was not forced into higher productivity by the markets. The state tried to solve this by setting up large co-operatives; by January, 1960, 55 per cent of the country's arable areas were farmed by co-operatives; while about 30 per cent of arable land was still in private hands.[9]

The earlier reforms laid the groundwork for the Second Five Year Plan, from 1961-65. The act for the Five Year Plan was passed by parliament on the same day as the Educational Reform Bill, symbolic of the fact that scientific planning depended on a population which was aware of the need for technological and scientific progress, together with higher social and cultural achievements. The results of the Plan, while mixed, were acknowledged to have been an overall success, particularly in the field of increased productivity, improved standard of living, and improved industrial output. However, in agriculture the progress was not very marked, and in housing only three-fifths of increase was accomplished by 1963.

The first half of the 1960s was generally considered a success by both Eastern European and Western experts. According to one authority, while the Hungarian reforms do not yet constitute an alternative model to the classical Soviet model, they are oriented towards a specific aim, the experience of which may be pursued by other socialist countries, seeking to surmount the drawbacks of a centralised system of planning.[10] Among the positive factors in the reform Richet catalogues the re-grouping of enterprises from vertical to horizontal; the changed system of directives; and the profit motive. At the same time, he considers the agricultural situation to have improved, particularly after the complete abolition of compulsory agricultural deliveries in 1965. This development, he claims, has created a climate of confidence in Kadar's government among the farmers. However, he considers that the price-fixing system is detrimental to the creation of a really flexible system, since prices are fixed according to value given out centrally - the same reason which Vajda gives but interpreted differently. The difference in ideological attitudes, therefore, accounts for different interpretations of success or lack of it.

Nevertheless, the Kadar plan is characterised by a pragmatic approach to problems of the economy, which makes it relatively successful. It was the success of the Second FYP which made it possible for the Hungarian economists to draw up the guidelines for the New Economic Mechanism (NEM), which was officially adopted by the Central Committee in 1968. The principal objectives of the NEM were as follows:

a.   to allow a more rational allocation of capital to branches of the economy; particularly to the most productive areas;

b.   to participate in the international division of labour;

c.   to construct a market structure which is flexible with respect to changing consumer demands;

d.   to link personal and enterprise revenues to economic results.

The reform of 1968 did away with the old system of planning on the basis of instructions. It allowed the enterprises to fix the production quotas. Old sectoral ministries were abolished; however, those ministries which were retained still had advisory powers, the power to dismiss managers and the powers of controlling the enterprises. The new system of pricing has evolved in a way which has been described as non-Marxist by another author.[11]
While Richet calls the reform a 'Kadar reform', both Vajda and another author maintain that it was the work of many experts (eleven work groups staffed by 130 experts worked for two years) and furthermore that it was no more than an extension of reforms already introduced elsewhere in Eastern Europe.

While the fundamental features of the Hungarian reform may be similar to those of the reforms already introduced in other Communist countries, the extent to which the reform has been carried is more far-reaching in Hungary than anywhere else in Eastern Europe except Yugoslavia ... In so far as immediate impact is concerned, it is noteworthy that Hungary's new economic mechanism was introduced in one stroke throughout the entire economy - a procedure quite contrary to that adopted by other countries, including the Soviet Union, where implementation of economic reforms has progressed gradually, from enterprise to enterprise and industry to industry.[12]

The new price mechanism is, according to Shaffer, a departure from Marxism-Leninism, because it departs from the theory of 'law of value' and concentrates more on 'use value'; there are also other unorthodox measures, such as interest charges on loans, regular land rent to prompt efficient land use, and price fixing is geared to demand. However, some of these measures stem directly from Libermanism and have been used both in the USSR and in other Eastern European countries since 1953. One must agree with Shaffer, however, that the wholesale introduction of reform throughout the whole country is a genuine innovation and must have a lot to do with the success of the reform. On the other hand, Hungary enjoys the advantage of a 'small economy' and a relatively highly-educated and large class of experts, coupled with a flexible ruling elite. The same type of reform could have been introduced in Romania, but was not because of the inflexibility of the governing circle; and was attempted in Czechoslovakia, but unfortunately became overwhelmed by political issues, which led to the virtual death of the reform movement (though after 1968, parts of the reforms were carried out in the interests of reviving the economy, and in this respect, one cannot talk of a complete standstill).

The difference between Hungary's economic liberalism and political conformism is such that Hungary felt obliged to send its troops along with other Warsaw Pact troops to Czechoslovakia in August of 1968. On the other hand, Romania, whose economic inflexibility has been well documented, refused to do so. The conclusion to be drawn is that one must not produce any generalised models on the basis of one or another kind of activity, because these activities are dictated either by need or by outside pressures.

Thus, whatever Hungary's preferences may have been in August, 1968, the fact was that since its increasing industrialisation, Hungary had been more dependent on imports and exports than almost any other country in the world. In 1968, exports amounted to two-fifths of Hungary's entire income; 37 per cent of her trade was with the USSR, 37 per cent with Eastern Europe. The USSR supplied all of her iron ore, fuel oil, fertilisers, and about two-thirds of newsprint, and half of other raw materials. The USSR was also the largest purchaser of Hungarian manufactured goods, including lathes, motor vehicles, railway wagons and textiles.[13]

While as a result of industrialisation, Hungary's standard of living has gone up constantly and the economy has taken on a new dynamic, this improvement has its converse side. In the first place, there has been a large exodus of young people from agricultural areas, and corresponding pressure on industrial jobs and accommodation in the cities. Secondly, the price mechanism has never been able to take care of the essential dichotomy between the planned economy and the demands of the market. Thirdly, the encouragement of small private enterprises has given rise to a very large second economy with corresponding price rises and inflationary pressures. Fourthly, agriculture, while apparently successful in its mixed private/co-operative form, has lagged behind industry. And fifthly, the whole economy is distorted as a result of having to depend on <u>all</u> imports of raw materials, and on the sale of almost <u>all</u> manufactured products. This last is perhaps best illustrated by a cartoon showing desirable Hungarian goods being exported, while a frustrated manager and customer exchange these words: 'what should we import?' The customer replies: 'the high quality Hungarian goods which we export'.[14]

The above assessment shows that perhaps it is best to rely on home-produced goods, to optimise production of things which are traditionally accepted and not to embark on artificial experiments of industrialisation. There is no reason to think that high quality food would be any less useful within the CMEA, or exported, than railway trucks or lathes. Such goods could be made in countries which cannot produce wine, southern fruit and vegetables or highly bred Arabian horses. One such country will be considered below.

4. An Industrial Socialist Model

In 1963, the GDR (German Democratic Republic, better known as East Germany) was the first CMEA country to introduce a comprehensive economic reform, under the name of New Economic System for Planning and Managing the Economy. The reasons for the introduction of reforms at such an early stage were complicated; in the first place, East Germany was the only country in the Socialist Bloc which had to suffer full exposure to comparisons with a sister country - West Germany - and was thus in an unenviable position of being <u>forced</u> to improve the standard of living of its citizens; secondly, - because Germany was the only country in the Bloc (not counting Bulgaria) which did not have any political upheavals since its setting up in 1949, and was therefore settled into a fairly stabilised system; thirdly, because owing to the above, it did not have any sudden changes in leadership and the leadership felt sufficiently secure to introduce a wide-ranging reform; and fourthly - perhaps most importantly, because in the CMEA plan East Germany was scheduled to lead the development of high technology, as the most industrially developed of all the CMEA countries. To these main motives, must be added some less obvious ones: these were the hope that the two Germanies would unite eventually, and that the Eastern, socialist half could not be any less developed than the Western half; the beginning of relations (both diplomatic and economic) with West Germany, though on an informal basis; and the wish of the Soviet leadership to strengthen Germany, as its most loyal supporter within the CMEA and the Warsaw Pact countries, against the unreliable Poles, Czechs and Romanians. The additional factor behind Soviet reasoning was the commitment that a unified Germany would be a socialist Germany; hence it was worth building up the German economy with this aim in view.

Germany felt the distortions produced by the Stalinist planning system more than the other Eastern European countries;

> its functional weaknesses aside, it was intended mainly to produce <u>extensive</u> economic growth. Thus, it could not help but be particularly dysfunctional in the GDR, where by the mid-1950s the most significant damages resulting from World War II had been overcome and further economic development had become increasingly dependent on the more <u>intensive</u> use of production factors. To a lesser degree, other CMEA members faced similar

problems, so that by the mid-1950s they, too, were wondering whether or not to follow the example of the Western capitalist states in establishing as goals the pursuit of technological progress, economic growth, and the related rise of a consumer society.[15]

The SED, the East German party, was particularly keen on implementing a scientific-political revolution, as it was assumed that it would be in line with the Marxist theory of developed communism: more consumer goods, less mechanical labour and a less labour-intensive economy were among the benefits cited in this respect. The marginal benefit was the relaxation of ideological control over the technocracy, as it began to develop systems theory, cybernetics and sociology to help the technological revolution to come about. The early economic reforms created a more flexible system of planning and management; a trend to innovation; gave more autonomy to individual enterprises and changed the financial accounting and the pricing system. Wages and bonuses were introduced which would reflect performance. The reforms were partially successful, but produced some significant drawbacks. The new automated plants were found to be very expensive to run; stress was registered among workers forced to service automated machines; a shift system was needed to make them profitable, and a resultant labour shortage made it imperative to gear more workers to industrial work. Because of shortage of male labour, women were encouraged to enter the industries on a larger scale, which provoked male discontent, being non-traditional in East German conditions. A rising divorce rate and a falling birth-rate were some of the results of this policy. These social problems produced a discussion in the highest party circles, and by 1965 the New Economic System for Planning and Managing the Economy (NOSPL) was expanded into the 'Economic System of Socialism' (Oekonomischen System des Sozialismus, or OSS). Under this system, economic planning was to be integrated with social planning; research was to be confined to selected large projects, so was investment. The result was that the industries not enjoying this priority were disproportionately disadvantaged and were unable to meet their production quotas. The favoured branches of the economy which depended on those less-favoured in many areas, were as a result also unable to meet their goals. This situation produced a worsening economic climate in the late 1960s, and a final coup de grace to the reforms was no doubt given by the Prague Spring.

The Fourteenth Plenum of the SED Central Committee in December, 1970, ended the economic reform and re-introduced centralised planning.16 As this author notes:

> There can be little doubt that the strikes which broke out in Poland at about the same time and toppled Wladyslaw Gomulka from power contributed to convincing the leadership of the SED that it had better refrain from further "experiments", and give priority instead to securing the domestic stability of its own system of rule, even if this meant accepting slower rates of economic growth.17

However, it must be remembered that this crisis of reform-making was connected not simply with events in Poland and Czechoslovakia, but also with the crisis of German leadership. After some three decades in power, Walter Ulbricht was about to retire. The new attempt to re-impose centralised control over the economy was as much his swan-song as a panic measure in view of the disorder in the Bloc. When Honecker replaced Ulbricht in May, 1971, the centralisation remained, but the implementation of reforms went on under different names; namely, reforms aimed at improving the social conditions of the population.

> The most important feature of the Honecker course in this respect is a planned rise in the living standard of the population. At the Eighth Congress the SED adopted special resolution to this effect. Willi Stoph reiterated the regime's intentions in his speech on the new Five-Year Plan, emphasising that its "primary task" was to raise the "material and cultural living standard" of the East German population. The Plan itself set forth the prospect of a considerably greater volume of consumer goods and services over the next five years. Housing construction is also supposed to be increased and improved: for example, the plan calls for the erection of

500,000 new apartment units by 1975... The East German leadership expects to achieve these improvements by restructuring priorities and inputs even while reducing the rates of expansion in overall industrial output and investments. Thus, industrial production, which increased at an average annual rate of 6.5 per cent in the last five-year plan period, is to be increased only 3.9 to 6.4 per cent over the next five years; similarly, investments, which increased annually by 9.7 per cent in 1966-70, are planned at a lesser growth rate of 5.1 to 5.4 for 1971-75.[18]

The East German economy could have expected to grow at a respectable rate, even if not at the extremely high rate of the 1960s, in the 1970s, had it not been for the rise in the price of crude oil in 1973. While the GDR increased its exports in the period from 1972-75 by a total of 17 per cent, prices for the goods imported rose by 34 per cent. As the GDR is poor in raw materials, this rise in the price of imported goods (even if subsidised to a certain extent by the USSR) made a great deal of difference to the economy. It also changed the direction of GDR's trade, with lesser emphasis on trade with the Eastern Bloc, and the development of trade with the West.[19] Thus, again, external conditions forced changes in an economy which could have hoped for every possible success.

5. Small Economies - A Separate Way

It has been seen above that various ways of introducing necessary reforms had been tried in Eastern Europe: the Czech way was a mixture of political and economic reform; the Hungarians applied the principles of 'humanist Socialism' to purely economic reform; the East Germans opted for what appeared to be a safe way, that of economic and administrative reform only. It has also been demonstrated that all these reforms had a measure of success; some being more successful than others, and that those with a larger admixture of political reforms came to grief. That is why the Czech reforms were halted, though only temporarily, after 1968; and that is also why the

45

Polish reforms will be discussed in the context of political, not economic reform at a later stage.

It is now relevant to see whether any other way of introducing reforms, without upsetting the established order and without provoking Soviet or Warsaw Pact reaction could be found. In this context, two countries must be investigated: Romania and Bulgaria, since they introduced reforms in a very specific manner, and were in many respects much more successful than the older industrialised countries like East Germany and Czechoslovakia.

Though statistics in respect of industrial growth can always be slanted, and though Western and Eastern statisticians distrust each other, some facts cannot be denied. The main one is that Romanian and Bulgarian industrial output grew much faster than those of the other Eastern European countries. Zauberman, who quotes official CMEA figures, says that: 'over the quarter of a century from 1950 to 1975 industrial output expanded by 19 times in Romania, 16 times in Bulgaria, 11 times in Poland, and between 6 and 7 times in the GDR, Czechoslovakia and Hungary'.[20] He also maintains that though Western economists have tried to recalculate the CMEA figures, and have arrived at annual growth rates rather below those of the official figures, the average annual growth rate was still quite impressive:

Annual growth rate of net material product over the years 1970-75; with 'O' as the official figure, 'R' the recalculated figure:[21]

	O.	R
Bulgaria	7.9	4.5
Czechoslovakia	5.7	3.4
GDR	5.4	3.5
Hungary	6.2	3.6
Poland	9.8	6.7
Romania	11.3	6.1

The growth of industrial output in some of these countries (as in Hungary and to a lesser extent in Poland) has caused problems in the agricultural sector. It is estimated that in the 1965-75 decade Bulgaria's agricultural labour dropped from 45 to 26 per cent, and Romania's from 57 to 37 per cent. This had a direct influence on the productivity in agriculture, and a less direct but even more serious effect on the shortage of industrial labour which had, up to 1970 or thereabouts, fed on the huge reservoir of rural manpower. In addition, the growth of other sectors of the economy, most notably the service sector, has meant that industry must increasingly compete with those sectors.[22]

Nevertheless, Romania has proved to be one of the more interesting models of development in many respects. Its unique situation stems from the political and geographical factors. Romania has no external border with non-socialist countries; has no Slavonic heritage to speak of; has lost its most fertile province to the USSR, after losing the war with the USSR (which it joined at the behest of Nazi Germany); and has had its considerable reserves of oil pumped dry in the years of Stalinist policy of plundering the satellites. Hence, Romania is both a victim and a beneficiary of its circumstances. It is small enough for the Russians not to be afraid of its independence; it is geographically isolated; it is not sufficiently wealthy to be exploited; and it does not suffer from the Great-Russian Panslavic syndrome, which has affected Soviet dealings both with Poland and Czechoslovakia. The Romanians, in addition, are not known to have fought against the Russians directly at any time, even in the Second World War, and they owe their independence to Russia.[23]

In view of the above, the Romanians felt early on that they had to develop their own pattern of socialism, one which had little to do with the USSR, but a lot to do with Romanian leadership. 'Romania is the only country that has managed to stake out a relatively autonomous position while at the same time remaining within the system', stated one writer.[24] A naive observer may well ask what system Romania remained within. It is true that it is both in the Warsaw Pact and the CMEA, but it has frequently refused to follow their policies. It is also true that it pays lip-service to socialism, and that the ruling party call itself the Communist Party of Romania. But the economic policy as well as the political leadership have little in common with the other countries of the Bloc. According to Farlow, the

Romanians use at least five major aspects of the ideological framework; they deal with the Romanian concepts of the nation, socialist international- ism, the laws of socialist development, national versus international communism, and finally, pro- letarian internationalism.

For the Romanian leadership, the nation is the only setting in which socialism can be fully contructed and a socialist revolution can only be successful because it is led by the people of one nation. Socialist internationalism is interpreted as co-operation between equally sovereign socialist states and non-interference in internal affairs; 'laws of socialist development' theory maintains that there is no objective general law of socialist development, but that such development depends on subjective socio-economic conditions; and the last three concepts are self-evident; they maintain that there are no barriers between national and international communism and that proletarian internationalism deals with equal relations between socialist parties.[25]

As can be seen, these concepts, many of which may be quite correct in the modern interpretation of Marxism, also happen to suit the Romanian leadership which wishes to maintain its independence of Moscow; wants to trade with non-socialist countries as much as socialist countries, and has made a bid to become a non-aligned country. On the other hand, it is very doubtful if they are really geared to the demands of the Romanian economy.

Romanian economic development has been based, since 1950, on the classical model of 'extensive growth'. A large proportion of national income has been channelled into investment, half of which has been directed to industry, while 80-90 per cent of industrial investment has been directed towards producers' goods. As a result, productive industry has grown faster than extractive industry, and trade surpluses obtained on fuels and raw materials before 1960 have been transformed into growing deficits. At the same time, there has been a dramatic shift in labour from agriculture to industry; industrial employment which has been 0.8 million in 1950 grew to 3.2 million in 1979; while agricultural labour declined by 2.7 million in the same period. This has decreased the production of agricultural goods, and according to one authority, the overall balance in agricultural production is hardly better in money terms in 1979 than it was in 1960. Conversely, the annual average growth rate of industrial output has been 12.9 per cent between 1950 and 1977.[26]

In 1967 Romania embarked on the strategy of 'import-led growth', aimed at raising domestic productivity through the acquisition of Western technology, principally via co-operation with Western multinational companies. It would appear that the co-operation ventures were less successful than had been anticipated, particularly in the field of repayment in terms of manufactured goods, and the bulk of technical transfer fell on direct purchases of machinery and equipment. Not relying on private banks, Romania joined the IMF and World Bank and borrowed from these sources as well. The trade with the Third World, which was one of Romania's objectives, allowed her to obtain fuel and raw materials in bilateral deals, which did not involve hard currency. But the trade with the West was less successful and increased Romania's indebtedness, particularly to France and Germany. This was due partly to Western discrimination against imports and partly to the poor quality of manufactured goods; nevertheless, Romania managed to increase substantially her exports of industrial consumer goods, mainly furniture, footwear and clothing; and unlike Poland, did not allow excess demand at home to lead to imports of consumer goods. Hence, despite the increase in oil prices in 1974, Romania appeared to be reasonably successful in reducing its deficits. The reason for this was partly that Romania was still a net oil exporter till 1977, by which time the domestic demand outstripped the supply, as a result of which, she had to become a net oil importer.

Additional problems were caused by Romania's refusal to become part of an integrated CMEA plan, which called for specialisation according to each country's capacities of labour fund and raw materials. Romania pursued her own policy of investment in energy-intensive industries, which necessitated not only imports of iron ore and coke and coking coal, but also more imports of crude oil; all of which (apart from two per cent from CMEA) had to be bought with hard currency.[27]

One may question whether Romania's attempt to 'go it alone' at any cost should be commended either in economic or human terms, but this will be discussed in the context of the post-earthquake situation, which brought to light the extent of Romania's difficulties. But there is little doubt that in terms of social upheaval, the position was very serious. In an interview with a journal, a professor of sociology at Bucharest University, stated that about fifty per cent of urban population in the cities had been born in the countryside, according to data from the 1966 Census. This meant that in the 1970s

in some areas of the country, agricultural work is done mainly by old people and women. Local demographic imbalances may therefore occur if there is a massive flow of rural residents to the towns at the expense of agricultural labour.[28]

While Stahl maintained that the Romanians could adapt to anything and that the training of the new industrial labour force was successful (though one may have some doubts in view of the admitted low quality of Romanian manufactured goods) he added that adjustment, assimilation and full integration of the rural work-force into urban social life is a much more difficult and slower process. The transition could be made easier by a large injection of social workers into the enterprise and district; but such social workers were rare, and usually inhibited from carrying out their duties by factory management. Hence, the problem was compounded by lack of understanding on both sides and by lack of trained personnel to remedy the state of affairs. Professor Stahl foresaw problems of delinquency and poor performance of the recently transferred peasant-worker.

Those managers ... are not fully aware of the fact that labour productivity, economic efficiency, and planning depend to an overwhelming extent on the social and professional integration of our citizens. In the long run, the money spent on organizing social services may prove to be a fairly profitable investment.[29]

Clearly, the plight of the Romanian population did not escape the leadership's attention. It is said that when Ceausescu met all the leaders from the Eastern European Bloc as well as Tito at the Helsinki Conference in bilateral talks, most of the discussion concentrated on economic matters. Similarly, though when meeting Western leaders he discussed international problems, he was also interested in renewed or increased co-operation with the West. An interesting insight into the leadership's appreciation of Romanian problems may have been provided by Ceausescu's irritation about the criticism of Romania's socialist progress:

> I am a Communist, and I cannot but mention with satisfaction that it is precisely due to the fact that Rumania is proceeding along the new road of socialist liberation, that my country, under the leadership of Communism has truly earned its independence and is creating a new type of life that guarantees its people well-being and happiness. Of course, there are different concepts about the organization of society, about the problems of democracy, and about other philosophical problems ... How can one speak of equality, freedom, and democracy between rich countries and countries where the annual per capita income is not even 100 dollars? To achieve, in fact, equality, meant to attain the material conditions necessary for it.[30]

This was not a rebuke to the West, as the RFE commentator interpreted it; it was a rebuke to the Soviet leadership, which refused to finance the Romanian 'independent road to socialism', and at the same time an acknowledgement that all was not well with the social and economic experiment in Romania.

However, things might have become easier had the leadership not been overtaken by a natural disaster. The Romanian earthquate on 4 March 1977, proved to be the equivalent of the oil embargo crisis for other Eastern European countries.[31] The careful planning and the suffering undergone by the people had been undermined by the earthquake. Resources had to be diverted towards repairing the earthquake damage; plans had to be abandoned; and, above all, the population was in for a second and much more grim phase of suffering. It is indeed good that as Professor Stahl has said: a Romanian adapts to almost anything - without this adaptability, Romania would not have survived; on the other hand, the adaptability allowed the leadership to stay in power, when it might have been better if new leaders had been able to step in with new ideas; or ideas better adapted for Romania's situation. This will be discussed later.

In the meantime, one has to look at Romania's neighbour, whose economic, political and social policy was diametrically opposed to that of Romania, and which has produced an 'economic miracle' without much publicity, and almost out of a hat. This country is Bulgaria. In an article entitled, <u>Bulgaria's Politics of Conformity</u>, a commentator states that Bulgaria has been least affected by the winds of change which moved Yugoslavia, Albania and Romania to challenge Moscow's hegemony in South-East Europe; 'the overall picture is one of constant, even increasing subservience'.[32] The author ascribes Bulgaria's 'subservience' in terms of historical affinity between the two countries, which dates back to Russian liberation from the Turks in 1878, and the strong cultural, linguistic and religious ties between the two nations, as well as the economic aid extended by the USSR to Bulgaria.[33]

In view of the close and ancient friendship between the Russian people and the Bulgarians, and the common religious ties, one would be inclined to describe the relationship as one of brotherly friendship, which may appear to a jaundiced observer to be subservience. In fact, the Soviet Union had a lot to gain from Bulgaria's friendship and economic well-being; but conversely, Bulgaria had a lot to gain from Soviet support and economic assistance. Hence the process is more one of symbiosis than of parasitism, and the real friendship between the governments is paralleled by friendship between the two nations. Naturally, this does not mean that the peoples and their governments are at one, but it does at least assure a degree of harmony virtually absent in other bilateral and multilateral Eastern European relations.

The reasons why the USSR would want Bulgaria to be friendly and prosperous are numerous and will be discussed more fully in further chapters of this work; at this stage it is sufficient to say that with Yugoslavia outside the Bloc; Romania in opposition to most Soviet policies; Greece and Turkey in NATO; and the increasing conflict in the Middle East, Bulgaria provides the USSR with an important bastion bordering onto a sensitive geographical region. Secondly, Bulgaria, the most agricultural and least developed country in the Bloc, has been assisted with a view to providing a showcase of socialist development; proof of what can be done in underdeveloped countries in other parts of the world. Thirdly, partly stemming from the above factors, Bulgaria has been the Soviet Union's most zealous ally in integrating its economy into a pattern which the Russians would like all the CMEA countries to follow, as an alternative to decentralising reforms in Eastern Europe.

Bulgaria, like other countries in the Bloc, embarked on a series of economic reforms in the 1960s. When the Bulgarian reform blueprint was announced officially at the end of 1965, it was viewed by Western analysts as moving further away from the Soviet model of a centralised command economy than other Eastern European countries. However, on further elucidation of the plan in 1966 and 1967, it turned out to be less 'advanced' than had been thought, but still removed from the Stalinist model. But in July, 1968, at the Plenum of the CC, the reforms were radically re-vamped and, according to one authority, there was a virtual retreat to the pre-1965 system.[34] The pre-1968 New System of Planning and Management of the National Economy had the same aims as the reforms in other countries: removal of excessive centralisation, providing material incentives, an improved pricing system, and so forth. The decree of November, 1968, was entitled: The Decree on the Gradual Application and Further Development of the New System of Management and Economy and repudiated decentralisation. Zhivkov, the Prime Minister criticised the system of 'planning from below' maintaining that individual enterprises cannot have an overview of the economy and that the scientific-technological revolution necessitated re-centralisation.[35] Needless to say, the lessons of the Prague Spring may have had some bearing on the reversal of the course; but it is notable that East Germany had also found that excessive decentralisation may limit the spread of high technology at about the same time. As a

footnote to the advantages of greater centralisation in highly technological fields, it may be
added that the period was also one in which a
record number of mergers were effected in the 'Free
World' where industrial giants were formed with the
same aim in view.
    The Bulgarian economy at this stage was still
highly agricultural, and therefore the leadership
turned its attention to industrialising the
agricultural work-force. This was to be done by
setting up agro-industrial complexes and
integrating them vertically into industry.
Speaking in terms of these in 1970, Dellin rather
contemptuously refers to the development as
'agrogorod-type units' and questions their
viability and efficiency.36 However, seven years
after their setting up, another analyst maintains
that they were a success, though a qualified one:

> The complexes are still far from problem free,
> and there is an urgent need for continued
> agricultural mechanization and "industrializ-
> ation". Great efforts have been made,
> however, and the performance of the
> agricultural sector appears to be showing some
> improvement. The Bulgarian example is
> increasingly being exported to the developing
> countries, and it appears that other East
> European countries are adopting some aspects
> of the model.37

The full extent of the agricultural revolution
which took place in the agro-complexes is discussed
by the author; here it will be sufficient to say
that scientific methods of production and computers
have been used to improve the methods of production
and the profitability of the factory farms. This
can be seen in some random figures quoted in the
paper, which show that some crops, like wheat,
barley, grapes and maize have doubled or trebled in
yields per hectare; that milk production in 1974
was about 60 per cent higher than in 1960, and that
egg production increased by about 44 per cent in
the same period. In a predominantly agricultural
economy, such successes are of great importance,
and the fact that several underdeveloped countries
have signed contracts with Bulgaria for help in
developing them, shows that the success is

not a paper one (Iran, India and Algeria in the mid-1970s). Hence, Bulgaria cashed in, admittedly with Soviet assistance, on a traditional skill, and managed to turn it to its own advantage, as well as becoming a showpiece of socialist development.

The second development was even more interesting. At the 1968 Plenum, Zhivkov expressed the party's desire to harness the ongoing world revolution in science and technology. Again, this would not create scepticism in East Germany, but Bulgaria was still classed as an underdeveloped country even by South-East European standards. Automated systems were to service 70 per cent of Bulgarian economy by 1975; in 1971 alone, the number of computers was to increase fivefold, the number of scientific specialists was to double between 1971 and 1975. Writing in 1972, the author doubted that this would be possible.

> Massive measures will indeed be required if Bulgaria is to have the skilled manpower necessary to operate a computerized society. At present, the absence of such manpower is a formidable roadblock to technological progress and even rational planning. ... Another major ostacle to Bulgaria's technological revolution is the enormous cost of building or purchasing electronic machines, technical facilities, and new plants, of planning and mastering information processing techniques, and of training the necessary manpower ... For all these reasons, one can safely predict that the road to technological progress will not be as smooth as Zhivkov and the BCP appear to hope.[38]

Further, the writer draws attention to the fact that it will be impossible to carry out this revolution with the present elderly and under-educated Bulgarian leadership. Some twelve years later, a note appeared in a newspaper seemingly proving that the Bulgarians were right, and the observers were wrong. It stated that:

> When the Communist Bloc leaders assemble in Moscow on June 12 for the first Comecon summit in 13 years, Bulgaria's President, Mr Todor Zhivkov may well be one of the more relaxed

> ... Mr Zhivkov will be able to report that Bulgaria has already launched an ambitious programme of economic reform, but has done so cautiously and within the bounds of Marxism-Leninism. His country's economy has been prudently managed and living standards have risen impressively without the accumulation of a crippling foreign debt. Bulgaria's ambition in the new Comecon scheme would be to emerge eventually as the Japan of Eastern Europe.

The correspondent further continues to praise the economic well-being of the people, the prosperous look of the capital and the countryside, the lack of dissent and of underground literature:

> When it comes to economic reform, it is obvious that Bulgarian leaders have carefully studied the policies pursued by the other East European countries, Yugoslavia included; they also know better than most where the Soviet Union is going wrong.[39]

There is more praise for the Bulgarian way in this note, penned by a fairly hardline Western journalist. There will be more private enterprise, decentralisation and improvement in the Bulgarian economy, since the reform called the New Economic Mechanism has only just begun to bite. However, sceptical one may be, it would appear that at this stage, despite the oil crisis and world tension, (or perhaps aided by them), the success of the reforms in Eastern Europe is at last beginning to show; at least in those countries which have avoided the upheavals of leadership changes and attempted revolutions. More will be said about those less happy countries in the next chapter.

CHAPTER TWO: FOOTNOTES

1. Edward Gierek, at CC Plenum of PUWP, 7th February, 1971, quoted by A. Ross Johnson: Polish Perspectives, Past and Present, p. 61.
2. Werner Klatt: The Politics of Economic Reform, Survey, Winter-Spring, 1969, p. 159.
3. Klatt: The Politics, p. 159.
4. Klatt: The Politics, p. 163, emphasis added.
5. Klatt: The Politics, p. 165.
6. For a brief account, see:
   Olga A. Narkiewicz: Marxism and the Reality of Power, Chapter Twelve.
7. J. Bognar, in the Introduction of Imre Vajda's: The Role of Foreign Trade in a Socialist Economy, p. 9.
8. Vajda: The Role of Foreign Trade, p. 14-15.
9. For exact figures of the above, see: Vajda: The Role of Foreign Trade, p. 16-30.
10. Xavier Richet: La Reforme Economique Hongroise: Analyse et Evolution, 1968-1978; NATO Colloquium, April, 1980, p. 85.
11. On the main points of NEM, see: Richet: La Reforme, p. 90-93.
12. Harry G. Shaffer: Progress in Hungary; Problems of Communism; January-February, 1970, p.51.
13. Shaffer: Progress in Hungary, p.57.
14. Cartoon from Ludas Matyi, reproduced in Shaffer: Progress in Hungary, p.52.
15. Hartmut Zimmermann: The GDR in the 1970s; Problems of Communism, March-April, 1978, p.3-4.
16. Zimmermann: The GDR, p.7.
17. Zimmermann: The GDR, p.7.
18. Peter C. Ludz: Continuity and Change since Ulbricht; Problems of Communism, March-April, 1972, p. 64-65. 8th Congress of SED was held in 1971.
19. Zimmermann: The GDR, p. 22-23.
20. Alfred Zauberman: The East European Economies; Problems of Communism, March-April, 1978, p. 56.
21. Figures by P. Marer: East European Economies Post-Helsinki, Joint Economic Committee US. Congress, 1977, quoted by Zauberman: The East European Economies, p. 56.
22. See: Zauberman; The East European Economies. p. 60-61.

,-8

23. See: O.A.   Narkiewicz: <u>Marxism   and   the Reality of Power,</u> Chapter 7.
24. Robert R. Farlow: <u>Romanian Foreign Policy: A Case of Partial Alignment;</u> <u>Problems of Communism,</u> November-December, 1971, p.54.
25. For a full discussion of these concepts, see: Farlow: <u>Romanian Foreign Policy,</u> p. 55-58.
26. Alan Smith: <u>Is there a Romanian Economic Crisis?   The   Problems   of   Energy   and Indebtness;</u> J. Drewnowski: <u>Crisis in the East European Economy,</u> p. 107.
27. For figures and tables concerning the above, see: Alan Smith: <u>Is there a Romanian Economic Crisis?</u> p. 107-130.
28. <u>Henri H. Stahl Discusses Townspeople and Peasants;</u> RFE Research, Rumanian Press Survey, No. 989, 6 March 1975.
29. Stahl: <u>Rumanian Press Survey,</u> No. 989.
30. <u>RFE Research,</u> Rumania/31, 14 August 1975.
31. For immediate after-effects of the earthquake, see <u>RFE Research,</u> Rumania/8,/9 and /10, March 11, 18 and 24, 1977.
32. F. Stephen Larrabee; <u>Problems of Communism,</u> July-August, 1972, p. 42.
33. For a much more objective and historically deeper analysis of the ties, see: Robert R. King: <u>Bulgarian-Soviet Relations: 'Socialist Internationalism in Action';</u> RFE Research; Background Report, Bulgaria/89; 26 May 1975.
34. L.A. Dellin: <u>Bulgarian Economic Reform - Advance and Retreat;</u> <u>Problems of Communism,</u> September-October, 1970, p.44-52.
35. Plenum of the Central Committee of the Bulgarian Communist Party, July 24-26 1968; quoted by Dellin: <u>Bulgarian Economic Reform,</u> p. 50.
36. Dellin: <u>Bulgarian Economic Reform,</u> p.51.
37. R.N.: <u>Bulgaria's Agro-Industrial Complexes after Seven Years</u> RFE Research, Background Report/Bulgaria/34; 14 February 1977.
38. Larrabee: <u>Bulgaria's Politics,</u> p. 49-50.
39. Hella Pick: <u>Bulgaria Points the Way for Comecon;</u> <u>The Guardian,</u> 30 May 1984.

Chapter Three

PATTERNS OF NORMALISATION

---

1. Czechoslovakia after 1968

In the early months after the quelling of the
Reform Movement in Czechoslovakia, it appeared as
though all the reforms were lost. Major purges
swept liberals and reformers from their positions
in party, government and the media.
Decentralisation of the economic management was
being replaced by centralised management. The
experiment of workers' councils on the Yugoslav
pattern was abolished, and the Czech attempts to
balance their Eastern European trade with Western
European links were abandoned in favour of a
strong slant towards relations with the Comecon.
But even the strongest opponents of the Husak
regime did not claim that this was a return to the
Novotny-Stalinist period. The reformers were
treated relatively leniently; no criminal
prosecutions of Dubcek and other party leaders
were begun.

> The party weekly Zivot Strany on October 8
> 1969, cautioned: "There can be no question of
> a return to the 1950s, of any kind of
> revenge". The comparatively gentle treatment
> accorded to Dubcek bears witness to the
> resolve of the Husak regime in this matter.
> Dubcek was appointed Ambassador to Turkey in
> December, 1969 and although he was
> subsequently recalled and stripped of his
> party membership, there has been no trial.
> The regime has initiated criminal prosecution
> for political activity only in the case of
> several lesser liberal figures.[1]

Other commentators were even more sanguine; one stated:

Let us now turn to the future of Czechoslovakia's reform movement. There are several reasons why one might speculate that, despite the present bleak situation in the country, the movement will in the long run be reactivated, or at least, that it will not be totally suppressed.[2]

Naturally, in establishing whether there would be a return to 'normalcy' or a continuation, albeit on a slower scale, of the reforms, it would be necessary to establish the concept of what was normal in Czechoslovakia before 1968. As a matter of fact, the country has had such a chequered history since 1945, that any historian would hesitate to establish the norm of 'normalcy'. Whatever happened after 1968, was not a return to the 1950s, but it was not a wild leap into the future either. Rather, it was a stumbling process, induced not so much by the regime's willingness to produce reforms, but dictated by circumstances, both internal and external.

On the internal side, it has already been noted that the Czech economy had been on the decline in the early 1960s. The economic reforms, introduced gradually in the mid-1960s were intended primarily to improve the national economy. Had they not been overtaken by the events of the Prague Spring, it is possible that the reformers might have succeeded. But even this is not certain. Here is what Taborsky has to say on the subject:

However, the NEM was experiencing severe start-up problems even before the Soviet invasion of August, 1968. Imperfections in the pricing mechanism and enthusiastic profit-seeking by enterprise managers combined to encourage production of high-profit, low utility goods at the same time that workers - enjoying bonuses which grew faster than productivity - found nowhere to spend their increased pay. Large profits accumulated in the hands of some enterprise managers, but the capital goods market was clearly inadequate to cope with the resulting demand. Large sums became mired in delayed construction projects, further fuelling inflationary pressures. The Soviet invasion only accentuated these dislocations and prevented the Czechoslovak government from grappling with the inevitable problems arising in the momentous transition from a centralized bureaucratic command economy to a more decentralized and liberal economic system. Economic performance faltered at the end of 1968 and fell short of the performance targets for 1969.[3]

Economic dislocation occurred, therefore, well before the Warsaw Pact troops entered the country. But the invasion produced more problems: social alienation was added to economic stagnation. We have ample evidence of a new trend in Czechoslovakia - an anti-Soviet sentiment, which has earlier been associated with Poland and Hungary, but had not registered any strength in Czechoslovakia.

> What is much more clear and certain is the deep and genuine anti-Russian feeling now general in the country ... it took the invasion of August 1968 to convert the Czechoslovak nation's basically good-natured attitude of superiority mixed with tolerance towards the Russians into a distinct and palpable hatred.[4]

The nation was feeding on hatred and hating itself. This applied to both the working class and the intellectuals; but the former had more clout in the dismal economic climate. A massive work slow-down was declared and was so effective that a visiting Italian delegation mistook the inactivity on a Czech plant for a workers' strike. By March 1970, the need to improve productivity forced the government to order extra shifts at weekends to make up for lost production.

But the intellectuals' alienation was perhaps more serious in its long-range effect: the country was deprived, either by resignation, dismissal or emigration, of its ablest economists, social scientists, journalists and writers. Even a country which had a strong intellectual base, like Czechoslovakia, could not afford such a drain on its intellectual resources without suffering the consequences of stagnation. Similar effects were felt in the party, where the top layer of able younger people were discarded, in favour of elderly cautious <u>apparatchiks</u> of the type Husak represented.

So, while the reforms were perhaps overhasty, not sufficiently considered, and not very successful, their sudden reversal did little for the Czech economic and social life either. Nor did it produce any normalcy within the Bloc. For, no sooner was Czechoslovakia declared to be 'normalised', than trouble began to brew elsewhere.

2. Personalities and Reform: The Polish Way

While the Czechs had been introducing reforms systematically, carefully and with the blessing of the party, only to be overtaken by events over which they seem to have had no control, and which destroyed a large part of their endeavour, the Poles had been in the throes of an economic and social crisis for some years. The Gdansk riots of December 1970 discussed earlier, were the culmination of several years of attempts to change the system both from above and from below. The difference in attempts at change is said to illustrate the national character: the Czech slowness and caution and the Polish tendency towards hasty violent solutions. But it also illustrates (and probably more cogently) the differences in the position of each country: while the Poles were fast becoming an industrialised nation, with a rising standard of living, the Czechs were slipping back from their favoured position of the most industrialised nation in the Bloc, and they were actually witnessing a slide in their standard of living in the 1960s. Hence, while one nation was violently insisting on retaining its gains and improving them, the other was attempting to rectify its deteriorating situation.

An admission of the fact that the Polish reforms had been half-hearted and that discontent had been growing for some time was given by Edward Gierek soon after he assumed the leadership:

It is quite obvious that the sources of the December crisis should not be sought only in the bitterness caused by higher prices and the way they were introduced. The crisis had been growing for years and had deeper causes.[5]

The early success of Polish industrialisation had become less obvious in the late 1960s, indeed by 1969 it may have seemed that all advantages had been lost. But this was not the case. Despite many difficulties, the general standard of living; of social and educational services, of housing had improved beyond recognition, compared with the state of the early 1950s. It was the sudden growth in prosperity, accompanied by the large influx of peasants into industrial jobs and cities which proved difficult to control. Remembering the words of the Romanian sociologist: it is very difficult for the rural dweller to adjust to the social conditions in the city, though he may learn to work in a factory quite easily, would have been a salutary lesson for the Polish authorities. The Polish crisis in 1970 was compounded by three factors: a large and unsocialised new class of workers; difficulty in providing this class with consumer goods which had become part of their expectations; and a rigid elderly leader, whose attitude had become inflexible and who had by 1970 come to regard himself as infallible. Added to this was the alienation of the intellectuals, whose apex came in 1968, during the student riots, and a dichotomy between the general population and the intellectuals and the two strata and the party. In other words, in place of the Czech concensus in favour of reform, in Poland one found groups poised against groups, and hardly any agreement on the remedy to the crisis.

In addition, the party was broken up between factions which fought bitterly with each other. It is perhaps little appreciated that apart from the political disagreements, there was also a great degree of economic disagreement within the top echelons of the party, which spilled over into a power struggle. An example of this is the front page of _Polityka_ in early 1970. This carries a large photograph of Gomulka on the right hand of the page, congratulating the leader on his 65th birthday. The main feature, though, is an interview with Maciej Szczepanski, the editor of the Silesian _Trybuna Robotnicza,_ whose paper has reached the highest circulation among Polish dailies; almost a million copies. The editor justifies the preponderance of material on economic data in his paper by stating that the paper is attempting to discuss matters closely

connected with the creation of a new economic
mechanism, which would be applied in the country
and in the region. The paper is also trying to
propagate new discoveries in science, to acquaint
its readers with modern technology and organisational methods, which would be relevant to the
development of socio-communal relations in the
region.[6]

This interview with the closest supporter of
the Silesian party secretary, Edward Gierek, could
not have been put alongside Gomulka's photograph
by accident. Nor is the subject matter devoid of
interest. It is a clear attempt to force Gomulka
into changing course or resigning - the Polish
retirement age is often 55 or 60 years - and this
was Gomulka's 65th birthday. Nor is it accidental
that the same issue of Polityka carries data which
shows that the lowest income families in Poland
spend some 62 per cent of their income on food,
while the highest income families spend only 32
per cent. Food and power struggle went hand in
hand in 1970; and food was the decisive factor in
the downfall of Gomulka. But without Gierek's
overt pressure to 'modernise' Poland, Gomulka may
have lasted longer, or other contestants may have
come to power. (Incidentally, Maciej Szczepanski
paid dearly for his support of Gierek; having
become the head of Polish TV and Radio, he was
arrested and tried for corruption after Gierek's
fall - another example of the underlings paying
the price of the leader's policies, while the
leader is left alone).

Gierek's arrival to power may or may not have
been helped by Moscow; certainly there were signs
for some time that the Russians have had enough of
Gomulka and were ready to try out a technocrat who
could turn around the ailing Polish economy, but
the USSR was very careful to avoid

> any impression of overt interference in Polish
> affairs. The new Polish leaders were promptly
> endorsed by Moscow, and in February 1971 the
> Russians even extended credits to help Gierek
> cope with the country's most urgent economic
> problems.[7]

But unlike Gomulka's accession to power, his
was not a triumphant or joyous occasion. Where
Gomulka had inspired enthusiasm in 1956 as a
liberator from Stalinism and a minor resistance

hero, Gierek had made his name as an exponent of the new technology, which he had introduced very successfully in Silesia. The fact is that Poland is not like Silesia; most Poles are not like Silesian miners; and the experience of Silesian economy may even unfit a manager for the management of the Polish economy.

Gierek's second problem was that it was suspected (though never proven) that his accession was engineered by the Russians. The Russians and the party were at this stage disliked more than ever; not since 1956 had there been such a distrust of both bodies. As a result Gierek had 'to cope with the fact that the credibility of the Communist regime had been seriously undermined ... The people, in short, demanded action rather than mere promises, and the new leadership could no longer count on their unlimited patience'.[8] As a result, Gierek had to try harder. His first moves were designed to bring about a broader support and to improve the economic situation of the population. They included the reform of agriculture, industry, education system; the development of a deeper understanding with the Catholic Church; an appeal to Polish patriotism through the reconstruction of the royal castle in Warsaw, and some political concessions to make the parliament more representative.

But courting the intellectuals, the Church and the patriots was not enough. (Not all patriots were courted either; General Moczar, a serious candidate for power yet again, was swiftly purged and his duties taken over by a dull functionary by the name of Stanislaw Kania.) The Poles wanted more food, and more food they got. It is estimated that the USSR provided a loan of 100 million US dollars in convertible currency and arranged for Warsaw to make special use of credit balances at the Comecon Bank. Imports from hard currency countries consisted in the first instance of consumer goods and food; meat in particular was imported in large quantities from the EEC.[9]

The second plank of Gierek's plan was equally predictable: more trade with the West; more imports of capital goods; a bid to industrialise the countryside and to improve the industries in the urban regions. By 1976 the Polish debt is said to have amounted to 10 billion US dollars.[10] The success of such large borrowing, of course, depended on the availability of cheap raw materials and cheap credits. This policy may have succeeded in Poland (and elsewhere in the Eastern European Bloc) had it not been for the events of 1973. While Western observers, like Zauberman, lay blame for their failure on the 'prevalent political philosophy in the area' and on the existing system of planning, i.e. 'the technical potentialities of planning instruments'[11]; the Eastern Europeans (like the Latin Americans in the 1980s) have put the blame fairly and squarely on the burden of rising interest rates, on the high cost of raw materials, and particularly oil; and on the increasing Western protectionism. The truth probably lies somewhere in between: given unlimited cheap credits and sufficient time, even the inept Polish leadership might have produced an economic miracle, while the Czechs would have at least returned to a pre-1968 level. On the other hand, given the best and most up-to-date technical means and personnel, coupled with the incentive of personal profit-making, they might also have become a model mixed-market economy. But in the circumstances, both factors were missing, and the time the leadership had was very limited, like the patience of the population. So in Poland the aftermath of the oil crisis produced several revolts on a scale which was unusual even in this country. In Czechoslovakia the ferment was slower but no less harmful; it led to further alienation of the intellectuals from the state apparatus and to an erosion of party influence among the people. In other countries of the Bloc, the problems were different, but on measuring their intensity, one finds that they were relative to the amount of debt: the higher the debt, the worse the problems. Since the high debt was the direct result of the chance concatenation of a new policy in the Bloc and a new policy of the oil-producing states (unless these were intentionally linked?), we must now stop and, before discussing further crises in Eastern Europe, briefly survey the impact of 1973 on the whole of the Bloc.

3. Effects of the Oil Crisis on Normalisation

In January, 1975 a communique of the Seventieth Session of the Comecon Executive Committee announced that the price of Soviet crude oil would be increased by approximately 30 per cent within the Comecon area. In the weeks that followed, it turned out that the price changes would apply not only to oil, but to other raw materials, agricultural products and industrial goods. In addition, the method of price calculation and the period of price validity have been altered. Up to 1975, the prices of a new five-year period (in this case 1976-1980) were usually valid for the duration of the plan. From 1975 onward, new prices were to remain valid for only twelve months, and the fixed average base year would become a moving average base year; thus allowing the prices to rise as the plan progressed.[12]

A Hungarian announcement in February, 1975, gave more details of how the arrangement would affect Hungary. The Soviet oil price would be 37 roubles per ton, in place of 16 roubles, the prices of imports from the Soviet Union were to go up by 52 per cent, while prices of Hungarian exported machinery and equipment would go up by 15 per cent; light industrial products by 19 per cent and agricultural products by 28 per cent. Further, since Hungary needed more Soviet crude oil in the current year, above its quota of six million tons, the extra oil (amounting to three quarters of a million tons) would have to be purchased with hard currency. However, because Hungary would find it difficult to finance such a large rise in prices and hard currency requirements, the Soviet Union would grant her a ten-year loan on extremely favourable terms; not just in 1975 but in each of the subsequent five years.[13] While Soviet loans would alleviate the situation in the Hungarian case for the time being, it was plain that most of the economic assumptions on which the Comecon FYP was based have become obsolete; and that plans would have to be amended to take account of the new situation. Possibly the most difficult point was that foreign trade prices which used to be stable and which acted as a framework for Comecon plans, were now fluctuating to the point where it would be impossible to plan for any long-term economic decisions with regard to investment, plant and other pressing tasks.

World inflation has thus had the effect of making the East European states even more dependent economically on the Soviet Union than previously. The need for various types of assistance in meeting the increasing cost of Soviet goods, as well as the siphoning off of funds that might have been used on the Western market, has decreased the range of alternatives open to these countries and provided Moscow with a new means of enhancing its control and co-ordination of their policies.[14]

It is quite true that the discussions in Comecon in the years 1973-74 were devoted to the problems of reducing the cost of R & D through integration of scientific research, and making specialisation a necessary task for each of the countries. But the most urgent matter was the improvement in the supply of fuel; both crude oil, gas and coal, and surveying of every area - however unlikely - for more fuel deposits. In the event, the USSR was forced to sell more of its fuel to those Comecon countries which had none, and the resultant problems may well have made it wish to have less influence over the Bloc and not to have to deliver its own precious hard currency oil and gas. Incidentally, the famous gas pipeline to West Germany was first begun as a pipeline to provide fuel-poor Czechoslovakia with essential gas supplies; not, as the Reagan Administration maintained, intended to make the West dependent on Soviet gas.

The severe impact of the increase in fuel prices can be shown in the fact that in some Eastern European countries the rise was not officially discussed. This is said to have been the case in Bulgaria; where, however, low prices for petrol were retained even after 1975, though Bulgaria imports up to 90 per cent of crude oil from the USSR. Still, since Bulgaria's trade had been concentrating on the Soviet Union before the 1973 crisis, (though it was increased to over 50 per cent in 1975) she may have been less affected by the events than other countries. The crisis was very obvious in Czechoslovakia, which had not yet recovered from the effects of the 1968 events. The increases in the price of oil and raw materials coming on top of 'normalisation' overshadowed almost all the other economic debates. The shortfall in oil was reported immediately in the winter of 1974-75, when heating

oil was in short supply; some industrial plants
were being switched to a double-fuel system to
allow the use of gas as well as oil, and
consumption of oil-related products was limited.
Here too, any consumption over the quota would
have to be paid for in hard currency, though all
of Czechoslovakia's oil was bought from the Soviet
Union. Another difficulty which was highlighted
by the oil crisis was the previous problem of
manpower and inefficiency. Since the need to
economise and improve efficiency was more urgent,
the problem assumed urgent and serious dimensions.
    To compensate for the losses suffered through
the debacle of the 1968 measures, the Czech
government began to make strenuous efforts to set
up a new network of foreign economic contacts.
Between 1973 and 1975 contacts were initiated with
Yugoslavia culminating in two important visits in
February, 1975, by Czech leaders to that country.
In the same period, relations with West Germany
were renewed. In January, 1975, a treaty of
long-term co-operation was signed, which set up a
series of economic, industrial and technological
ventures between the two countries. This was done
despite the fact that Czechoslovakia had a trade
deficit with West Germany and the foreign trade
minister, Barcak, complained that discriminatory
measures were used by the West Germans. The
agreement was all the more important since after
it was signed, the EEC took over the
responsibility for concluding all ordinary trade
agreements of its members states. Similar
attempts were made to develop links with France,
again with some trade and diplomatic gains.
However, none of these measures seem to have been
capable of compensating Czechoslovakia for the
losses suffered through the fuel crisis.[15]
    The political effects of this standstill were
to be seen in the formation of a new protest
movement, the Charter 77 movement, later on in the
decade. On a national basis, the country suffered
through the split in relations between the Czechs
and the Slovaks, which was accentuated by the new
federal system. Both will be discussed later on
in this work. But the problem which caused most
difficulty in the mid-1970s was the economic
stagnation, a stagnation which was apparent, even
though the statistics seemed buoyant. One analyst
suggests that despite very high investment in
industry (35.6 per cent of the GNP in 1973), the

GNP did not rise in relation to such investment:

> given an investment share falling somewhere between 35 and 40 per cent of the GNP, one is entitled to expect a rate of growth of the GNP about three times higher than the one actually achieved. This presents a puzzle which seems to be greatly disturbing Czechoslovak officials as well ... Minister of Finance ... writes: "we must give an answer to the question why, given a rate of investment exceeding 30 per cent, which is one of the highest, there exists a continued hunger for new investments".[16]

Holesovsky's view is that the basic method of financing the investment - through taxation - is not very conducive to making rational decisions on investment and implementation. Further, there is a lack of skilled labour once the investment is implemented. He quotes the fact that in 1976 investments in industry alone were so large as to produce 13,000 new vacancies and 200,000 unfilled vacancies created by 'attrition' in older capacities.

The overall picture of Czechoslovak economy is one of a slow and steady decline in economic efficiency throughout the 1970s, accelerating towards the end of the decade. 'With the symptoms of crisis, not explosive but persistent like a toothache, we have been witnessing the reappearance of statements, analyses and recommendations which marked the economic debate after 1964 ... However, the discussion, if it deserves that name, is muted. It lacks the free-wheeling nerve and the brio of its predecessor.'[17] The would-be reformers look wistfully towards Hungary but do not even dare to mention this name. The author concludes that even in a well-ordered and technologically advanced country like Czechoslovakia, there are two, mutually antagonistic trends in economic functions: on the one hand, the scientific planners draw up very good plans, with the latest instruments; on the other, the implementation is done in a completely different manner, on a day-to-day basis by managers only interested in fulfilling their quotas, and worried by shortages and breakdowns. Hence, the difference between the investment and real growth is explained by poor implementation which is no fault of anyone in particular, but the fault of an essential split within the system. This will be seen even more clearly in the matter of an economy which is much more badly managed than that of Czechoslovakia: the Polish economy.

The Polish problem was much more serious and more difficult to treat than the Czech problem, and that, despite the fact that Poland did have large supplies of fuel; the coal mines in Silesia. It was also essentially different from the problems experienced by Hungary and Bulgaria. The main reason was that unlike the other countries, Poland had been in a state of relative turmoil throughout the period, while Bulgaria did not experience any revolutions, Hungary had one only in 1956, and Czechoslovakia had one major shake-up in 1968. In contrast, Poland had had changes in leadership in 1956, an upheaval in 1968, change of leadership in 1970-71 and a continuing series of disorders in 1976, finally culminating in a series of leadership changes in the 1980-82 period. Lack of political stability gave rise to the belief that Poland's main problem was bad government. In fact, a close analysis will show that each upheaval and change of leadership was caused by an increasingly deteriorating economic condition. One must come to the conclusion that the Polish case is one of economic difficulties, rather than political discontent; though, naturally, the former leads to the latter.

A closer look at the deteriorating economic situation is necessary. Here is what a serious Western analyst has to say about the decade:

In the second half of the 1970s Poland experienced a serious deterioration in economic performance, in spite of the massive accumulation of capital and the large scale import of Western technology and machinery undertaken under Gierek's leadership, especially in the first half of the decade. In particular: ... the growth rate of income produced ... declined steadily from an average 9 per cent per annum in 1970-75 to 6.8 per cent in 1976, 5 per cent in 1977 and 3 per cent in 1978; early income statistics indicated a negative growth rate of -1.9 per cent ... but have now been revised downwards to -2.3 per cent ... negative growth was unprecedented in post-war Poland, indeed throughout Eastern Europe with the exception of Czechoslovakia in 1963. ... The decline in national income distributed ... is even sharper ... while up to 1976 income distributed grew faster than income produced, in subsequent years - primarily due to the burden of repayment of debt incurred in earlier years - income distributed grew more slowly than income produced. ... Part of the decline in performance is due to a fall in agricultural output and adverse natural conditions (particularly in 1975, 1976 and 1980) but an equally significant steady decline can be observed in industrial production, from an average of over 10 per cent in 1971-75 to 8.3 in 1976, 6.3 in 1977, 3.6 in 1978, a modest 1.9 increase in 1979, which picked up in the first half of 1980 but ended with -1.2 per cent by the end of the year. ... The growth of labour productivity had declined since 1976 and actually became negative in 1979-80; the productivity of fixed capital started to grow more slowly from 1973 and steadily fell from 1975 onwards. Continued trade deficits, especially with Western countries ... led to mounting hard currency indebtedness. In 1971 net external debt amounted to $1.2 billion, matched by central bank reserves estimated at $1 billion. By 1979 external debt (excluding short-term loans) had risen to $20.5 billion ... taking first place among Comecon countries. ... A more than fivefold increase in imports from the West was matched by a less than fourfold increase in exports, leading to consistently negative balances from 1972 onwards; the burden of debt service (amortisation and interest) grew by 20 times over the decade, absorbing an increasing share of export earnings, from 12.4 per cent in 1971 to 75 per cent in 1979 and 81.8 per cent in 1980.'[18]

This bad state of affairs was underestimated, according to Nuti, who states that the increasing use of short-term debt, the increasing cost of debt-servicing, the undisclosed amount owed to the Soviet Union and other East European countries, brought the total amount to just under $27 billion

in 1980 and absorbed all export earnings, against
the IMF practice of allowing a maximum of 40 per
cent debt service ratio, as the manageable limit.
Inflation rose dramatically, from -1.2 in 1971 to
8.5 in 1980, while the relative stability of food
prices (stemming from fear of a popular protest)
demanded large and rising subsidies from the state
budget. The situation was further complicated by
shortages of consumer goods which indicated a
flight from domestic currency, and the consequent
shortages of materials and semi-finished products
for industrial enterprises; these were exacerbated
by the increased import of machinery and the
rising dependence on Western intermediate
products, which followed Gierek's policy of
technology transfer from the West.

This economist does not believe that Gierek
was to blame for all of the problems associated
with the Polish economy in the 1970s. Some
factors were inevitable; agricultural production
suffered because of particularly bad weather
conditions, which were even described as the seven
biblical years of poor harvest; but this had to be
added to years of lack of investment in
agriculture and transport, loss of manpower and
bad food pricing policy.[19] Nuti maintains that
international factors played a major role in
Poland's economic crises; because, despite being a
major fuel producer and exporter, the industrial
growth policies left her unprepared for the oil
crisis, world recession, inflation and rising
interest rates. The crisis was much worse because
the managers were not yet used to the import-led
growth policy, after what had been a de facto
autarkic policy practised by Gomulka and the
Stalinist leadership before him. The oil crisis
started just as Gierek's policy began to develop
fully. In addition, Nuti maintains that the
programme was both over-ambitious, badly planned
and badly executed; thus, while in principle, it
could have worked, in practice the general
incompetence, negligence and corruption of
individual managers combined with the
disillusionment of the population at large, made
it unworkable.[20] All these troubles gave rise
to a political crisis, which, in turn, led to a
complete collapse of the economy in 1980.

While Poland was grinding to a halt, other
Eastern European economies were experiencing some
difficulties, but on a different scale. It has

already been seen that the more isolated, or autarkic the economy was (like Bulgaria's or Poland's before Gierek), the more chance it had to survive. In this respect, one country is the odd man out of Eastern Europe. This is Romania. Romania's case is all the stranger because it seems to have accumulated all the undesirable features which are said to have made Poland unmanageable: it has a highly centralised economy; strengthened by an administrative reorganisation in the period of 1973-78, which concentrated economic power in the hands of a small group of individuals; it is governed by one man and what amounts to his 'family', albeit an extended family; it has been involved in a strategy of 'import-led growth' since 1967, when other Eastern European countries were still well behind in borrowing foreign capital; and, above all, it has a problem of corruption, against which measures are taken at all times. Further, Romania, again like Poland and Czechoslovakia, has expanded its industries at the expense of its agriculture (a traditional Romanian source of export); like Poland, she has been at odds with the Soviet policies, not only on economic integration, but also in the sphere of foreign relations.[21]

There were some differences, though, in the way in which Romania tackled her problems. These seem to be bound in a strange manner with the fact that the country is run by one man, with as little delegation as possible. Instead of this being a drawback, as it would be in Poland or Czechoslovakia, it seems actually to provide more concensus (or resignation?) in Romania. The second advantage Romania had was connected with the former: despite excess demand for consumer goods, Romania did not import large quantities of these from hard-currency countries like Poland did. Ceausescu's strong position enabled him to tell the people to cut down on their demand, rather than having to satisfy it, as the Polish leadership was forced to do. The third advantage was the fact that Romania used to be a net oil exporter till 1977, and she avoided the first phase of the oil crisis:

As a net oil exporter Romania did not suffer from the immediate macroeconomic problems resulting from the price rise, and

74

consequently tended to isolate herself from the general problem of relative price changes. In the sixth five-year plan Romania still concentrated investment in energy-intensive industries, the result of which was to increase domestic demand for oil at the time domestic supply was falling, so that finally Romania became a net oil importer. Simultaneously Romania responded to natural disasters and diminished domestic resource availability not by cutting back plans, but by pursuing taut planning policies, as a result of which macroeconomic problems started to bite.[22]

Following the decision to import raw materials including crude oil from hard-currency countries, in defiance of CMEA policy, Romania had by 1980 a large deficit in trade in fuel and raw materials and the trade surplus with Third World countries till 1977, became a large deficit. As a result, Smith concludes that Romania is facing far larger problems than those faced by other Eastern European countries except Poland, and is, in the 1980s, confronted by a crisis. However, it must be admitted that this is not reflected in her status as a borrower. Romania is a member of the World Bank and the IMF, and has had few problems about obtaining extra loans, despite her estimated indebtedness which is on par (on a per capita basis) with that of Poland.

One must ask, therefore, what it is that makes Romania the favoured Eastern European country in the eyes of Western bankers, while Poland has been the subject of strictures, refusal of loans, rejection of proposed membership by the World Bank and IMF, and the subject of an economic boycott by the USA, which has led not only to an industrial standstill, but also to the ruin of farmers and widespread hunger among the people in the period of 1981-83. It is not top-of-the league in opposing Soviet policies; that place has always been occupied by Poland. It is not the most democratic country in the Bloc; this place is probably best attributed to Hungary. It is not the least corrupt, most productive or most efficient country. This is East Germany. The only conclusion one can reach is that the reasons for supporting Romania are political; and that the support suits not only the West (which has little to gain in practical terms, except Romania's participation in Los Angeles Olympics), but also the USSR. Romania has become the broker in East-West relations, particularly in Middle Eastern politics, and in banking diplomacy. In a way which may have been quite unintentional, she may also have become a test-case of the viability of a highly centralised economy. If the centralisation works in Romania, against virtually all odds, then why should it not work elsewhere as well? Hence, Romania's case is much more important and interesting than that of Bulgaria, and may yet demonstrate some dramatic developments. The _rapprochement_ between the Romanian rulers and the USSR just before the CMEA summit in June, 1984, may be significant, but so far, does not seem to have produced any new developments.

East Germany is one of the countries on which the development of the socialist economy must hinge. A highly industrialised, and well-disciplined country, which has had the advantage both of large Soviet and Western material help, one, moreover, which lies at the heart of East-West disagreements since the Second World War (for despite protestations, the West - or to be more precise, the US, cares little for the Eastern part of Europe, except in election years), it is of crucial importance to both the East and the West. It is perhaps hardly surprising that the assessment of the GDR ranges from the ecstatic to the most pessimistic. It is hard to distinguish fact from fiction, but certain statistics do help. East Germany had been listed among the top ten nations of the world in terms of gross national product by the end of the 1960s and had become the economic pace-setter within the CMEA. Industrial production _per capita_ clearly surpasses that of the other socialist countries, taking over the leading role of the CSSR. By mid-1970s _per capita_ national income exceeded that of the United Kingdom and New Zealand. In 1965, a Unesco study ranked the GDR's child-care facilities as the best in the world. East German education and health facilities are also comprehensive and generally accepted to be excellent. On the other hand, the housing shortage remained a problem and it is only hoped to overcome it in 1990. So is the shortage of consumer goods; cars, electronic equipment and luxury goods are either in short supply, or only to be bought for hard currency.[23]

Because of its intensive industrial growth and shortage of raw materials and fuel, the GDR suffered considerably as a result of the oil crisis. Already in deficit in its trade with the Western industrialised countries in 1973, the GDR was hit by the rise in oil prices immediately, and has only succeded once, in 1978 in increasing the value of exports more than that of imports. It has therefore developed a considerable deficit with Western countries and the USSR. In addition, the GDR is faced by the following problems: its work-force cannot be increased in the 1980s and its age structure shows that with the retirement of a large proportion of those now working, the work-force will rapidly decrease. Secondly, it is a high user of raw materials and fuel, in relation to the consumption in industrialised countries. Thirdly, its main difficulty is to increase its volume of exports to the West, in order to lower its indebtedness. And fourthly, the work-force must become more productive, in order to compensate for the high cost of imported fuel and raw materials.[24]

The difficulties of facing this situation were summed up by the Secretary General of the party, Honecker, in December, 1979 when he stated that 'we are not only facing an aggravation of the situation, which is complex anyway. We are faced with a new situation'.[25] The theme of difficulties is taken up by another analyst, who stresses that the work-force shortages will continue, particularly as a result of many women working part time and retiring five years earlier than men. The employment ratio in late 1970s was 99.7 per cent for men and 87.6 per cent for women. In the 1980s twice as many women as men will become eligible for pensions; this will mean that many more men will enter the working force; that there will be a surplus of men by 1990, and that after 1990 the population will stabilise and then decline. The second difficulty is that a decrease in unskilled and semi-skilled workers is expected. By 1990, eight per cent of all the employed are expected to hold university degrees; twelve per cent diplomas from technical institutions and 60 per cent trade school certificates, compared with the figures for 1980 of: six per cent, ten per cent and 58 per cent

respectively.[26] The remedies to be tried range
from reducing the stress on growth to shortening
the working week. At the Eleventh Conference of
the CC. it was pointed out that some people within
the political leadership think that 'the less
economic growth there is, the better this is for
the national economy'.[27] There is also a
concerted effort to increase the productivity of
individual workers, by raising wages, improving
bonuses and keeping prices of goods steady. If
there seems to be some contradiction in the above
outlined aims, it may well be that there are other,
less well aired, aims behind this expression of new
ideas. The fact is that the East German leadership
is proud of its achievement in being the flagship
of the Bloc; and may also be considering the future
of a united Germany. In this context, keeping the
population satisfied and the country's economy in
good shape, even in difficult global conditions,
may be an index of wanting to demonstrate abroad
that a socialist economy can be efficient, humane,
concerned and economically and ecologically sound.
It is also worth showing that the population has a
steady growth - a case not at present demonstrated
- in comparison with the falling birth-rate of West
Germany. The reduction in working hours may be an
attempt to make more women work full-time and yet
bring up larger families. The stress on lower, but
more efficient and ecologically approved, growth
may well be the answer to the pollution prevalent
in the 'free market' areas of West Germany, where
little or no attention is paid to air or water
pollution in relation to market forces. The rise
in wages and decrease in the working week at a time
when West German industrialists are talking of
cutting the wages of those workers who are still in
employment and are refusing to cut the working week
(as witness the Metal Workers' Union's strike in
the summer of 1984) is a demonstration that
socialist economy is less buffeted by the winds of
the free market and that planning for the future
can pay off. Naturally, one cannot safeguard
against every possible future eventuality, but
within its narrow parameters, the East German
leadership is doing all it can to provide a
demonstration - or, if one prefers the phrase, 'a
propaganda coup' - of the superiority of planned
economy.
    This brief survey of the economic state of the
Bloc countries in the 1970s and their prospects

for the 1980s may have provided some useful
comparisons. It can be seen from this that the
world oil crisis and subsequent depression have
affected them all, and that most have had to make
sacrifices, which occurred just as the standard of
living was steadily rising. It also showed that
foreign credits, while useful during the boom,
proved to be fatal during the depression, or at
least fatal in one case, which has had a near
revolution as a result of the curtailment of
credits. Nevertheless, countries which borrowed
little or which had retained the confidence of
Western bankers, have come through the recession
in better shape than others. The survey did not
demonstrate that socialist economies cannot be as
efficient or more efficient than free or mixed
market economies; on the other hand, it did not
produce any evidence to the contrary. This seems
to indicate that efficiency is an index of good
management and foresight as much as of the
economic system - with some luck thrown in.

In order to get a picture of how badly the
economies of these countries were affected,
compared with the 'free market' economies, one
would have to survey the Western and Third World
economies. This is not the purpose of this
chapter. However, even a glance at the British,
French and West German economies will show that
deepening unemployment, falling standard of living
and de-industrialisation have affected them all,
bringing in their wake industrial and social
unrest and a wave of crime, delinquency and drug
abuse. On the other hand, the Eastern European
economies have experienced a falling standard of
living and, in some cases, industrial unrest, but
industrialisation (with the exception of Poland,
which is a special case) has proceeded, though at
a slower pace than before. There does not seem to
be any comparison with the Third World countries
which can be carried out, even though some Eastern
European countries (such as Bulgaria) used to be
classed as so undeveloped as to virtually belong
to the Third World. However, the case of
agriculture in all the Bloc countries is a
different proposition. There, stagnation and low
productivity have plagued most of them. But this
has less to do with socialist economy, (indeed,
the most stagnant of them all is Polish
agriculture, which is mainly in private hands),
than with low capitalisation of agriculture and

with the loss of young workers to industry.

If any lessons are to be learned from the above, it may be this: in the first instance, the leaderships which undertake over-ambitious tasks will usually find themselves in trouble; either vis-a-vis their populations or foreign bankers, or, in the worst case, with both. Secondly, that it is probably better to base one's main efforts on the traditional product (be it agricultural, raw materials or manufactured goods) which has been accepted by the work-force for generations, than to go for a highly desirable new product which it is impossible to produce in the circumstances. The third lesson must be that planning has its place, but that planning cannot (and has never been intended to) take account of every probability. To take but one dramatic example: has anyone foreseen in any planning models the earthquake which shook Romania in the 1970s? Similarly, has any planning model foreseen the quadrupling of oil prices? Fourthly, it does not pay to neglect agriculture, even in a country which is only partly agricultural like East Germany. That is not to say that one has to invest enormous sums of money in order to build food mountains, as the EEC has done; it merely means that agriculture should be well looked after, provided with enough capital to be supplied with machinery and fertilisers, and, most importantly, in the case of Eastern Europe, that labour should not be siphoned off to industries. The correct balance between agriculture and industrial development is one of the factors which Eastern European leaderships (probably spurred on by the Soviet model) have consistently neglected, and they have found this out at their peril. The loss of hard currency for grain and cattle fodder has been a constant and worrying drain of capital on the economies; one which could have been avoided with proper foresight and planning; or at least the need for which would not have been so urgent had proper measures been taken in time.

The last lesson is perhaps best expressed through the opinions of a well-known economist, who stated as early as 1978 that:

> East European authorities have envisioned in trade with the industrialized West possibly much greater benefits than those foreseen in the traditional view of foreign trade as a

means of obtaining essential producer goods simply to achieve plan targets. In the first place, East Europe's leaders have looked upon sales in Western markets as a means of gaining convertible currency, which, in turn, it was hoped, would widen the area of manoeuvre. This hope would appear to have dimmed in the late 1970s as members of the family reconcile themselves to the fact that the aim of multilaterality in trade - without supranational planning - is unachievable. Secondly, trade with the West has been viewed as an opportunity for the East European economies to increase their short-term supplies of capital-forming goods by means of long- and medium-term credits. In fact, by the end of 1975 the net indebtedness of the six East European countries in convertible currency amounted, according to Western estimates, to nearly $20 billion ... Finally, trade with the West has been seen as a very major vehicle for acquisition of new technology ... On the Western side, the recession and unexpectedly slow recovery of the 1970s have stimulated a search for export markets in Eastern Europe, whose economies enjoy a solid reputation for having absorptive markets and being dependable in the repayment of credits. At least in this respect, the non-cyclical economies of the East have been the beneficiaries of the cycle which affected the Western trading nations.[28]

The wisdom of hindsight would make one add a rider: Western institutions would have done better and the world would be in less danger of a global banking collapse, had they adhered to lending to the Eastern Bloc, instead of lending many times over to the Latin American countries. The debt of Eastern European countries in the late 1970s and early 1980s pales into insignificance compared to the Latin American debt. Moreover, the Eastern European governments are servicing their debts and have not so far (mid-1984) declared a moratorium on servicing, unlike the Latin American governments. Political consideration aside - and they will be discussed in the next chapter - on analysis, one wonders who has suffered more in the recession; its makers, the 'free world' or its unwilling recipients - the Socialist Bloc.

CHAPTER THREE: FOOTNOTES

1. Edward Taborsky: Czechoslovakia: The Return
    to 'Normalcy'; Problems of Communism,
    November-December, 1970, p. 33.
2. Galia Golan: The Road to Reform; Problems of
    Communism, May-June, 1971, p. 19.
3. Taborsky: Czechoslovakia, p. 37-38.
4. Golan: The Road to Reform, p. 21.
5. At the Eighth Plenum of the PUWP - CC, Trybuna
    Ludu, 8 February, 1971; also see: Ross
    Johnson: Polish Perspectives, p. 60.
6. W Poblizu Miliona, Polityka, 7 February 1970,
    p. 1 and 6.
7. Adam Bromke: A New Political Style; Problems
    of Communism, September-October, 1972, p. 2.
8. Bromke: A New Political Style, p. 2.
9. Michael Gamarnikow: A New Economic Approach;
    Problems of Communism, September-October,
    1972, p. 23.
10. According to Zauberman: The East European
    Economies, p. 68 and note 46.
11. The East European Economies, p. 69.
12. RFE Research; Background Report/73.
13. Nepszabadsag, 23 February 1975; quoted in RFE
    Research/73.
14. RFE Research/73.
15. RFE Research/73.
16. Vaclav Holesovsky: Czechoslovakia: Economic
    Reforms; NATO Colloquium 1980, p. 64.
    Emphasis in text.
17. Holesovsky: Czechoslovakia, p. 65.
18. D.M. Nuti: The Polish Crisis: Economic
    Factors and Constraints; Jan Drewnowski (ed)
    Crisis in the East European Economy, p. 19-21.
19. For a detailed examination of the agricultural
    situation up to 1970, see O.A. Narkiewicz:
    The Green Flag, Chapter 11, and A. Korbonski:
    Politics of Socialist Agriculture in Poland,
    1945-1960.
20. See: Nuti: The Polish Crisis, p. 28-35.
21. For a detailed statement of Romania's economic
    problems, see: Alan H. Smith: Romanian
    Economic Reforms; NATO Colloquium 1980, p.
    35-37. The statements about problems of
    'probity' are made in text, specific measures
    are mentioned in notes.

22. Alan Smith: <u>Is there a Romanian Economic Crisis?</u> p. 110.
23. See: Jurgen Tampke: <u>The People's Republics of Eastern Europe</u>, Chapter 5.
24. Doris Cornelsen: <u>GDR: Industrial Reform; NATO Colloquium 1980,</u> p. 73-74.
25. Report to the Politbureau; quoted by Cornelsen: <u>GDR</u>, p.73.
26. Herwig E. Haase: <u>GDR: Prospects for the 1980s; NATO Colloquium 1980,</u> p. 165-169.
27. Haase: <u>GDR</u>, p.165, emphasis added.
28. Zauberman: <u>The East European Economies,</u> p. 68.

POLITICAL CHANGE AND THE LEADERSHIP

---

1. The Growth of Dissent in Eastern Europe

The Czechoslovak leadership which succeeded Dubcek
and the reformers had to deal with problems of
various kinds, many of which were structural,
others - the result of the hasty reform and the
even more speedy overthrow of the reform. But
their biggest problems were concerned with their
relationships within the Bloc. It has been seen
in an earlier chapter that the relationships with
non-Bloc countries were taken up on a small scale
in the early 1970s, and that they produced a slow,
but relatively steady recovery and a degree of
acceptance of the Husak government among Western
Europeans at any rate. This was strengthened when
it became clear that purges on the old scale were
not envisaged and when some liberalising measures
were introduced; such as the introduction of a
federal structure of the Czech and Slovak nations.
    However, the situation was much more difficult
vis-a-vis the Eastern European Bloc. Not only did
the Czechs refuse to forget that they had had
their reforms blocked by an invasion of the Warsaw
Pact countries in August, 1968; they now also had
to rely on the very same countries for economic
help. It is debatable whether the reforms would
have accomplished the goal of prosperity and
democracy, unless large amounts of foreign loans
were poured into Czechoslovakia. It had already
been pointed out that many of the reforms were on
the verge of collapse even before the invasion,
and that only the invasion saved their
reputation. But the post-invasion chaos, the
changes in the apparatus, the industrial go-slow,
had deteriorated the Czech economy even more; and

help was urgently needed. Help could only come from the USSR, and perhaps to a lesser extent from East Germany; the problem was that the traditional Czech dislike of the Germans was now reinforced by a new and perhaps unexpected dislike of the Russians. The additional problem was the suspicion among the Czechs about the government's motives. Since there was no doubt that somebody had kept the Russians informed about the reformers' plans, and that somebody had helped the Warsaw Pact troops to land and cross the borders, the government, so obviously in the USSR's good books, was the prime suspect; particularly as several hardline ministers were included in it; even if Husak himself escaped part of the blame. The people also blamed themselves for 'behaving like Czechs' as the Poles liked to put it; i.e. putting up passive resistance instead of taking up arms.

A combination of those factors was bad for the morale of the nation; not very good for the government and somewhat ominous for the future. However, the Czechs are nothing if not realistic, and the pressing needs of the present made them push the past into some kind of limbo, if not forgetfulness. In the late summer of 1969, Husak, who had been the First Secretary of the CPCS since April 1969, finally beat his breast in repentance and admitted that the reform was un-Marxist and incorrect. In October, 1969, a joint Soviet-Czechoslovak Declaration was signed, which all but thanked the Soviet Union for the invasion. And in May, 1970, a Soviet-Czechoslovak Treaty of Friendship, Co-operation and Mutual Assistance was concluded, which solemnised the relief aid which the Russians have been sending the country unofficially since the invasion. In view of the go-slow and the administrative and transport dislocation, massive supplies were needed simply to keep the basic services going and the basic foodstuffs reaching the people.[1]

The policy of giving small concessions and improving the standard of living, while simultaneously stifling intellectual dissent worked for a time. This was particularly so, because the general opinion was that the reforms helped the intellectuals rather than the 'people' and there was little grief for those intellectuals, (many of whom very able people) who had emigrated abroad or who had been deprived of their lucrative posts. Just how much support the reforms had among the ordinary people is difficult to say. According to surveys, the majority of the people would have voted for the Communist Party in the middle of 1968, but these replies could mirror the natural caution of the Czechs. Also, there was some conviction that the reformers had gone too far: the invitations to Western 'cold warriors', the coquetting with the 'free market' and the wish to leave the Warsaw Pact made many people uneasy. The public opinion polls show that the people felt that though they had something to gain from the reforms, they were really the intellectuals' plaything. It may be that Dubcek never used his Rolls-Royce equipped with a refrigerated bar and television; but it was Husak who returned it to the manufacturers in Britain.[2]

At any rate, for a few years everybody kept a low profile and made good the ravages of 1968-69. The first occasion for demonstrating dissent was given by the Helsinki Agreement in 1975. In 1977, some 250 signatories (all of them intellectuals) signed a document which became known as Charter 77, calling on the Czech government to implement the human rights part of the Helsinki Act. This was further intensified by an appeal from eleven former members of the Central Committee to Western European Communist parties for help in ensuring that the Czechoslovak authorities would act in accordance with the Helsinki Act.[3] But the Chartists did not form a committee as such, and did not formulate a political programme in earnest. This may have been because there were so few intellectuals left to protest in Czechoslovakia (many Western European and American chairs were filled with the emigre professors), or it may have been because of the fact that:

> In Prague, there was an unpopular government, but one that felt itself rather more firmly "in the saddle" than did that of Poland's Edward Gierek. This sense of security was due to Soviet support, political resignation on the part of the populace, and a different set of economic facts. "Consumerism" has flourished in Czechoslovakia, sweetening the bitter pill of "normalization". Thus, there was unfertile ground for the seeds of protest, and by all indications, mass response to the chartists has hardly been overwhelming. To be

sure, the number of signatories grew rapidly
from the initial 250 or so (by mid-1978, to
more than 1,000 signatories), and at each
phase those identifying themselves as workers
grew as well. But the total of the latter
never reached the point where it was more than
a modest minority of all signers. Moreover,
some portion of the "worker" signatories were
former students or former members of the
intelligentsia - precipitated by political
reprisal into the working class - rather than
"authentic" proletarians.[4]

It has been the opinion of many Western
analysts that the Czech 'chartists' lacked broad
issues to coalesce their protest. Unlike in the
case of Poland, they could not find any
significant mass base willing to offer support.
Conscious of their isolation, the government tried
six Charter 77 activists in 1979, and in October,
five of them were sentenced to a total of nineteen
and a half years imprisonment.[5] To be a
dissenter in Czechoslovakia after 1970 needs a
great deal of commitment, and a cause; the most
successful of the dissenters were either prominent
writers, who felt that they were being censored,
or religious individuals (particularly Catholics)
who felt they or their children were being
discriminated against because of their belief.
This last issue is a very particularist one in
Czechoslovakia, (unlike Poland) and the former one
is particularist anywhere in the world. Hence, it
must be considered that the Czech dissent is a
particularist cause, and that it would take an
economic upheaval of the Polish proportions, or
larger, to make it into a major issue.

2. Political Opposition Builds Up

The coming to power of Gierek in 1970 gave
rise to a new wave of prosperity in Poland, based
on ample and cheap foreign credits. The 1970
events showed the essential dichotomy in the
Polish society; as in 1968 the workers did not
come to the aid of the intellectuals, so in 1970
the intellectuals left the workers to wage their
struggle alone. The 'pacification' of the
rebellious workers in 1971-72 was quite

successful. A range of methods was used to repress the workers' leaders; starting with dismissals, through transfer of ringleaders to other work places and ending with stressing the hooligan element of the riots.[6] The 1973 oil crisis brought about a deteriorating economic condition in Poland which made the party recast its policy.[7] The party launched an ideological offensive because of economic success in 1972 and stopped it because of lack of economic success in 1974; this is the view expressed by Bromke. But, in fact, the problems did not surface fully until after the reform of the local administration misfired badly. At any rate, the statement that

> despite signs of rapidly deteriorating economic conditions, the party proposed amendments to the Polish Constitution that would bring the document closer to the Soviet model. These proposed changes were regarded by the opposition as a violation of the implicit compact between it and the government. The result was a deluge of formal protests, signed by some 40,000 people in all, including many intellectuals. The Catholic Episcopate and Cardinal Wyszynski personally threw their great authority behind the opposition. Under popular pressure the party modified the most controversial constitutional amendments, but the harm to the Communist regime had already been done,

does not even begin to explore the situation.[8]

As in Czechoslovakia, so in Poland, the Helsinki Accords encouraged the Poles to increase their opposition to the government. Again, to quote Bromke:

> To begin with, the opposition became emboldened by the improvement in East-West relations and by the example of Soviet dissidents' use of _detente_ as a protective umbrella for their activities. In the eyes of many Poles, the Final Act of the 1975 Helsinki Conference on Security and Co-operation in Europe reduced the chances that the USSR would intervene in their country as it had in Czechoslovakia in 1968. The Carter Administration's early pronouncement about human rights heartened them as well.[9]

In fact, as the Jachniak-Ganguly essay on
local government reform proves, the country was in
a state of administrative chaos by 1975, because
of the reform, and hence it was easy to set up any
number of dissenting movements. The anarchic
situation analysis is confirmed by a
constitutional expert who states explicitly:

> The unreformed system of political and
> economic decision-making was unable to cope.
> The absence of either Stalinist or socialist
> market disciplines meant that more problems
> were created than were solved. Gierek's
> system was neither strong enough to impose its
> will in many areas, nor decentralised enough
> to allow enterprises... to take their own
> local decisions. The burying of a real reform
> programme by 1973 was therefore paralleled by
> Gierek's efforts to strengthen the
> administrative and economic machines to enable
> them to face up to the coming social storm.[10]

What is clear is that Gierek had neither the
cadres nor the time (nor, perhaps, sufficient
experience) to reform the whole system, after
years of maladministration and tinkering. That is
why he was attempting the impossible, and that is
why the opposition grew stronger, possibly
emboldened by some signs from abroad that, while
the USA had overlooked the invasion of
Czechoslovakia, a similar invasion of Poland would
not be tolerated. The advent of a Pole into the
high reaches of the Carter Administration in 1976
may have strengthened this belief. These events
pose a query: since the disturbances both in
Czechoslovakia and in Poland were caused by a
deterioration in the economic situation, why did
not the Soviet leadership act in time to help the
Polish economy as it had done in Czechoslovakia in
1968? It would have made more sense to provide
help before rather than after the disorders.
There may be several reasons for this. The most
likely one is that the Gierek leadership had
deliberately kept the Soviet leadership ignorant
of the real state of affairs, for fear of being
deposed, or at least having to make changes in the
economic and political course. The second reason
may have been that by then Brezhnev's
administration was already suffering from the

famous 'immobilisme' which made all decisions difficult. The third reason may have been that the Soviet Union was at this stage in serious difficulties itself, trying to solve the problems caused by the oil crisis, and that it was simply unable to provide generous aid to Poland, on top of the generous aid it was already providing to all the East European Bloc in the shape of cheap oil and other raw materials. This is not to say that the Polish disturbances could have been completely avoided had help been forthcoming earlier, but it does mean that the intellectuals may have had to carry out the protests without the participation - and later on, the leadership - of the workers.

The 1976 food riots were the upshot of the economic crisis, as a result of which the government suddenly increased food prices for basic foodstuffs on 24 June. On 25 June there were violent riots in several centres; on 26 June, the government swiftly withdrew the price rises.[11] The brutal repression of the workers which followed in the wake of the government's capitulation drew widespread protest; this time from the intellectuals. In July 1976, Jerzy Andrzejewski, a prominent writer, praised the workers as fighters for true socialist democracy, and promised to help them. In consequence, a Committee for the Defence of the Workers (KOR) was formed on 27 September 1976. The original fourteen members comprised very old pre-war academics and political leaders; middle-aged resistance movement participants and the largest group consisted of the ex-1968 student protesters - among the best known of whom were Jacek Kuron and Adam Michnik.[12] KOR was composed of people who were either Marxists, or ex-Marxists, or liberal Social Catholics; hence, its approach was left wing. Another organisation, formed in March 1977, was rather different. It comprised members of the former Christian Democratic Party and newer crypto-CD groups which succeeded the CD. Christian Democracy never had a strong following in Poland,[13] and the government was doubtless less worried by this than by KOR. It is also problematic whether the government was over-worried by another organisation which was formed in the autumn of 1977; the anti-abortion Polish Committee for the Defence of Life and Family, which according to Bromke soon took on the tinge of National Democratic pre-war politics; the Polish Communists always welcomed diversions in the form of anti-semitism to validate their own policies. On the other hand, the student SKS, a new solidarity committee (Studencki Komitet Solidarnosci) founded in Krakow in May 1977, may and should have been more worrying, particularly since it soon claimed an organisation in each university in the country and one of its papers bore the title of 'Bratniak', highly reminiscent of the extremely right-wing student fraternity organisations of the pre-war period. All these organisations - and many others, which are not mentioned here for lack of space - claimed widespread membership, issued their newsheets, often in samizdat forms, and are said to have sprung up spontaneously and to have increased their following as a result of government persecution.

The question of the government's strength of purpose must be queried here; did the government really try to wipe them out, or was it rather hoping that their very number and opposing aims would make them fight each other and forget their main enemy, the Communist party? Or, even more deviously, did Gierek hold this Polish revolutionary movement as a trump card in his desperate attempt to force some concessions either from the USSR or from the Western banks? Each hypothesis is possible, and it is even possible that all of them were correct. At any rate, as one author says:

> The period between 1976-80 was characterised by the unparalleled growth of a plethora of dissident groups in Poland. Their real aims and significance and their degree of popular support are difficult to assess, but they can, in retrospect, be seen as having incubated a wide variety of the forces of contestation which emerged in Summer 1980. The authorities played a cat and mouse game in harassing the dissident leaders, but no real measures were then taken to suppress them as Gierek wanted to show his liberalism to his Western creditors. He also regarded this dissident activity, much of which had been infiltrated by the authorities, and some of which had been manufactured by the police agencies, as safety valves for political and social tension.

But there is no doubt that he underestimated, very badly, their capacity for encouraging and aggregating latent opposition. Their potential as battle-hardened information and leadership-core networks during the crisis which over-whelmed Gierek in Summer 1980, as well as the support which they received from Polish _emigre_ organisations, which also became a significant force in the 1970s for the first time because of their rejuvenation with the 1968 generation, are factors which only became clearer after the event. Gierek's tolerant and easygoing treatment of dissident groups was one of the main secret reproaches and charges later laid against him by the PZPR, Soviet and Socialist Bloc hardliners.

- in other words, Gierek did nothing until it was too late, and there may have been deeper reasons for his inactivity.[14]

Whatever the reasons for Gierek's apparent tolerance, a more aware government would have been alarmed by the policy outlined in 1976 by a writer under the assumed name of Marek Turacz, in which the author maintained that open insurrection against the government would bring about a Soviet intervention. The only way to produce change would be through exerting popular pressure, taking the form of a long-term systematic campaign; in place of the usual Polish revolutionary upheaval, the writer called for everyday demonstrations of civic courage.[15] Writing in mid-1978, Bromke maintained that the government could afford to tolerate the opposition, because it was mostly composed of the intelligentsia.

Two attempts to organize a free trade union movement - the first in Katowice in February 1978, and the second in Gdansk the following April - were confined to a handful of individuals and were both met with immediate and severe reprisals.[16]

Also, it had to be taken into account that the opposition had at least 20 _samizdat_ papers with a total circulation of at least 20,000 copies monthly, and that to write, publish and distribute such a volume of semi-underground press would need a wide network of supporters. What the writer does not mention, is that it also required

considerable sums of money and machinery and paper
- all scarce in Poland. Hence, the movement
hardly seems spontaneous or unsupported in other
ways than locally.

Bromke believes that Gierek's motives in
tolerating the opposition were rather different:

> Resorting to mass terror would have disastrous
> political consequences for the Gierek regime.
> It would intensify the alienation of
> intellectuals from the Communist government
> and would lead to a new rupture with the
> Catholic Church. Furthermore, it would also
> adversely affect Poland's external relations
> with the West. The disruption of this trade
> is something which the country, in its present
> economic situation can ill afford, for any
> further deterioration of the standard of
> living could lead to what Gierek fears most -
> namely, new unrest among the workers... It is
> very doubtful that Gierek could weather such a
> political storm. In this respect, the
> opposition's assumption that he will refrain
> from wholesale terror at all cost seems to be
> quite correct.[17]

This paragraph seems more of an outline for
further action than a call for restraint. On all
the above counts, except for the last one on the
workers' unrest, the author is mistaken. The
Western banks were desperate to maintain order in
Poland, but were against dissent which led to
go-slows and reduced productivity. They were
against improving the workers' standard of living,
because this meant that Poland could not pay her
debts. The Church was desperately trying to avoid
getting embroiled in any confrontation with the
state, and in particular in having to side with
the opposition against the state. The
intellectuals were alienated in any case and
little could be done to mollify them. The only
valid argument is that the workers' unrest, caused
by higher food prices or lower wages, would
produce another 1970 or 1976, which would unseat
Gierek. The direct conclusion could well be that
someone wanted to unseat Gierek (and there were
plenty who did, and not outside the Eastern Bloc
either), and that this was the - very dangerous -
path they chose. It was also a well-tried path.
Like the Czech workers, the Polish workers do not

easily relate to intellectual freedom; on the
other hand, they relate very quickly to the price
of sausage.

One more hypothesis is advanced by Bromke:
this is that the peaceful character of the protest
was being undermined by the hardliners in the
party (who wanted Moscow to intervene) and the
extremist elements - mostly young - in the
opposition who were tired of the long-drawn out
struggle. Indeed, he quotes the example of the
1830 and 1863 insurrections, which were led by
hotheaded young people against the advice of their
elders. One would have to be wary of this
hypothesis; it seems much more in line with the
hopes of the emigration that there would be a
full-scale, military confrontation between the
USSR and the Polish people and that there would be
a political advantage to be drawn from this ouside
(and inside) the Bloc. It would be very wrong to
expose the people of Poland to danger against
which they would have to defend themselves with
their bare hands. The position in 1980 was rather
different from the position in 1830; the Kingdom
of Poland was in some ways similarly placed to the
Polish People's Republic but this is merely
incidental. The Poles of 1830 who were prepared
to fight were mostly classes which were losing
their favoured position in life because of the
Kingdom's problems; in 1980 it was the people who
still had a favoured position which they could
lose if they fought, who decided the course of
action.

Nor is it really safe to bank on the last
proposition which Bromke advanced: that the

assumption underlying the opposition strategy
is that in a climate of East-West detente the
Soviet Union would be reluctant to intervene
with force in Poland. This assumption is also
probably accurate. The Soviet leaders seem to
be well aware of the grave consequences such a
step would produce for them in the
international sphere. In the existing,
strained state of East-West relations, it
might well spell the end of detente. In order
to avoid this risk, Moscow would probably
accept substantial reforms in the present
system in Poland as long as they were carried
out in an orderly fashion and under the aegis
of the PUWP.[18]

This assumption, if it was a serious one, carries the gravest danger in it: it underestimates Soviet leadership and its motives to the point of folly. As far as the Soviet Union is concerned, detente is a convenient temporary state of armistice between East and West; but the Eastern Bloc is socialist because of a decision made by the wartime allies between 1943 and 1945. For the Russians this is a permanent state, not to be tinkered with. Any assumptions that the USSR would give up what it considers to be in its rightful sphere of influence for some tenuous gains, like the import of high technology, must have absolutely no understanding of what motivates Soviet leadership. One can only hope that this dangerous delusion does not lodge in the minds of Western leaders as well as in those of political analysts.

3.   Revolutionary Consequences of Dissent

In the autumn of 1978 a brief reign by Pope John Paul, an obscure Italian cardinal before his election, ended with his sudden death. On the 16th October 1978, the College of Cardinals elected Karol Wojtyla, a relatively new cardinal, better known as the Archbishop of Krakow, to be the new Pope. This event and what followed was later described in the following terms by a journalist:

> Some 30 years after the establishment of a Communist regime in Poland, a Pole is elected Pope. A few months later he returns to Poland, where he is greeted like a hero by millions of his fellow countrymen. Until the 16 October 1978... this would have sounded like the plot of an improbable movie. We know better. Although Wojtyla's election was impossible to predict, it was a natural enough event in a Europe that has been gradually growing together again after its division at the end of the Second World War.[19]

Frankland then goes on to discuss the difficulty of governing 'the well-informed and impatient Poles', though the people put up with the system partly because of the geo-political situation, but much more because of the genuine social and economic change which the regime brought. Socialism brought industrialisation and development and caused a social revolution; not many Poles would argue for a restoration of the pre-war system, or even a modern capitalist regime. But, notes Frankland, if the Polish intellectuals are dissident, it is not only because they are impatient and well-informed;

> if they are the strongest dissident group in Eastern Europe, it is because of the survival of the Catholic Church. A Pole who is a Catholic - and most Poles are - is not necessarily a dissident. But he is certainly a man of divided loyalties for how can he be both true Christian and true Marxist-Leninist? The answer is that he can be true Christian and true Pole, even by the Polish government's standards, and it is along these lines that the Polish compromise is being shaped.[20]

To press the point, the magazine carries a cover photograph of Adam Michnik, with the caption: 'It's a tense life, bucking the system ...'
The linking of the two, apparently unconnected, events: the growth of the dissenting movement and the election of a Pole as Pope, may appear to the innocent observer to be sinister. It may also imply - as indeed Frankland does - that the Church in Poland was striving for a revolt, or at least a stronger degree of dissension. This attitude gives the Church too much credit for a situation not of its own making and generally not much to its liking. The Church, particularly in Poland, is a conservative institution. It has survived many onslaughts not by pushing the Poles into revolutionary situations, but by warning them against revolutionary situations. If the odd parish priest or even a bishop speaks up for dissent in principle, this means as much as when an Irish priest speaks up for the IRA - individual views, not those of the hierarchy. On the other hand, as the only non-political institution left in Poland, the Church feels obliged to speak up in favour of human rights: where people are ill-treated by the police, where wages are insufficient to keep a

family, where local authorities close a church or a church-run creche; in these instances the intervention is quick and determined.

It would appear that the Church and Polish Pope had little direct influence over the August, 1980 events. They were foreshadowed for several years (indeed, hardly averted in 1976) by a long-term and a short-term problem. The long-term problem is discussed in a remarkable document, produced by the DIP Group of Experts,[21] first published in English in 1981. The document demonstrates on the basis of a questionnaire in the winter of 1979-80 that the population has lost faith in the government; that the leaders had no credibility; that it wanted the full truth about the economic situation; that it objected to the manipulation of facts; and that it felt the government and party did not relate to ordinary people.[22] If these were serious demands, then on this basis every government in the world would fall; few of them would agree to share all their worries with the population, and none would stop at manipulating the truth. But the rising expectations and the political naivete of the Poles, stemming from having been educated in what amounted to a political hothouse, away from political strife normal in a multi-party state, may explain this demand for what is obviously not realistic. Thus, the long-term problem was insoluble, though a more sensitive and less beleaguered government may have at least tried to persuade the population that it was doing its best under very difficult circumstances. In fact, the government was not doing its best; if Sanford is to be believed, Gierek simply went deeper into the bunker after 1976, because he knew there was no way out - it was merely a matter of time before the disturbances broke out.

The short-term problem was simple: the price of food had to go up to pay the debt off. This had proved impossible in 1970 and 1976; it proved impossible in the atmosphere of 1980. When the government rather surreptitiously raised the price of meat in the shops on 1 July, a series of strikes broke out immediately; according to government sources, by late August the strikes involved 640,000 workers.[23] It may have been the last straw for Gierek that the Silesian miners joined the strike in late September 1980; so far, the miners had been his staunch supporters, and the main reason why he had lasted in the leadership for so long. The other reason was less obvious, but even more important: there was literally no one in the Polish ruling circles who could take on Gierek's job. The miners' strike was reported in the Guardian under the jubilant title of 'Miners Strike Puts Paid to Silesian Mafia.'[24] The miners' strike ended the possibility of debt repayment; though the Katowice region accounts for 2.1 per cent of Poland's land surface, in 1980 it accounted for 18 per cent of Poland's GNP. Gierek's last card had gone; whether he did suffer a heart attack in early September or not, as reported, he was by then a man of 67, worn out by his long, and apparently unsuccessful career in managing Poland's difficulties. He was replaced on 6 September 1980 by Stanislaw Kania, who had been a full member of the Politbureau since 1975, and was in charge of overseeing the security forces. He has been classed as an apparatchik, and a 'moderate'.

The main achievement of the striking workers, apart from getting large pay rises, had been to set up the independent trade union, Solidarity. This was registered with the courts on October 24 1980, though the court changed the union's statutes unilaterally. The long drawn out fight with the courts continued for several months, but finally the trade union was legalised. The second achievement was getting large loans from both the West and the East to help Poland get over her debt problems. The Wall Street Journal reported on 13 October 1980 that US$670 million were obtained from the US, US$690 million from the USSR and 1.2 billion DM from a West German banking consortium.[25] The third achievement was most certainly sympathy in the West. On 1 September 1980, President Carter, then in the final stages of his electoral campaign, expressed the 'admiration of Americans for the workers of Poland'. 'We have been inspired and gratified by the peaceful determination with which the crisis was solved.' He further stated that the strikers had set an example for all those who cherished freedom and that they had won a victory for human rights.[26]

But the sceptics who questioned the victory and looked for further developments, may have been justified by other, less optimistic signs. First of all, everything happened very quickly. Gierek had said he would not use force; none of his negotiators insisted on concessions from the workers; indeed the government granted concessions almost immediately. Reporting on the agreement in the South of Poland, the correspondent of the Guardian noted himself that the negotiator 'surprised the miners by giving in to virtually all their demands with a swift "Tak" (yes) and not even trying to strike a compromise.'[27]

Secondly, Moscow was not happy, though it was well understood that both Gierek and his successor, Kania, were advised, maybe even ordered, to avoid friction and certainly to avoid bloodshed. It could have been that the Russians genuinely hoped that they could grant some concessions, lend Poland some money, the situation would improve and worse trouble could be avoided. If this was the case, they would have done better to smooth the situation out several months earlier; October was far too late. Perhaps the best commentary was provided by the American Communist leader, Gus Hall, who blamed weaknesses of the leadership in Poland for the disorders, and enumerated some of the causes as bureaucracy, lack of communication between the party and workers, and ideological backwardness.[28] Moscow may also have been banking on the fact that the Poles would soon get tired of their new plaything, and that their organisational difficulties would break the movement up.

Indeed, it seemed that the strike was so disorganised that it could not last for long. In September, 1980, Lech Walesa himself was complaining that 'the strike took place a year too early... We weren't prepared for it. If it had taken place next year, we would have had the statutes drawn up. Now we have chaos.'[29] Chaotic or not, the strike seemed to have gained support according to this report. Anna Walentynowicz, the prime mover behind the strike, was at this stage in charge of finances. 'She hands out small packets of zlotys to the neediest and is one of the 19 members of the union's organising presidium.' But such support as there was, seemed to be very localised, because it was decided that: 'for some time to come, the headquarters of the new independent union will remain in Gdansk rather than move to Warsaw as its greatest strength comes from the nearby shipyards.' Financial matters also played an important role. Since the official trade union stated that the workers will lose their social benefits if they defect to the independent union, hence: 'most of the issues thrashed out at the endless meetings in the Hotel Morski are practical, organisational ones in which money plays an important role. The union is advising workers not leave the old union until it can provide them with the same social benefits.'[30]

From all these separate snippets of information, one can draw the following conclusions: the strike started too early; the organisers were not prepared for it; the strike had localised support, but the organisers were not sure how much support there was outside the focal point - Gdansk. Indeed, they were right, because the other most important group of workers - the miners - were very reluctant to join it, till the last moment when victory seemed to have been won. Even Warsaw, despite its large industrial population, was not a certainty. Further, the strike had serious logistical difficulties and the organisers had financial problems. There clearly was some money, otherwise Mrs Walentynowicz could not have handed it out, but there was not sufficient to compensate the new members for the loss of considerable benefits accruing from the official trade union.

Despite all that has been said about the Poles' lack of organisational skills, it cannot be maintained that the organisers could have ignored all these problems at the outset. Neither Walesa, nor his advisers, like Kuron, were ignorant or unintelligent. They must have known that these problems were obvious. The question remains: why did they continue to press for a general strike; why did they persuade the rest of the working population to join it; why did they halt the industrial production in Poland almost completely, though the debt problems would only be aggravated by such actions? There are two possibilities: the first one, that they hoped that large amounts of money (possibly in the shape of large, long-term credits) would flow into Poland, thus relieving the situation and giving the whole country some breathing space. This seemed a logical thing to expect, since Poland, Hungary and Czechoslovakia had managed to get rather more help from the USSR in 1956 and 1968 after disturbances

than they would have done without disturbances.
And some credits did flow into Poland immediately
the strike began to bite, but such credits were
but a drop in the ocean compared with the Polish
overall debt. The organisers may have
miscalculated one thing: the financial situation
in the West and in the USSR in 1980 was nowhere as
good as it had been in the late Fifties and
Sixties. It is possible that the lack of
information the Poles had may have contributed to
this miscalculation, but one would expect some
knowledge of the recession to filter down to the
strike organisers, particularly since many top
figures in the party and in the government, while
not exactly encouraging the strike, were on
excellent terms with the organisers. This is not
to say that the whole plot was thought up by
Gierek or the CC of the party as a way out of a
difficult situation; but there may have been some
collusion, or eye-shutting on the part of the
leadership.

The second hypothesis was suggested by the
Guardian's correspondent in Poland:

> One interpretation of events in Poland is that
> the Polish workers have been engaged in a
> sophisticated exploration of the outer
> boundaries of Soviet tolerance. Despite the
> invasion of Czechoslovakia, the limits have
> already been stretched considerably over the
> last decade with Romania doggedly pursuing its
> own independent foreign policy and Hungary
> quietly introducing a free market mechanism in
> its domestic economy. The crucial question,
> therefore, is not whether the limits can be
> pushed out any further, but where does the
> ultimate breaking point come?[31]

Naturally, one would be very doubtful if the
Polish shipyard workers, despite the strides made
in the Polish educational system, thought up such
a sophisticated scheme themselves, particularly as
their worries about the cost of living were
overwhelming them at this particular stage; but it
is always possible that someone else thought it up
for them, and they were the blind executors of
somebody's policies. On the other hand, the two
hypotheses are not mutually self-exclusive: it
could have been a case of the USSR trying to test
the limits of Western generosity (particularly in

the wake of Afghanistan and the boycott of the
Moscow Olympics), while some elements in the West
were trying to test the limits of Soviet
patience. All this done at the expense of the
Polish workers, whom Carter congratulated on their
heroism, much as Roosevelt and Churchill were
congratulating the heroes of the Warsaw Uprising
in 1944, without as much as lifting a finger to
help them. This last, at any rate, was the
version which, once Solidarity was crushed, was
put about by party and government circles, and
this was one of the most important factors in the
process of 'pacification', after the Jaruzelski
coup d'etat (as it may well be called) in
December, 1981.

There is some evidence that such intentions
may have been present among at least some
political activists in the West. Writing in The
Times, Arrigo Levi suggested that Poland should be
given help with her debts, but on condition that
more political pluralism be allowed. Quoting a
discussion with President Carter's adviser, Helmut
Sonnenfeld, Levi suggests that Sonnenfeld had said
that no open encouragement to the Poles should be
given, in order not to damage the chances of
success;

> But we ought to make our further financial
> support of Poland's efforts to develop its
> export and to restructure its industry
> dependent upon the acceptance of change by the
> Polish regime and by the Soviet Union. I
> agree with that recipe. I would add that we
> ought to make detente itself dependent upon
> Soviet good behaviour, while reaffirming our
> full dedication to detente itself as a system
> of balance and stability in Europe. Detente
> is also the only policy instrument we have to
> influence events in Eastern Europe during
> these very critical times, when great changes
> may occur.[32]

4. Dissent goes Underground

This work is not concerned with the account of the
Polish August and its aftermath, since a large
amount of literature has already been published in
this connection[33]; what we are at present trying
to do is to establish the chronology of events and

their consequences. As had been stated, earlier, when Gierek was forced out of office, the dearth of talent was so great that Kania had to be appointed the First Secretary of the party, despite his complete lack of experience in government and lack of any charismatic qualities. A series of prime ministers followed one after another, without anyone being able to solve the crisis. Meanwhile, the dissent grew, absorbing not only industrial workers, but the intellectuals, people in the media, students, and finally, the peasants. Faced with these growing problems, the government was forced to act. A new leader, who would be popular, was absolutely necessary. Unfortunately, the only popular leader in Poland at this stage was Lech Walesa, closely followed by Pope John Paul II. Neither of these was eligible, since neither was a party member. (An interesting question arises whether Walesa would have been appointed had he been a party member; this might have solved most problems immediately, and it must have been a question discussed by the CC endlessly, as they tried to guess who would be capable of stifling the dissent).

For lack of a popular leader, an acceptable leader was sought. None could be found. Finally, somebody remembered that the army could save the party, and that Polish uniforms still carried some weight in the country. A man in uniform might be better than a civilian; the only possibility was General Wojciech Jaruzelski, whose great advantage was that he had a middle-class background, and who, thus (or so it was hoped) could talk to the intellectuals, who could then persuade the others to drop their action. Jaruzelski had been Minister of Defence since 1968 and the CC's Eighth Plenum held on 9 February 1981 appointed him Prime Minister. Significantly, in May, Cardinal Wyszynski died and the new Cardinal Glemp did not carry the same weight in the country as the old dignitary. The first Congress of Solidarity was held in September and October 1981. When the government refused to give in to the demands of the Congress (many of which had been agreed earlier in separate accords) Solidarity threatened a general strike. A tape recording of Walesa and other leaders discussing the inevitable confrontation and calling for the overthrow of communism was released by the authorities.

Immediately the Congress was over, Kania resigned as First Secretary and was succeeded by the Prime Minister, General Jaruzelski. The election was held at the Plenum of the CC on 18 October 1981, and Jaruzelski was elected by 180 votes to four.[34] After several attempts at patching up the quarrels, the government introduced an emergency bill banning all strikes, which led to Walesa threatening a general strike and the release by the authories of the above mentioned tape.

Finally, having not succeeded by peaceful persuasion, Jaruzelski introduced martial law and a state of emergency on 13 December 1981. It was announced that the Council of State had acted in order to forestall a Solidarity coup, and had decided to set up a Military Council of National Salvation, which would be headed by Jaruzelski. Thus, Jaruzelski had taken supreme power as a military dictator, Prime Minister and First Secretary of the Party. It is little wonder that, after the internments and repressions started in earnest, his nickname bore the joint acronym of the security police (ZOMO) and Latin America: General Zomoza. Attempts to dress this coup in Pilsudskiyte colours, as though it was based on the 1926 coup, failed completely. With the coup and the military rule, Poland had the distinction of being the first state with a Socialist government, which was ruled by the military. Those Solidarity leaders who were not interned, went underground. In the meantime, the struggle for Solidarity's original aims was tranformed as it was taken up by politically-motivated students and dissidents from the KOR-type of organisations.

5. International Consequences of the 'Normalisation'

The growth and apparent initial successes of Solidarity had some repercussions throughout Eastern Europe, though not on a very large scale. These will be discussed later on in this chapter. But the most dramatic effect was in the West. Western media had had wide access to all deliberations and events in Poland; they hailed the development of the first free trade union movement in the Socialist Bloc as a breakthrough; one serious newspaper leader even talked of the 'crumbling of the Soviet empire'; others discussed the introduction of pluralism by consent.

Hence, the consequences of the Jaruzelski <u>coup</u> came as a shock. What was expected, should steps be taken against <u>Solidarity</u>, was a solution similar to 1968. It takes some imagination and an understanding of the Russian mind to know that they hardly ever do the same thing in the same way. Rumours had been circulating in Poland that a Soviet invasion was imminent. These were most likely scare tactics employed by the government to curb the most unruly <u>Solidarity</u> members. On the other hand, there were substantiated rumours of Polish army uniforms being transported in large numbers across the Polish-Soviet borders.[35] But an internal <u>coup</u> carried out with the knowledge and approval of the party, though without the approval of the parliament, was not anticipated. Yet it would have been easy to reach for history books and see that a similar <u>coup</u> was carried out by Marshal Pilsudski in 1926, though for different reasons. The unfortunate part was that Jaruzelski, a small, stocky, somewhat corpulent man in dark spectacles, whose only claim to distinction was the fact that he had taken part in quelling the Gdansk disturbances in 1970, could not play the part of a liberator in the same way as Pilsudski had done. His only card was to maintain that he had saved Poland from a Soviet or Warsaw Pact invasion, a card he played long and hard without much success.

The West was outraged. A check through a range of liberal newspapers in the two weeks which followed the <u>coup</u> shows that each day a large front-page article was devoted to the Polish situation. On 15th December, <u>The Guardian</u> carried a large headline saying: '<u>Poles rally to resist curbs of martial law</u>' and listed a series of strikes, protests and arrests. Foreign press representatives had been told to stay in Warsaw. However, it further stated:

> With a news black-out imposed throughout the country, it has obviously not been easy for anyone outside of the martial law authorities to gauge the extent of resistance to the emergency measures that have been imposed. Certainly the call for a general strike put

out by members of the Warsaw branch of
Solidarity on Sunday was largely
unsuccessful. In Warsaw essential services
and transport were still functioning.

It was only further down in the article that
the correspondent noted that:

On Sunday night the Polish Primate, Cardinal
Glemp, made a plea to the Polish nation to
avoid "fratricidal struggle", even though the
authorities had replaced "dialogue with the
use of force". He left no doubt of his
critical attitude to the decision to impose
martial law. But, delivering a sermon in a
Jesuit Church in Warsaw, which was
re-broadcast several times, Cardinal Glemp
argued: "Nothing is more valuable than human
life. That is why, even if I became a target
for insults, I shall plead, even on my knees,
do not start fighting, Poles against
Poles".[36]

The following day this correspondent reported
that strike leaders had been arrested in several
Polish cities and it was believed that Walesa was
under house arrest. A report smuggled out into
Holland stated that in Gdansk, the occupation
strike had collapsed; thousands of workers left
the Lenin Shipyard when told to go home by the
authorities. They appeared to have lost faith in
Solidarity, added the report. A report from
Washington stated that:

President Reagan reacted strongly last night
to an American news agency report that the
Soviet Union was ready to offer military
assistance to Poland if the Warsaw Government
could not quell the unrest. "That sounds more
like intervention than anything we are
saying... That would be very serious. We've
said that very many times - the whole Western
world has said - intervention by the Soviet
Union would be taken very seriously".[37]

The Soviet Union called a meeting of the
Warsaw Pact leadership on 19 December 1981, at
which it was expected that Jaruzelski would tell
his allies that the Poles could manage to stifle
discontent by themselves, and appeal to

Soviet Bloc countries for aid with food supplies, detergents, medicines and some industrial products. One Western correspondent suggested that the coup was made easy 'by the general sense of hopelessness and fatigue which the food shortages of this autumn have created among the population.' But with almost all the Solidarity leaders arrested in Gdansk, including apparently one who had been abroad since 1971, and who had been smuggled back to Poland a year earlier, it is difficult to see what the population could do. In addition, the Church appeared to be conducting high level discussions with the government on resolving the crisis.[38]

In fact, it was acknowledged in the West that the Polish economy, already in serious crisis before Solidarity was set up, had, thanks to the actions of the new unions, all but collapsed. Indeed, some Western commentators had it that it was not the Soviet leadership, but the Western bankers who demanded that Poland returns to a stable form of government, fearing for their loan repayments. This may be far-fetched, but it is interesting that the same liberal newspaper which was reacting strongly to the suppression of Solidarity ran a leader which amounted to a grateful acknowledgement of the coup. That is how parts of it read:

> Poland has, for the first time in almost 18 months, a government that is prepared to govern and, so far, the nation has not errupted... So far the signals are ambiguous but tend towards an attempt at accommodation, albeit on pretty brutal terms, rather than to outright repression... The Western response, meanwhile, has, quite properly, seemed distinctly muted. There have been low key reminders of the package of (non-military) sanctions which the free world has had on the shelf since early this year, in case of Soviet intervention... It is well that both the General and the Warsaw Pact should know that the West expects something more from Jaruzelski than curfews, military patrols on the streets and crushing diktats from military headquarters. It is equally important that the Polish people hear yet again (thank heaven for the BBC's external services, Radio Free Europe and the rest) that there is not the

slightest chance of any form of military aid
for them from NATO if they do decide to take
to the streets. There must be no repetition
of the misunderstandings and the romantic
rumours which encouraged doomed resistance in
Hungary a quarter of a century ago. But the
West can and should do more than issue
warnings to influence the course of events.
It could give urgent and specific promises of
aid to help Poland out of chronic economic
crisis. That aid should have been forthcoming
months ago. Had it been, Poland might not,
today, boast the dubious distinction of being
the first European Communist nation to suffer
direct military rule. In the short run Poland
needs massive injections of food, fuel, raw
materials and medical supplies to keep things
ticking over at all during the cruel months to
come. So far the EEC has made utterly
inadequate supplies available. Those supplies
have been supplemented by generous... help
from relief agencies and Polish exile groups.
In the longer run Poland needs to reschedule
its monumental $27 billion debt to the West.
Most of the debt is to commercial banks which
have to pay some minimal regard to banking
criteria. Rescheduling is now delayed because
Poland is unable to pay even the $500 million
which the banks have demanded as a sign of
good faith. All of which has led to the
distasteful spectacle of some Western bankers
almost welcoming the smack of firm military
government and a good clobbering for
"irresponsible" trade unionists and the
foolishly optimistic suggestions that Soviet
military intervention would mean the Kremlin
taking responsibility for Polish
indebtedness. The truly urgent need now is
for an offer of relief aid on an unprecedented
scale, coupled with Western governmental
guarantees to commercial bankers to cover
their Polish loans. (If Poland did default,
Western governments would have to pick up the
pieces anyway to preserve the stablility of
the banking system).[39]

Reading this article, with the wisdom of
hindsight after the default of Latin American
countries (a de facto if not technical default),
one could only state (were this not an impossible

hypothesis) that it might have been written by
General Jaruzelski. One might equally well
suppose that the solution for a Latin American
style of government may have come from Western
bankers, rather than from the Soviet Union. It
might have been accepted by the Soviet leadership
under pressure of having to deal with the Polish
crisis, and possibly even having to send in the
army. The military dictatorship may have seemed
cheaper and preferable. In the event, the
Jaruzelski coup provided a dangerous precedent,
not so much for Poland or the smaller Bloc
countries, but for the Soviet Union itself. If
the Russians have learned about free trade unions
from the Poles - and they have - they could
equally well learn about military coups to replace
immobile and inefficient governments. The Soviet
leadership could also well ponder on the next
action of the Jaruzelski government: the arrest
of most of the Gierek ministers and advisers,
including (apparently) Gierek himself, and the
trials of some less politically important figures,
such as Szczepanski, on charges which may well be
true, but which could equally well apply to any
leadership in the Bloc.

Moreover, the Polish problem had spilt over
into other countries, not least within the Soviet
Union itself. Most certainly, the really
frightening thing would have been if Soviet
soldiers, having been sent to intervene in Poland,
had instead crossed over to the revolutionaries.
Such improbable events have happened in previous
Polish revolutions in the nineteenth century, and
could not be discounted. There was also evidence
that in the Ukraine, a free trade union movement
had been created under the impact of Solidarity.
However, the Ukraine is not typical of the whole
of the Soviet Union, particularly since a large
part of it has a significant percentage of Polish
population, and since the Ukrainian protest
movement had always been more interested in
nationalist, rather than democratic causes. The
very strong movement of dissent among ethnic
Russians is mostly of an intellectual or religious
nature[40], and the only free trade union founded
in 1978 has, according to Reddaway, not made any
inroads into the general mass of workers.
Reddaway concludes, probably rightly, that trade
union dissent has no influence on Soviet

leadership, whereas religious, nationalist, and intellectual dissent are of enormous importance.[41]

There are, however, some areas of the Soviet Union where Polish dissent is invariably taken up by the broad masses; these are the Baltic countries, most particularly Lithuania, which, like the Ukraine, has a large percentage of Poles within its territory. In the event, while religious dissent by Catholics was the strongest in Lithuania, the Solidarity theme was swiftly taken up by the most prosperous and enterprising of all the Baltic republics: Estonia. In Lithuania, despite the lack of strong support for Solidarity, the authorities feared that the

> convergence of nationalism and religion that threatened to overthrow Poland's socialist system seemed most likely to be replicated in Lithuania, where a widespread and strong movement sought such rights as recogniton of the Catholic Church;... as legal entities... In all three republics, party and security officials claimed to perceive an additional threat from Baltic emigres in the West and from Western intelligence services.[42]

It is doubtful that Solidarity had much influence over the Romanian, Hungarian and Czech workers, but there is strong evidence of intellectual co-operation between the Polish leaders and the dissenters in those countries.[43] More evidence can perhaps be found in Yugoslavia that the Polish movement influenced working-class discontent, but Yugoslavia is prone to dissent of the nationalist kind to an extent in which it is almost impossible to distinguish any other kind of dissent.

And perhaps the most important dissent came from Eurocommunist parties; most cogently from the founder of the Historic Compromise, Enrico Berlinguer himself. But the Italian ties with Poland are very specific, and this may have had some bearing on the reaction. By and large, one can state that the revolt was nipped in the bud, before it had time to be taken up in other countries of the Bloc. Moreover, since many of them have only just recovered from serious shocks of various kinds, and some were on the way to greater prosperity, it did not cause too many ripples. On the other hand, had the revolt gone on for six months longer, the situation may have been different. In view of this, it is perhaps not surprising that the Soviet Union opted for the desperate solution of a military dictatorship, rather than allow the rot to spread.

CHAPTER FOUR: FOOTNOTES

1. Taborsky: <u>Czechoslovakia</u>, p.40.   The same
    article also gives detailed changes in the
    party; p.32, and notes Soviet shipments of
    relief supplies; p.38.
2. Public opinion polls analysed in H. Gordon
    Skilling: <u>Czechoslovakia's Interrupted
    Revolution</u>, and J.A. Piekalkiewicz: <u>Public
    Opinion Polling in Czechoslovakia</u>; for the
    news of returned Rolls-Royce: <u>Daily
    Telegraph</u>, 17 February 1983 as quoted by
    Jurgen Tampke: <u>The People's Republics</u>, Ch. 7,
    note 44.
3. Trond Gilberg: <u>The Political Order</u>;
    S. Fischer-Galati (ed): <u>Eastern Europe in the
    1980s</u>, p. 145.
4. Walter D. Connor: <u>Dissent in Eastern Europe:
    A New Coalition?</u>; <u>Problems of Communism</u>,
    January-February, 1980, p.9.
5. <u>RFE Czechoslovak Situation Report/33</u>, October
    24 1979; as quoted by Connor: <u>Dissent</u>, p.9.
6. See: George Sanford: <u>Polish Communism in
    Crisis</u>, p. 33-34.
7. There are two views about this development -
    both coming from the same author, Adam
    Bromke.   He maintains that the regime was
    emboldened by the economic success and hence
    increased its ideological pressure on dissent;
    see: <u>Poland under Gierek: A New Political
    Style</u>; <u>Problems of Communism</u>, September-
    October 1972, and states the opposite in: <u>The
    Opposition in Poland</u>; <u>Problems of Communism</u>,
    September-October 1978.
8. See: <u>The Opposition in Poland</u>, p. 38.   On the
    reform of local government and the dislocation
    it caused, see: Danuta Jachniak-Ganguly:
    <u>Spatial Planning in Poland and Local
    Government Reorganisation, 1961-75</u> in: Jack
    Hayward & Olga A. Narkiewicz: <u>Planning in
    Europe</u>, p. 147-168.
9. <u>The Opposition in Poland</u>, p.38.
10. Sanford: <u>Polish Communism</u>, p. 34.
11. For a brief description of the situation,
    see: O.A. Narkiewicz: <u>Marxism</u>, p. 182-83.
12. See Bromke: <u>The Opposition in Poland</u>, p.
    39-40, who also analyses KOR's gradual change
    of tactics.

13. In pre-war Poland Christian-Democratic parties were broken up into several groups; the three parties which called themselves 'Christian' or 'Catholic' in parliament in 1926, comprised 14.7 per cent, as against 26.6 per cent for National Democracy (right wing), and 26.5 per cent for Populist parties. See: M. Pietrzak: Rzady parlamentarne w Polscew Latach 1919-1926, Table 3, p. 98-99.
14. Sanford: Polish Communism, p. 35.
15. Bromke: The Opposition in Poland, p. 45. Bromke implies strongly that Turacz may have been Adam Michnik himself.
16. Bromke: The Opposition in Poland, p. 48.
17. Bromke: The Opposition in Poland, p. 50.
18. Bromke: The Opposition in Poland, p. 51.
19. Mark Frankland: The Poland that Pope John Paul left behind; The Observer Magazine, 3 June 1979, p. 56.
20. Frankland: The Poland that, p. 58.
21. Poland: the State of the Republic.
22. See p. 155-165 of Poland: the State of the Republic.
23. Sanford: Polish Communism, p. 48.
24. Michael Dobbs: The Guardian, 2 September 1980.
25. See Jan B. de Weydenthal: Workers and Party in Poland; Problems of Communism, November-December 1980, p. 20 and note 67.
26. Jonathan Steele: US plays it cool despite Pravda attack; The Guardian, 2 September 1980.
27. Michael Dobbs: Poles try to legislate new found freedoms; The Guardian, 4 September 1980.
28. Mark Frankland: Moscow marks out Polish danger areas; The Observer, 7 September 1980.
29. Leslie Colitt: Squalor and hope at the Hotel Morski; Financial Times, 16 September 1980.
30. Leslie Colitt: Squalor and hope.
31. Michael Dobbs: Why Polish summer is not the same as Prague Spring; The Guardian, 4 September 1980, emphasis added.
32. Western Role in Aiding a Polish Compromise; The Times, 18 September 1980.
33. Perhaps the best account is Neal Ascherson's: The Polish August, but the reader can choose from a large selection of literature.

34. See: Sanford Polish Communism, p. 226. Sanford also gives the background to the crisis, including discussions between Kania, Jaruzelski and the Soviet leadership; Solidarity, the Church, and dissent within the party.
35. These rumours stemmed from transport and railway sources who were in a position to know that this was happening. To the best of the author's knowledge, that information never appeared in print.
36. Hella Pick; The Guardian, 15 December 1981.
37 Hella Pick and Harold Jackson: Polish Workers Fight on under the News Black-out; The Guardian, 16 December 1981.
38. Hella Pick, Martin Cleaver, Jonathan Steele and Foreign Staff reports; The Guardian, 17 September 1981.
39. The Guardian, 15 December 1981, emphasis added.
40. See: Peter Reddaway: Dissent in the Soviet Union, Problems of Communism, November-December, 1983.
41. Reddaway: Dissent, p. 14-15.
42. V. Stanley Vardys: Polish Echoes in the Baltic, Problems of Communism, July-August 1983, p. 25-27.
43. Walter D. Connor: Dissent in Eastern Europe: A new Coalition? Problems of Communism, January-February 1980, p. 1-17.

Chapter Five

LEADERSHIP AND PARTY UNDER STRESS

---

1. An overview of leadership changes

The system introduced in the USSR when setting up
the government and party apparatus did not provide
for flexible changes in the leadership. Though
there are frequent and extensive elections, these
do not allow for a major test of a government's
popularity, which exists in Western-type
parliamentary systems. While the Socialist states
are right to maintain that theirs is a true
democratic electoral system in some ways (i.e. in
so far as the widespread network of elective
institutions involves millions of citizens), they
suffer by not being exposed to a multi-party
system which allows for a larger degree of
discontent to be expressed through the ballot
box. It is well known that this problem is
understood by the Socialist governments, and this
is why in the newer countries of the Bloc, a form
of multi-party system is allowed; though such
parties are always parties 'friendly' to the
ruling party, and hence have been dubbed by
critics of the system as mere puppets of the
regimes. This is not true, but what is true is
that, when a major party is established
institutionally, it plays the same role as an
established church: it gives the non-established
institutions a very minor role in the system, and
tends to draw in the most ambitious and the most
power-seeking elements.
  Because of these shortcomings, the Socialist
states have to look for mechanisms of change which
are not brought about by the ballot box, and
because of them, the problem of top leadership is
crucial. Change has to be engineered from above,

though not without consultation with the grass-roots. Leaders have to appear to be popular, and if they do not manage this, they have to be removed. On the other hand, leaders who become too popular threaten the middle-leadership and efforts are made to depose them. Perhaps the most dramatic example of this was the period of Khrushchev's rule when he became the most popular leader in the USSR and instituted changes which threatened the middle leadership. It was impossible to remove Khrushchev by a coup d'etat, or to have him indicted on some crimes; yet removed he had to be because of the threats he posed. It took both manoeuvring and a vote in the Central Committee, as well as Khrushchev's undoubted deterioration in health, to depose him. He was succeeded by a man who had been described as a boring bureaucrat; a man with few friends, but one who had acquired a reputation for good administration and care for his subordinates. Leonid Brezhnev's popularity had to be built up over the years, while Khrushchev, with his colloquialisms, his easy manner and explosive views, became popular overnight, even among his adversaries abroad.

Thus, shorn of the possibility of choosing leaders by popularity polls, assisted by television exposure, the Socialist governments are reduced to attempting to forecast who would be the most suitable leader with regard both to efficiency and to charismatic qualities. This is not an easy task and it is hardly surprising that so many failures emerge. On the other hand, it perhaps speaks a lot for the system that many leaders are not only efficient, but also popular and manage to retain the trust of the CPSU and their own party, without losing the trust of their people. This is of course relative, but it would probably qualify on a par with leaders elected through the Western-type parliamentary elections. The difficulty of the task also explains why leadership changes are avoided and only used as a last resort. Hence, classifying the regimes as 'totalitarian' or 'authoritarian' in the manner of some political scientists is rather erroneous, though it may have been applied with some truth in Stalinist days. Since de-Stalinisation the leaderships have been very careful to avoid the stigma of violating 'socialist law' and 'socialist morality' and of undertaking only such illegal acts as are absolutely necessary for the survival of the government. Notable examples of this are the effort to make the invasion of Czechoslovakia justifiable (by being invited to invade) and the military coup in Poland legalised by the Council of State. Both acts were, by implication, against the law and in both cases the necessity to act overrode the wish to remain within the realm of legality; but ample provision was made to appear not to have transgressed the law.

It is perhaps wiser to look at Eastern European leaders neither through the prism of Stalinism, nor through the experience of Western parliamentary systems. Additionally, it is better not to generalise about the leaderships of all the six Eastern European states, since on analysis they each show different characteristics. And finally, it is very dangerous to assume that because a particular leader happens to have won popularity abroad, he is also popular at home; or even that he is a good leader. Two examples may be quoted here: one is Poland's Gierek who was popular both with Western bankers and Western governments, and who yet (partly because of this) managed to ruin Poland economically; the other is Ceausescu of Romania who is a popular figure in the West but little more than a clan leader given to nepotism and oppression at home.

On looking at the difficulty of assessing leaderships, one is tempted to assume that it is their quality which is of most importance. In fact, when comparing the various leaderships in the Bloc, it is striking that it is the length of being in power which appears to have the most bearing on the success of a leader. One glance at Table I will show that the rate of success is directly related to the length of tenure, if by success we define political stability and economic growth. The country which had most changes of leadership over the last three decades, Poland, is the least successful on both counts. On the other hand, USSR during the Brezhnev period experienced growth, built up new industries, recovered some agricultural impetus, began to build the most powerful navy in the world, and developed rocketry to a great extent. It allowed dissent to flourish, permitted emigration of 'non-ethnics' on a large scale, signed the Helsinki Accords and developed its own brand of juvenile delinquency,

TABLE I

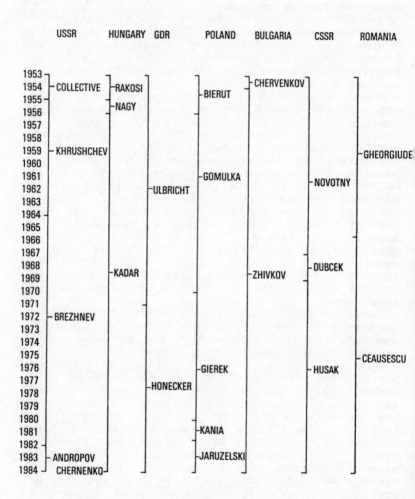

This table is intended as a guide to the length of each leadership; for exact dates of accession and resignation, consult appropriate sources.

modelled on the American pattern. These developments, unique in the USSR, were signs of a relaxed style of government and a secure leadership. This allowed Brezhnev to get over the invasion of Czechoslovakia, invasion of Afghanistan and two major changes of regime in Poland without much difficulty at home. Even though towards the end of his life, Brezhnev was much less mobile than any leader in Eastern Europe and was a very sick man for the last four years in power, there appears to have been no move to dislodge him, while Khrushchev was removed for a much less serious reason in connection with the Chinese problem and the Cuban missile crisis.

The same criteria applied to other countries in the Bloc will show that East Germany (stable leadership with one natural change-over when Honecker took over from the ageing Ulbricht) is the most prosperous and politically stable country; Hungary, which has had one leader since 1956, follows it closely, and the poorest and least developed country in the Bloc, Bulgaria, has overtaken one of the most developed and industrialised countries, Czechoslovakia. Bulgaria had had one leader, Zhivkov, since 1954, whereas Czechoslovakia had suffered almost the same fate as Poland though Husak has been in power for a period of almost fourteen years; previous changes, however, have meant that the country has never really recovered its will to progress.

The difficulty of governing Eastern Europe is not limited to the lack of real elective processes. It is complicated by the fact of dual, sometimes triple responsibility. While General Jaruzelski and Leonid Brezhnev may be unique in concentrating all the top jobs in one person, it is a well-known phenomenon that government and party jobs are often merged and that one and the same person has to respond to many different problems. Naturally, this is not possible. There is ample evidence to prove that even in Stalin's times, responsibility was shared out among several bodies; that Khrushchev was deposed because he tried to take too much power too quickly and that Brezhnev delegated easily and naturally. In the same manner, Andropov came to power as a compromise between two wings of the Politbureau, and had to share his duties with other people even before his last illness. Each leader in each of the countries of the Bloc has had to follow a similar pattern of power-sharing. But there is one exception to this: when things go wrong, there is only one person (and his 'kitchen' cabinet) to blame; the notion of ministerial responsibility (never known in Russia) does not enter into modern socialist leadership's concepts of power. Thus both Gomulka and Gierek had to take all the blame for the mismanagement of economic affairs, even though the former was hardly a qualified economic expert, and the latter had very limited economic expertise. Similarly, in Czechoslovakia, Novotny had to take all the blame for the Stalinist purges, even though most of the excesses occurred during the Gottwald period.

There is additional disadvantage in this arrangement; that of international relations' problems. Mostly through ignorance, though sometimes through ill will, it is assumed in non-Socialist countries that each leader, and particularly the Soviet leader, has unlimited power. This became very clear when the American administration attempted to read the behaviour of Chernenko after Andropov's death. Mr. Chernenko was polite to Vice-President Bush at Andropov's funeral - that meant that he wanted to begin the Geneva talks again. The following month, Chernenko gave a tough anti-American speech. This meant that he had changed his mind. The following month he received American media people and spoke warmly about friendship of the peoples; this meant that he was again leaning towards <u>detente</u>. As a result all contacts in international matters are concentrated on personalities, instead of, as is really the case, considering who actually makes decisions in the Socialist Bloc.[1] The answer to this is complicated by the fact that what is true of the USSR may not be necessarily true of other countries in the Bloc. One also has to bear in mind the fact that much of the supposed evidence from such countries as Czechoslovakia, Poland and Romania comes either from edited government and party versions of top meetings, or from exiled dissenters, and from gossip picked up by journalists in private conversations. While this may also apply in some cases to information forthcoming from Western countries (e.g. the leaks coming from unnamed sources in some administrations) one cannot agree that such sources of information can ever be very satisfactory.

The results are plain to see in mid-1984: international links between the super-powers have broken down; the Eastern European Bloc is left exposed on the one hand to the arbitrary rulings of the Soviet government and on the other, to the vagaries of the Western bankers and trading barriers; and no one knows how to remedy the situation. Some proof of this unsatisfactory state of affairs was given by a British newspaper; the Reagan administration is said to have begged the Soviet government to resume arms control discussions away from Geneva:

But the Kremlin has not yet responded to the American offer which was made through diplomatic channels. Officials clearly hope that President Reagan's recent overtures, together with the renewed dialogue on such matters as scientific exchange, may eventually lead to a more positive response from Moscow. Disclosure of the US offer to resume talks with the Soviet Union in secret came in testimony by Mr Richard Burt, the Assistant Secretary of State for European Affairs, before a House foreign affairs committee. It is the first time that the Administration has publicly acknowledged willingness to depart from the Geneva forum to move arms control talks forward.[2]

Admittedly, the Reagan administration is desperate to resume talks in the run-up to presidential elections in November 1984, and obviously it has to take some of the blame for the breakdown of the Geneva talks. On the other hand, the Soviet government has to take its share of the blame not so much for walking out of the Geneva talks, which was forecast by Leonid Brezhnev in November 1979[3], when he clearly stated that should medium-range nuclear weapons be employed in Europe in larger quantities, the chances of reaching an agreement on limitation of nuclear arms would be seriously undermined; the blame lies in making it appear that Brezhnev, and Brezhnev alone, had the final say in the continuation or breakdown of the negotiations. It is hardly surprising that the Reagan Administration, perhaps the most naive in foreign affairs ever, aware of the fact that Brezhnev was seriously ill and still convinced of the old analysis of 'power struggle

121

in the Kremlin', should consider that either during the power struggle or with the accession of a new leader, it would be able to bend the Soviet Union to its will. It must be stressed that while the Reagan Administration may appear to be the worst informed of all the American administrations, the problem is not confined to right-wing Republicans. American critics of the Establishment claim that the 'Riga-Syndrome' and the 'Cold War Syndrome' have dominated American foreign policy since 1917, with the brief interlude of the Second World War,[4] independent of which administration was in office.

But an objective observer cannot but state that the Soviet system has encouraged these attitudes not only by its sporadic militancy or by its ambiguity, but much more by making it difficult to establish with whom a foreign government has to deal. The simplistic calls for the establishment of a multi-party system made by Western politicians cut no ice with the Russians - with one or two exceptions, Russia and the USSR have never had a multi-party system and would be hard put to introduce one now. If there was to be yet another revolution in the USSR, it would only produce another single-party system. Traditions die hard everywhere, but nowhere so hard as in Russia. Foreign governments should adjust to the permanence of single-party state system and act accordingly; foreign banks already think such a system is good because their debts are guaranteed. But the USSR and the Eastern European Bloc should think hard about improving their decision-making processes and their system of accountability. While it may not be a large step, a system of ministerial accountability would not be impossible to introduce, with some limited parliamentary control imposed on individual ministers. The second step should surely be a very much more developed division of labour; the party may rule, but the specialists must be allowed to make decisions in their spheres and to be responsible for them; not simply to suffer if things go wrong. Lenin introduced this system in the USSR in 1918, though it was phased out during the late Twenties. This system is also in existence in Hungary, in so far as economic decisions are concerned. It has not yet led to any anti-socialist conspiracies, though the economy is geared to some free-market practices.

An extension of the system to other countries and other fields would benefit everybody, but most of all the Eastern European countries.

Finally, the personalities and backgrounds of the leaders must be taken into account in making changes. The modernisation of leaderships cannot be denied. By modernisation one means that the single-minded tyrants, whose origins stemmed from underground struggle and terror tactics (Stalin and Rakosi come to mind) have been or are being replaced by technocrats, more interested in economic progress than in ideological rectitude. The change in the leadership reflects another change: that in the party cadres. It is to these that we must now turn.

2. Party Cadres and Technocratic Elites

While party leadership evolved because of changes in party cadres, these, in their turn, depended on the new elites, which developed in the Socialist Bloc since 1945. The new elites were of mixed origins; in some countries, as in Poland between 60-80 per cent of the middle classes have been eliminated during the war. In others, like Hungary, the old elites were not acceptable to the new communist regime. In yet others, like Czechoslovakia, the old elite, which survived the war, was not necessarily opposed to communism, and sometimes actively supported communist policies. In East Germany, depleted of skilled manpower in all areas, the party had to rely on whoever could be found to carry out skilled jobs. Therefore, just as the East German army was built up on the basis of the old officer corps so much of the technocracy, at least in the first two decades of the GDR's existence, had been brought up in the Nazi era. Other East European countries: Romania, Bulgaria, and Albania had such small elites before the war that they had to be built up from scratch after 1945.

The task of analysing these developments on a general Eastern European basis is not within the scope of this work. However, it must be stressed that, given such different backgrounds, and given the urgency of the new tasks, the work of building up new technocracies and bureaucracies was extremely difficult and demanding. How and in what spirit this was done depends on interpretation. According to one historian, the greatest degree of support for the Communist Party (apart from Yugoslavia and Albania) in Eastern and South-Eastern Europe, was in Bulgaria. In October 1947, while opposition parties were still legal, though under pressure from the Communists, the Patriotic Front - a coalition of Communists, Peasant Party and Social Democrats - polled nearly 70 per cent of the vote in the elections for the Constituent Assembly.[5]

A similar situation existed in Czechoslovakia, where it could rightly be claimed that even after the 1948-1949 events, the population was not dissatisfied with the regime, and may even have been fully mobilised behind it. But Czechoslovakia had a different history, a different war and a different economy from the other Eastern European economies. It had clearly been picked as a model of a developed socialist state after the war, and even the Stalinist purges of the early 1950s did little to upset the acceptance (with or without enthusiasm) of the regime by the population in general. It was not until the economic problems began in the mid-1960s that the support for the regime was severely eroded.[6]

Hungary and Romania were, like Bulgaria, ex-enemy states, and agricultural states. A series of brutal regimes did nothing to reconcile the population to the Communists, and the peasant population was alienated by the Stalinist collectivisation procedures. In Bulgaria, collectivisation was not resented because private smallholders had been few in number, whereas most of farming land was owned by large landowners. In Hungary and Romania, smallholders of peasant origin were in the majority and collectivisation was not welcomed. A similar position obtained in Poland. East Germany cannot be assessed in terms of any certainty, because the situation there was so abnormal immediately after the war as to defy any classification.

One must, therefore, enquire into the possibility of developing a socialist regime in a situation of post-war disintegration, partial or complete occupation by foreign troops, in countries with a large agricultural population, a small working class and a very depleted middle class. The first task of such a regime apart from policing the dissidents, which was done fairly thoroughly in the Stalinist era, would be to produce a new technical intelligentsia (to borrow a Soviet term); to build up industries; and to transfer the population from the countryside to industrial areas, where socialisation would be quicker and easier.

Of the three above tasks, only the first one was done well and on a large scale. Industrialisation and the influx of peasant population into the cities, as carried out in the Stalinist period, produced bad results which have continued in the post-Stalinist period, particularly in Poland, Czechoslovakia and Romania. In a way it was fortunate that the new technical intelligentsia had been only in their teens in the 1950s, because by the time they had arrived into responsible positions, Stalinism was over and they could start the necessary reforms in a more liberal atmosphere. It was the new intelligentsia, as well as the junior army officers and the junior civil servants, who formed the bulk of the renewed Communist Parties in Eastern Europe. As Stalin managed to build up the new Soviet intelligentsia in the 1930s, so the Eastern Europeans repeated the process in the 1950s. One authority notes that after 1953, and even more after 1956,

The economic and intellectual elite became increasingly articulate and found expression through the Communist cells in their professional organisations. Orthodox officials in charge of cultural activities, such as Adam Schaff in Poland or Hendrych and Koucky in Czechoslovakia, succumbed to the ideas they were supposed to be combating. It became obvious that men and beliefs were not as unchangeable as had been supposed. After Djilas and Imre Nagy, there were Czech and Slovak officials making the leap from Stalinism to humanistic and democratic socialism... The disintegration of personal power and the collapse of the belief in the infallibility of the supreme rulers... are reflected in the Central Committees, which tend to become, if not the centre of power, at least the arena in which internal struggles are fought out and resolved. This renewal, this rediscovery of identity, spread from the top down through the lower ranks. Even in Kadar's pacified Hungary, a party theorist admitted that the Stalinist model of party unity, prohibiting all discussion and requiring absolute obedience, had become an anachronism.[7]

As Fejto notes, in all countries of the Bloc the social composition of the parties had been substantially altered by the influx of new generations of officials and graduates, who were more interested in pragmatic solutions, or were downright opportunistic, rather than devoted to ideology. The top levels of the party were now staffed by technocrats and these new people were creating the new criteria of efficiency and 'consumerism' which were to improve the administrative processes. According to the figures provided by this author, the Hungarian party district committees in Budapest had 46 per cent of members with diplomas in 1967; nearly 40 per cent of Yugoslav party members in 1965 were officials, managers and office workers, as against 15 per cent in 1947. The tendency to subordinate politics to economic considerations of efficiency and prosperity was being propagated by all the parties in the Bloc, including the CPSU. 'And whether one likes it or not, it implies the transference of some decision-making power to the experts, managers and technocrats, who are not necessarily Marxist.'[8]

However, such optimism was clearly somewhat premature. The Prague Spring had undermined the intelligentsia; particularly the economists who were in the foreground of the radical Reform Movement, to a certain extent. The intellectuals in the universities, the media and the literary world were also under suspicion, particularly in Poland (with Marxists like Adam Schaff and Leszek Kolakowski choosing to leave the country after 1968) and in Czechoslovakia, where they were forced to choose between demotion, emigration or even face imprisonment. The trend towards Humanist Socialism so much to the fore in 1968 had proved to the leaderships that 'consumerism' could go hand-in-hand with political liberalisation, and political liberalisation could lead to demands for a multi-party system. The new technocratic elite, while less suspected of political liberalism, suffered on account of economic liberalism. It has already been noted that the enterprise manager who was given directives to make profits, proceeded to make profits in his own field regardless of the global economic situation. Unfortunately, the system is unable to accommodate plurality of decision-making or political parties, because of its structure; piecemeal changes on the Czech or Hungarian pattern merely manage to accentuate the problems.

Further, it must be noted that despite the changes in leadership, leaders are never appointed in the prime of their youth. In 1980, a writer comparing the ages of leaders in the Socialist Bloc found that all but one of them (Romania's Ceausescu) were born between 1892 (Tito) and 1913. Though Tito and Brezhnev have since died, those who have remained, and indeed the man who succeeded in USSR after Andropov's death, Chernenko, still have an average age of nearly seventy.[9] Now, there is nothing particularly wrong about having older, experienced leaders in principle. But as Kux so rightly pointed out, those leaders are often in poor health, and suffer from exhaustion. Since Kux had written this, two Soviet leaders have died. In Poland, the two deposed leaders, Gomulka and Gierek, both in their sixties, were said to have suffered heart attacks (which may or may not have been diplomatic illnesses). The newly appointed Soviet leader, Chernenko, is in obvious poor health, and those Eastern European leaders who are still in power and not obviously ill - Husak, Kadar and Zhivkov - have shown distinct signs of ageing in the last few years.

The result is that owing partly to their strenuous jobs and partly to their age, they have tended to delegate their responsibilites more and more. But because they have grown up in a closed circle and because they (rightly or wrongly) hardly ever dare to trust anyone, they appear to delegate responsibilites to those nearest to them; in practice, this usually means their families. This may not be quite so blatant as the situation in North Korea, where the party's First Secretary actually nominated his son to be his successor, but it is very far from the ideal succession on merit.

The following conclusions can therefore be drawn up on the basis of this brief assessment: firstly, that the original parties and leaderships which had to be strongly motivated by ideology, and which were largely Stalinist into the 1950s, or even later in some countries, were replaced, under the impact of de-Stalinisation and for economic reasons, by technocratic elites, which had been educated in a socialist system. However, as these elites grew older in the late 1960s and in 1970s, they followed in the footsteps of other elites everywhere; instead of ensuring the succession on meritorious grounds, they made sure that their children or other closely associated persons had access to succession, if not the actual succession. Conversely, it could be argued that since their children had had the best opportunities to succeed and the best education, they may have been the obvious candidates for succession. But this argument carries no weight in ideological terms of socialism under which each citizen should, in theory, have the same chances of success. Secondly, the assessment shows that the painful process of selecting a leader, or leadership, may eliminate some of the lottery which exists in parliamentary systems (i.e. election by the media, opinion polls, or simply through the sheer weight of capital), but it does not ensure that the best person will succeed, because of peer envy. Thirdly, the elected leader needs to be well known to his peers, if not to the population at large, and hence he arrives at his post too late in life to provide continuity or dynamism. Fourthly, instead of promoting the able, such a leader will of necessity promote the mediocre; again peer envy plays a large part here. And last, but not least, the leadership of Socialist countries is but a reflection of the party membership; that membership had never been open to all and sundry, but has been closely circumscribed by Lenin's dictum about the 'vanguard of the revolution'. This has meant that party membership is kept down to a certain limited percentage of the population, and while grass-roots pressures and ideological demands make sure that a certain percentage of less priviledged citizens is included (such as national minorities, women, workers from the bench and small farmers), the majority of party members are top or middle technocrats, officials and intellectuals.

While this state of affairs is well known on a country-by-country basis, it is still not sufficiently appreciated how steady the membership numbers and quotas are kept on a comparative basis. It is a useful exercise to look at the figures of party membership in relation to the numbers of population in the six countries under investigation:

TABLE II[10]

Country	Population	Party membership
Bulgaria	8,944,000	825,876
Czechoslovakia	15,420,000	1,600,000
East Germany	16,724,000	2,202,277
Hungary	10,691,000	852,000
Poland	36,556,000	2,327,349
Romania	22,649,000	3,300,000

It can be seen clearly that with two exceptions, the membership in each country is kept as near to ten per cent of the population as can be done. Of the two exceptions, one is Poland, where a membership of over three million before the birth of Solidarity had been whittled down to less than two and a half million through resignations and purges; and Romania, which encourages a larger membership than the other countries in order to give the regime a higher degree of legitimacy and to give its loyal citizens a greater measure of reward.

Having thus demonstrated that the parties are the seat of the elites, it will be interesting to see who these elites are and how they behave, compared with the earlier 'conviction' Communists. A brief survey will show that they behave differently in each country in the context of their national policies, but that, taken globally, they bear remarkable similarities to the elites in the capitalist countries. They strive for better housing, better education for their children, expensive cars and retinues of secretaries and servants. They often work long hours, they are afraid of being sacked and they succumb to the executive illness of stress and coronary disease. Should the worst happen, they are in the same position as a redundant Western executive; they lose their privileged positions, grand houses and chauffeured limousines. They have to take menial jobs and their children are often forced to leave the university. The West considers this to be political persecution, but how does it explain the case of a sacked managing director, whose only fault was that he had dared to say 'no' to the chairman, or who was dismissed because a son-in-law had to be found a job? And while statistical data of comparison is not available, in times of recession, or even in periods of boom, the Western executive is perhaps more often at risk than his Eastern European counterpart. The Western executive defends himself by being deferential, trying to be mediocre and sending his wife out to work to protect himself. The Eastern European executive does exactly the same and is probably generally protected by his behaviour. And, as at work, so in the party; the yes-man predominates and gets promoted; the bright analytical person becomes a political dissident. While many studies of the Soviet and Eastern European executives have been made in the West,[11] little effort is given to discovering that the party is a Socialist substitute for the membership of the country club, the golf club, a Masonic lodge or an established church. Each of these organisations performs the function of making the elite meet each other in surroundings outside their working place. The old boys' network in the West is not much different from the Ukrainian mafia and the Leningrad clique in the USSR, or the Natolinians in Poland.

But instead of making mechanical studies of party membership, class origins or promotion ladders, all one needs to do is to see what happens to the displaced chief executive in any Eastern European country in the post-Stalinist era. Khrushchev was displaced and went to live in retirement in a comfortable country house, where he dictated his memoirs, gave interviews to Western journalists and died a disenchanted old man. Dubcek was sent off to Turkey as Czechoslovak ambassador, and after a decent period of time elapsed, was recalled and given a minor job in the provinces. Gomulka was sent into retirement to a country house, where he died of a heart condition in a few years. The Stalinists did not do too badly in Poland either; the former Prime Minister, Cyrankiewicz, was well known to haunt the best hotels in the province where he retired and could be seen every evening in the lounge, waiting to be recognised. East Germany's Walter Ulbricht, received a purely honorific post after it was decided that he was no longer fit to lead the party; a cue which may have been followed by West Germany's Social Democrats in the case of Willy Brandt and Helmut Schmidt. Arguably, these people were the top people in their countries, but a look at lower rungs of the elite will show that similar patterns obtain. In many Eastern European countries there is even pressure to take early retirement from the age of fifty onwards; the executives receive two-thirds of their salary and retain many of the perks of their former job. Thus, some of the features of elitism equal or even surpass those in the West. The system rewards those who serve it, and only punishes those who have transgressed greatly or who have to be made an example of, because the regime has been singularly unsuccessful. This may strike the Westerner as unjust, but it can be compared to the trial of John DeLorean in Los Angeles on a charge which the defence contended has been fabricated in order to frighten the population of the dangers of drug trafficking. Though DeLorean was acquitted, his trial may be on par with that of Maciej Szczepanski in Warsaw, when he was tried to demonstrate the iniquities of the Gierek regime.

However, some examination of how the system works and who its supporters are will be necessary to explore the thesis of middle-class elitism in the Socialist Bloc. While exact classification is not possible because of the national divergences within the Bloc, we will try to divide the parties into those which are conformist and where the leadership has been in power for a period of time and those which have a history either of consistent non-conformism or of sudden revolts.

3. The Conformist Elites

One of the longest periods of uninterrupted leadership is undoubtedly that of Todor Zhivkov in Bulgaria. He has been the First Secretary since 1954, which makes him at present (1984) a leader for more than a generation. This thirty-year period beats even Stalin's record of a quarter of a century and means that (despite longevity due to drinking yoghurt) few Bulgarians remember life without Zhivkov. Yet it is worth remembering that Zhivkov's rule has not been without difficulty and that throughout his period of leadership he has had to fight off rivals and to make many compromises. A protege of Khrushchev, Zhivkov was nearly demoted in 1962 and it was only after a hasty visit by Khrushchev in May of that year, that he managed to consolidate his leadership at the Eighth Congress in November 1962. However, an analyst maintains that though he managed to retain power, 'he has never really succeeded in establishing a relationship of legitimate "authority" either within the party or among the population'. He had to fight off a military plot against his leadership in 1965, only a few months after Khrushchev's deposition; had to purge a rival in 1966, and had to put up with severe CC criticism in 1971. By switching his loyalty to successive Soviet leaders and by keeping a constant watch on potential rivals, Zhivkov has managed to retain his post and entrench himself sufficiently to survive.[12]

Since this article was written, Zhivkov has remained the only Eastern European leader to be still in power and this has obviously given him the status of the 'grand old man' of the Bloc. His leadership is no longer questioned, but no doubt it is questioned how long he will retain his power in the changed circumstances of the country and the party. Bulgaria's bid for a technological revolution may have been accomplished under Zhivkov, but it is doubtful if he was the prime leader of the movement. The bare facts of the matter are that Bulgaria had been brought into the twentieth century in the 1970s and hence her leap into the future seems much more dramatic than would that of a more developed country. Some figures from mid-1970s demonstrate this amply. The Bulgarian population's occupations underwent a sharp restructuring in the first half of the decade, as the following table will show:

TABLE III

Social category[13] (or occupation) in percentages	1970	1974
Blue collar workers	47	57
Collective farmers	28	15
Socialist intelligentsia	23	27
Others	2	1

The change in occupation was directly reflected in the changes in party membership, which will be seen in the following table:[14]

TABLE IV

Changes in party membership between 1971 and 1976

Occupation or sex (in percentages)	10th Congress April, 1971	11th Congress March, 1976
Blue collar workers	40.1	41.4
White-collar workers	28.2	30.2
Collective farmers	26.1	23.0
Women	25.2	27.6

By the end of 1975 there were 788,211 party members, 88,735 more than in 1971, which meant that every eleventh Bulgarian belonged to the organisation. 'The marked increase in the number of white-collar workers (which includes all categories of the intelligentsia) may be related to the scientific-technological revolution, which is producing an ever-increasing number of qualified technological specialists... (It is) claimed that, on average, every third engineering or technological worker is a party member. On the other hand the decrease in the number of collective farmers is a function of the migration from the countryside and of the mechanisation of agriculture that has set large numbers of agricultural workers free.' The age structure of the party was shown to be good; about 70 per cent of members were under 50-years old and 72 per cent of newly admitted members were under 30. But the social structure was not very satisfactory; despite constant calls for the recruitment of technological intelligentsia, blue collar workers and women, the 1976 figures still show an over-representation of farmers and under-representation of women and blue collar workers. It was suggested that membership should be 'regulated' and a strict selection of candidates should be introduced. A call was also made for purging those members who were unsuitable and giving preference to those with higher educational qualifications.[15]

An ironic note was added to these views, when complaints were made that cadres were chosen on the grounds of personal friendships, nepotism or favouritism, and Todor Zhivkov himself twice castigated those members who used the party as a vehicle for further promotion. This, despite the fact that only a few months earlier, Zhivkov's daughter, Lyudmila, has been appointed as head of the Committee on Art and Culture, and the deposed chairman was 'kicked upstairs' to become a chairman of the Central Committee Art and Culture Department.

Miss Zhivkova was then 33-years old, some twenty years younger than her predecessor and has for some years been playing the part of Bulgaria's First Lady. She used to accompany her father on official trips to foreign countries and has several times acted as his personal envoy, when she accompanied the Foreign Minister on his trips to Egypt and West Germany in early 1975. While Miss Zhivkova has obviously had a very good academic career, having graduated in history at Sofia and having taken a postgraduate degree at Oxford, her public career was clearly pushed so fast that even the Politbureau was embarrased. Radio Sofia reported that the Politbureau had decided to agree to the proposal that she become the Chairman of the CAC, the exact wording as given by RFE has it that it was decided 'to agree to propose to the CAC Plenum that (she) be elected chairman of the CAC.'[16]

If being a child of well-placed parents is an advantage, it can also be a disadvantage if the parent falls into disfavour. When Boris Velchev was removed from the Central Committe of the party and from membership of the Politbureau (he had ranked second only to Zhivkov since mid-1960s) in May 1977, his demotion was preceded by a vicious attack in the literary press on his son, a well-known film director. In this, Ilya Velchev was accused of being intolerant of criticism; of relying on his father's reputation to have his work accepted and of deviating from socialist artistic criteria. While the comments from RFE Research point out that Velchev Senior may have been removed as a result of too favourable a view of Eurocommunism, it is assumed that his son was attacked as a prelude to his father's demotion.[17] Nepotism can work both ways; but in a small country with a relatively small elite and a well-ensconced leadership, the disfavour of the leader can prove much more dangerous than in a larger, more tolerant system. Nevertheless, it is worth noting that socialist countries are not free from the usual human weaknesses of selfishness, self-seeking and greed, nor are the elites as monolithic and self-disciplined as they are made out to be. On the other hand, there seems to be no reason why normal human characteristics should be missing in Bulgaria any more than say, in Belgium; it is simply that nobody would turn a hair in Belgium if a father appointed his son to a top position at a very young age. The fact that Bulgaria's socialist principles should act against nepotism is no more valid than the assumption that in a capitalist system promotion should be on the basis of efficiency and not birth. Whichever way we look at the position, we cannot escape the essentials of human nature; they can be minimised or rationalised, but they are seldom eradicated completely. We will discuss the 'rationalisation' theory later on in this chapter.

There are other parties which have a conformist pattern, even if not in the same manner as the Bulgarian party. One such party is the Romanian party. While the government and the leadership of Romania have for over twenty years been a thorn in the self-image of the CMEA and Warsaw Pact organisation, not to speak of a serious embarrassment to the USSR, the party itself has been, with some exceptions, very obedient. The question may well be asked why this is so. If the leadership displays independence and dissent, one would expect the same to happen within the party ranks. The standard answer in the West is that Romania is a very strict police state which does not allow for dissent. It is true that the policing of Romanians is done on a large scale, but this has been the case during the Fascist period and hardly stopped dissent, particularly among the left. A closer look at the Romanian party will explain the position better. Unlike the other parties in the Bloc, the RCP has actually gone out of its way to enlarge the party. In 1975, active party members represented 17.35 per cent of the country's adult population, and 23.67 per cent of its active labour force. The total number of party members at the end of 1975 was 2,577,434; their occupational pattern was broken down as follows:[18]

Workers	50%
Peasants	20%
Intellectuals & White-collar workers	22%
Women (as of 1974)	25%

The situation in 1975 compared favourably with that of 1969, when the percentage of workers in the party was 42.6 per cent, and that of peasants, 28 per cent. The number of women in 1965 was said to have been 21 per cent.[19] Despite the improved situation by mid-1970s, the CC meeting of July 1975, declared its dissatisfaction with the: 'unsatisfactory educational level of members...' 'too many party members with employee status have no higher education and it was decided that such persons should in future be admitted to the party only in exceptional cases...'

> Working people will not normally be granted party membership unless they have at least seven or eight grades behind them. Those with only four grades will be accepted if they have exceptional professional or political qualifications. Evening courses will be organised for party members lacking proper formal education - especially for the younger ones - which will enable them to complete their studies at least to eight-grade level.

The CC further warned the party officials to be careful about admitting peasants, both in the co-operative and private sectors, as party members. On the other hand,

> Particular attention should be paid to increasing the number of women admitted to the party... Engineers, economists, technicians, valuable scientists, those who work in the cultural field, and teachers... will also be welcomed as members.[20]

Some further light is thrown on the general standard of RCP membership by the dissatisfaction shown about the ideological attitudes of the members, 'some of whom have a retrograde attitude to work and an inadequate view of their responsibilities to their families and to society... Further efforts will therefore be made to help all party members to become familiar with communist ideology and ethics, and to develop their militant, combative and revolutionary spirit.'[21]

If the rank-and-file of the fast expanding RCP appears to be lacking both in education and in socialist awareness, the top layer has an overwhelming percentage of the highly educated membership. According to figures given, the leading political activists, who were also top members of the meritocracy were invariably people with high qualifications:[22]

Directors, deputy directors
of ministries, central
enterprises and foreign
trade units with higher education ... 98%

Members of party county
bureaux with higher education ... 81%

Members of executive committee
of county people's councils
with higher education ... 68%

Leaders of national units with
higher education ... 91%

This is sufficient to show that in Romania, the elite governs a large body of under-educated or uneducated party members, whose only road to a degree of prosperity is to follow the directives of the leaders. The party, while ostensibly dominated by people of working-class origins, must surely, in a country which has only begun serious industrialisation in the 1960s, be a party of peasant-workers or peasants; hence the low degree of educational attainment and low female participation. This dichotomy between the leaders and the membership has given rise to what one author describes as a 'worker-party conflict'. The contention is that as communist policies promote growth and competition, they bring conflict in their wake; and that the process of modernisation and industrialisation has required a proliferation of educational and training institutions which bring about 'political socialisation patterns', i.e. that differing opinions, viewpoints and interpretations arise and 'there is nothing to suggest that Communist states are immune to the emergence of... (such) phenomena.'[23] This author further claims that in order to explain these conflicts (real or imagined) the ideologists have invented the term of 'developed socialism', an intermediate stage between capitalism and communism; and that it is claimed that such conflicts will disappear once full communism is operational.

In fact, whatever the truth may be about such conflict in other parties - which will be discussed further on in this chapter - Nelson himself admits that

> Romania seems to be at an earlier point in the dynamic chain. By and large, its industrial labour force is just beginning to question party hegemony, broadly expressing its dissatisfaction through opinions that diverge from accepted priorities of the Romanian Communist Party... Conflictual behaviour - such as the 1977 strike in the Jiu Valley or the more limited work stoppage at the "23 August" enterprise in Bucharest during 1980 - is still the exception.[24]

Nevertheless, since by the 1980s the work-force will be in short supply, and highly paid, but deprived of good housing and other privileges of the elite (luxury consumer goods and high quality cars, such as Mercedes-Benz which are the prerequisites of the top management), the author considers that growing conflicts will ensue, particularly as it has been made clear by the party that the burdens of development must fall primarily on the industrial labour force.

4. The Non-Conformist Elites

The predictions about future Romanian conflict may well prove true, but the contention that the transitional period always brings about conflict seems to be unproven. Additionally, while the Bulgarian and Romanian Communist parties are highly conformist, they are totally different from the ideal of a Marxist party, in so far as they are composed of a majority of members who are of recent peasant origin and who, despite their 'petty bourgeois' mentality, are prepared to put up with socialism, developmental or otherwise. The reasons for this conformity will be discussed later, but their origins do not lie solely in the low educational standards of the membership. There is one conformist party which is much nearer the Marxist ideal - the SED in East Germany - and here conflict appears to arise when developmental socialism has long been forgotten. In fact, the conflict rarely arises among the workers, whose standard of living has been increasing rapidly; the strongest signs of discontent are among the intellectual elite; and even among top party officials.

And it scarcely needs to be repeated that the gravest conflict of all has arisen in a party which was not only strong, highly educated, but also traditionally accepted: the Czechoslovak party; while at the other end of the spectrum a near-revolution occurred in a country which, while strongly agricultural, did not accept the party's leadership for various traditional reasons, and where the party lived on the fringe of society: in Poland. The Czechoslovak party had been one of the strongest Communist parties outside the USSR in the inter-war period. It had genuine support, mostly among the industrial, Bohemian workers, rather than the agricultural population in Slovakia, and it was well known to be pro-Soviet at a time when most other Communist parties were being purged by Stalin in the 1930s, and when Communist regimes were being opposed in Eastern Europe in the late 1940s. The educational standards in Bohemia were generally high and the working-class population strong and highly socialised. There was no problem about large working-class membership even after the Communist coup in 1948.

By 1960 between 75 and 77 per cent of the party were said to be of working-class origin, though it was admitted that only some 25 per cent were at this stage 'workers from the bench.'[25] Unlike in Romania and Bulgaria the farmers did not flock to join the party, which was one of the main complaints of the leadership in the 1950s. On the other hand, like the workers, the intellectuals had joined the party in great numbers and apparently with enthusiasm. During the 1956 events in Poland and Hungary, the Czech leadership was extremely worried that similar problems may

arise in their country. They need hardly have
worried. Taborsky complained as long ago as 1961
that the

> Czech revisionist camp is sorely lacking in
> forceful leadership. Among its adherents
> there is no one anywhere near the calibre of a
> Gomulka or even a Nagy ...; the availability
> of a proper leader at the crucial stage of
> developments in October and November 1956
> might have made a difference. This is
> particularly so because of the rather
> unfortunate Czech habit of waiting for a
> signal from above and depending too much on
> the leader. Among the major traits of the
> Czechoslovak mentality are a down-to-earth
> realism, a mistrust of doctrinaire
> shibboleths, an overdose of caution, a dislike
> for doubtful risks, and a lack of romantic
> heroism. When confronted with what he thinks
> to be a superior power, the average Czech
> resorts to devious maneuvering, covered up by
> a pretense of submission, rather than to an
> outright frontal opposition. He prefers to
> bend and preserve his strength rather than
> break in a gesture of bold defiance. He is
> ready to rise and fight for his cause and
> conviction as much as any one else, but ... he
> is ready to do so only if he sees a realistic
> chance of success.[26]

A very similar assessment of the Czech party's
character is provided by a more modern writer, when
he maintains that the party has always upheld the
Moscow line, when confronted by a choice
between reformist tendencies and foreign
diktat; thus it followed the Soviet policies from
1920 onwards and with a brief break in 1968, it
returned to them after the Prague Spring.[27] It
has already been discussed why the Prague Spring
occurred at all, earlier on in this work, and there
is reason to believe that part of the problem was
the worsening economic situation. But this does
not explain the fact that the Reform movement was
led and sustained by the elite of the Communist
Party, people who were least likely to suffer from
a lowered standard of living, and by the most
privileged intellectuals whose standard of living
was less likely to fall than that of the
workers. And in fact, both Taborsky and Kusin

(who are opposed to the regime) as well as Tampke (who is prepared to make allowances) agree that Czech workers 'accepted' the government and that they were very passive during the summer of 1968, only getting into fray after the Warsaw Pact invasion.[28]

It is clear that the Prague Spring was engineered by the established elite for its own purposes and national pride was only hurt after the Warsaw Pact interfered grossly with the (real or imagined) independence of the country. The puzzling reason for the elite's revolt is perhaps best explained by Bradley, who maintains that the reformists (whose only aims were economic) were overtaken by a party struggle, during which Dubcek attempted to unseat the Novotny leadership.[29] The unusual combination of economic reformers and party opportunities was then overtaken by the enthusiasm of the intellectuals for change, and possibly with some help from the Czech emigres in the West, the situation got swiftly out of hand.

While 'normalisation' in Czechoslovakia was a painful business, and is still, some sixteen years later, not complete, it was achieved in line with the Czech character, cautiously and by the use of the 'carrot and stick' techniques, the carrot predominating over the stick. Kusin sums the process up in three words: coercion, consumerism and circuses. The coercion means a large police force, both secret and riot; but the strongest weapon is the filling of some half a million top positions with either party members or those who can get party approval. The party has been purged; during 1970 alone some one and a half million members were individually screened by special committees. About half a million were deprived of party membership and about 150,000 resigned in protest. One third of office holders in the party were eliminated and only 26 survivors of the pre-1968 Central Committee were in the 137-member Central Committee in 1971, at the Fourteenth Congress. How has the CPCS reacted to all these events? With the exception of those who were deposed or who left voluntarily, it seems to have survived, and Husak has become the great conciliator. Even staunch opponents of the regime wonder at this:

> Presiding over the whole assortment of ideologists, party activators, quasi-

technocrats, CMEA integrationists, and nonentities comprising the Communist leadership in Czechoslovakia today, is Gustav Husak, who is simultaneously party General Secretary and President of the Country. In his name... and under his unquestionably skilful political leadership, the CPCS wiped out the reformism of the Prague Spring and achieved dubious fame as the harshest and domestically least tolerant member state of the Soviet Bloc in the 1970s, not excluding East Germany and Bulgaria. Having defeated reformism, Husak gradually evolved from the Great Normaliser into a consensus preserver and advocate of a status quo that was largely of his own creation. He has doubtless acted in the Soviet interest and perhaps even aspires to replicate in Czechoslovakia the role Leonid Brezhnev has so successfully played in Moscow. But Husak is a derivative, subordinate political figure... Informed foreigners returning from visits to Czechoslovakia talk about Husak's waning influence in all except one aspect of party politics. He is still able to hold the party Presidium in a state of uneasy equilibrium. But the price is "no innovation". No one appears courageous enough to make a radical move, lest the Presidium's balance be lost or lest he find himself exposed to a concerted onslaught by the others.[30]

An exactly opposite situation occurred in Poland, where the Communist party (under its more modern name of PUWP) has never enjoyed the respect of CPCS or the apathetic climate in Romania and Bulgaria. The reasons for this are traditionally explained in terms of Polish Catholicism and anti-Russian sentiments. Such statements involve explaining why the Communist Party of Italy, a country probably more Catholic than Poland, enjoys great vogue; and why the traditionally anti-Russian East Germans hold their party in great respect. Some authors explain it in scientific terms; too few people have been allowed to join the elites.[31] Others, with more reason, point to the fact that the party has been less successful in ensuring economic progress than the parties in other Socialist states, even though Poland has greater economic potential. I have already considered those and other reasons, such as private agricultural enterprises in a previous work[32], and do not propose to repeat them here. However, there are two reasons I would wish to add to those already mentioned; both of which are often overlooked. The first is that the traditional Polish distrust of the Russians (well founded) was reinforced in very recent times; the Hitler-Stalin Pact in 1939 and the Soviet annexation of half of the then Polish Republic has not been forgotten or forgiven, neither has the treatment by Stalin of the Polish population in those provinces. This was strengthened by the non-intervention of Soviet troops in the Warsaw Uprising, whatever justification there may have been. The second reason is more subtle and less easily proven in scientific terms, but nevertheless it is probably the most powerful one. Like many other nations, the Poles have been and still are very snobbish. The Republic of the Gentry is not dead yet, even though the gentry may only be represented at present by the dictator, General Jaruzelski. But unlike many other nations, the Polish middle classes are intellectual snobs, much more than social snobs, modelling themselves in this respect on the French. The fact of the matter is that the 'right people' have never joined the Communist Party in the past or at present. Alone of almost all European countries, Poland has not produced a single 'orthodox' Communist philosopher or writer, though many Marxist thinkers like Kolakowski and Schaff have developed revisionist theories. The Polish party has always suffered from an invasion of really underprivileged proletarians, or plain opportunists. It was further compromised by the Stalinist element in the 1940s and 1950s and by what can be only described as a Fascist element, as exemplified by Moczar.

All these factors have meant that the PUWP is the least stable and the least socially secure party in the Socialist Bloc and, as a result, tends either to compromise too much or to over-react in emergencies. The instability of the party is well illustrated by a writer who examined the turnover in the PUWP and came to the conclusion in mid-1970s that:

> In comparison with other East European Communist Party elites, turnover within the Polish Central Committee may well be quite high.

143

This was reflected in the age of the CC membership, whose average age in 1971 was forty-five. By 1964 only 24 per cent of those who had been members in 1959 were in the CC. By 1971, 61 per cent of members were newcomers since 1964. The author calls this 'a rather remarkable example of party rejuvenation.' One would rather, particularly in view of the turnover of the top leaders and the disasters the party encountered, call it an example of strong and sustained instability.[33]

Hence, in Poland, unlike in other countries of the Bloc, the problem is not so much of poor party leadership, but of a basic lack of leadership, the main cause of which is its lack of social and intellectual influence. The Polish case is extreme and will be discussed later on in this work in another context. It has simply been introduced here to demonstrate that non-conformism in the Polish party stems from exactly the opposite sources than that in Czechoslovakia. Where the CPCS has traditionally enjoyed the support both of the population and of the Kremlin, the Polish party has had to jockey even for the minimum of support in the country and its nationalistic tendencies have made it even more suspect in Moscow. This may explain why the revolutions which happen in Poland are always different from those which occur in other countries in the Bloc.

CHAPTER FIVE: FOOTNOTES

1. See: Marc D. Zlotnik: <u>Chernenko Succeeds;</u> <u>Problems of Communism,</u> March-April 1984, p. 17-31.
    Some inkling of the decision-making processes has been given by Churchward in <u>Contemporary Soviet Government</u>, and the 1970 edition of Schapiro's <u>The Communist Party of the Soviet Union</u>, but the lack of confidential data, such as records of the meetings of the CC (though Andropov has introduced the publication of truncated reports of the meetings,) does not allow us a good insight into the workings of the inner circle of the government and party.

2. Alex Brummer: <u>Kremlin offered secret arms talks by Reagan diplomats,</u> The Guardian, 27 June 1984.

3. See; <u>Reply of Comrade L.I. Brezhnev to questions by the correspondent of Pravda,</u> <u>Pravda</u> 6 November 1979.

4. See: Daniel Yergin: <u>Shattered Peace,</u> and Jerry W. Sanders: <u>Peddlers of Crisis</u>.

5. Jurgen Tampke: <u>The People's Republics</u>, Table 1.1, p.22.

6. Tampke: <u>The People's Republics</u>, p. 93.

7. Francois Fejto: <u>A History of the People's Democracies</u>, p. 348.

8. Fejto: <u>A History</u>, p.350-51.

9. Ernst Kux: <u>Growing Tensions in Eastern Europe,</u> <u>Problems of Communism,</u> March-April 1980, Table 1, p.25.

10. Figures according to <u>Checklist of Communist Parties in 1983,</u> <u>Problems of Communism,</u> March-April 1984, p.45.

11. Perhaps the best known is J.F. Hough's <u>The Soviet Prefects: the local party organs in industrial decision-making</u>.

12. Stephen Larrabee: <u>Bulgaria's Politics of Conformity,</u> <u>Problems of Communism,</u> July-August 1972, p. 43-44.

13. I have transcribed the term 'social category' into 'occupation' to conform to the Western categories, because it complies more with the actual state of affairs. A farmer who becomes a blue collar worker has changed his occupation, hardly his origin or social belonging. Table compiled from <u>RFE Research/51 Bulgaria</u>, 23 February 1976, Table 2.

14. Table compiled from RFE Research/51, Bulgaria, 23 February 1976 Table 1.
15. RFE Research/51, Bulgaria, 23 February 1976, p. 3-5.
16. RFE Research/18, Bulgaria, 26 June 1975, p.5-6.
17. RFE Research/14, Bulgaria, 16 May 1977, p.1-4.
18. Scinteia, 24 April 1976 as quoted by RFE Research/15 Rumania, 7 May 1976.
19. Scinteia, 8 August 1969, as quoted by RFE Research / 126 Rumania, 18 August 1975.
20. RFE Research/126, Rumania, 18 August 1975, p.5.
21. RFE Research/126, Rumania, 18 August 1975, p.6.
22. Extracts from RFE Research/126 Rumania 18 August 1975, Table, p.7.
23. Daniel N. Nelson: Worker-Party Conflict in Romania, Problems of Communism, September-October, 1981, p.41.
24. Nelson: Worker-Party Conflict, p. 43.
25. See: Edward Taborsky: Communism in Czechoslovakia, 1948-1960, p. 34-35.
26. Taborsky: Communism, p. 128-129.
27. Vladimir V. Kusin: Husak's Czechoslovakia and Economic Stagnation, Problems of Communism, May-June 1982, p. 24-25.
28. See: Tampke: The People's Republics, p. 107, on the basis of research by H. Gordon Skilling and Alex Pravda.
29. See: Bradley: Politics in Czechoslovakia, Ch. 6.
30. Kusin: Husak's Czechoslovakia, p.37.
31. See: Sanford: Polish Communism in Crisis, p. 10-11, where the use of schematic terms such as 'Central Political Elites' and 'Supporting Communist Intellectual Elite' is suggested to explain the lack of popularity for the party.
32. The Green Flag, Ch. 11 and 12.
33. See: Donald Pienkos: Party Elites and Society: the Shape of the Polish Communist Party Central Committee since 1945, Polish Review, No. 4, 1975, particularly p. 39-40.

THE CMEA'S ECONOMY AND WORLD RECESSION

---

1. Politics and Economics of the Comecon

Probably the only certain thing about the CMEA (Council for Mutual Economic Assistance) is that its statutes, organisation and internal arrangements are extremely imponderable. The result of the involved procedures and legalistic devices has made the CMEA a body which is as complicated as the EEC and probably equally distrusted. One must question whether Europeans in general (Western or Eastern) are capable of economic co-operation without the usual tariff barriers, customs difficulties and competitive practices. The Thatcher government's demands for 'our money' are very similar to the Ceausescu government's demands for 'our freedom to trade', and probably equally well, or ill-founded, depending from which side one is observing them. It must be admitted that despite almost four decades, during which both organisations have existed, the will to do deals in good faith has been missing in both the EEC and the CMEA; and apart from the normal difficulties of communication between the various nationalities and the acknowledged economic difficulties which always exist in such organisations, it is perhaps overlooked that the European nations hardly ever liked to co-operate with each other, except when their borders were not adjoining, or when they were in dire difficulties owing to some disaster, like a war.

Hence, because the economic organisations have always been investigated by economists or political scientists, with scarcely a glance at sociology or even anthropology, their real - as against their theoretical - nature has never been well understood. Grand phrases about the elimination of war because of the EEC, or about the brotherly help of the USSR to the smaller economies ring hollow, or downright funny to a social historian who is attempting to reconstruct the past and perhaps get a glimpse into possible future prospects.

We do know some facts about the CMEA; it is an organisation of states with the same political systems, in one area of Europe. This is true even if the organisation has accepted the membership of some non-European countries; such membership is relatively speaking, very marginal. The CMEA was set up originally to offset the bilateral trading patterns with the USSR which had been used till 1949; in these patterns the smaller economies suspected that they received a raw deal and envisaged that they would be able to drive a better bargain in a larger multilateral organisation. On its side, the USSR intended to press the smaller economies harder in the areas of socialisation; particularly with regard to collectivisation and rapid industrialisation. The conception was partly correct, partly faulty: late Stalinism was hardly in a position to provide liberal policies for countries ruined by war and not particularly happy to be excluded from the generous provisions of the Marshall Aid. Therefore, hasty collectivisation and industrialisation could only do harm at this stage. On the other hand, the correct part consisted in the appreciation that the countries in the Bloc had a large, and largely misused economic potential, and that better use could be made in almost every field of their economies.

The problem of the relations between the smaller states in the Bloc and the USSR was very serious; however, perhaps more serious was the fact that the CMEA was set up in response to what the East saw as a 'Western threat'. One leading economist has pointed out that the original plans after the war were to set up a united economic system throughout Europe; the ECE, a UNO body, was set up in Geneva in 1947 with just such an aim:

> as a regional organisation ... and was to be concerned with initiating and participating in concerted measures aimed at securing the economic reconstruction of Europe. The aim

was to create an instrument of co-operation between all the states of Europe, Eastern, Central and Western. Unfortunately, by the time it began to operate, the Cold War had become a reality and the world had been divided into two camps.[1]

The path of Western European unity did not go any smoother than that of the Eastern Bloc. The UK and the Nordic countries did not join the original Western bodies; and the military organisation, designed to parallel the economic unity, was joined by many powerful non-European countries, such as the US and Canada. (The case for Turkey, a member of NATO, is rather curious; Turkey is not a European state either culturally or politically, though it has been approaching some of these aims during the Kemal Attaturk period. But it can be paralleled by the description of Greece, always acknowledged to have been a Balkan, and therefore a South-East European state, as a 'Western European' country.) All in all, the Western Alliance produced some strange bed-fellows, and it can hardly be said that the West is any more consistent in its membership patterns than the East.

The point which is rarely made is taken up by Swann in detail. This is the basic aim of the economic organisations: are they to be purely commercial - such as the EFTA alliance - or do they have to have a political content. Neither the EEC nor the CMEA have ever had the courage to tackle this problem head on; though the changes in attitudes in the West[2] could quite easily be matched by similar arguments within the CMEA. One need only look at the language which expresses the aims of the CMEA as integrational, while at the same time assuring the individual countries of their independence:

The member states of the CMEA construct the foundations of their inter-state relations on the basis of <u>full equality, the protection of sovereignty of each state as well as the protection of national interest, mutual gain and brotherly assistance</u>. This basis ensures a fruitful co-operation of socialist states in the building of socialism and communism, and simultaneously retains the Leninist principle of peaceful coexistence of states with different social systems and agrees with international socialist principles.[3]

The underlying problems which gave rise to this strong emphasis on sovereignty and national interests (that is, problems of a political rather than economic nature) produced a compromise situation with regard to decision-making procedures. The CMEA decisions which are not agreed to by a member country, need not be implemented by the said country. But the member who disagrees may still, at a later stage, join the contested programme if he so wishes. The decade of 1960s was a period of attempting to introduce a division of labour system between all the members, but by 1969 this problem had not been solved, mostly due to each member's insistence on retaining his own independent decision-making processes. It became obvious that in order to encourage the division of labour system, harmonisation and mutual co-operation, they had to be seen by members as profitable and economically stimulating. The Twenty-third Special Session of the CMEA, which took place in Moscow in April, 1969, set up the new 'Complex Programme of Further Deepening and Improving Co-operation and Development of Socialist Economic Integration of the Member States of CMEA'[4], but by 1984 the problem is, if anything, more serious than in the 1960s.

One of the results of the insistence of member-states to retain their independence in economic matters was the increasing trade with the non-Socialist world, which in turn led to the serious indebtedness of many of the Eastern European countries. The original debt, acquired between 1970 and 1973, may have been possible to absorb; the rise in oil prices, raw materials and interest rates after 1973, negated any positive results that such trade may have initially produced. Like the EEC, which is stuck on the horns of the dilemma of large agricultural subsidies and enormous military expenditure by NATO countries, (both linked to the desire to strengthen the right-wing farmers' lobby and the anti-Soviet lobby, and both continued because of US pressure), so the CMEA is stretched between the impossible aims of retaining national independence in economic matters with the necessity of abdicating this independence to the USSR in political and military matters. The EEC compensates for this by deflationary policies when times get hard - as in the 1973-84 period; the CMEA's attempts, very timid ones, one must admit, to deflate, usually produce a social outburst on a large scale. Western Europe's deflationary policies have, in the end, to be paid for by the USA, often in the form of allowing large European imports at the expense of domestic manufacturers; Eastern European debt can only be paid for by the USSR.

Eventually, the <u>reductio ad absurdum</u> of this situation is that the two super-powers, which have tacitly and openly supported the setting up of organisations with a quasi-colonial status, find - like the older colonial powers before them - that instead of bringing in benefits, the satellites are a considerable burden. And the follow-up to this is punishment; in the US the right-wing senatorial lobby has expressed a strong interest in withdrawing from Europe in June, 1984, as the involvement is too expensive; in the USSR the anti-<u>Solidarity</u> lobby made sure that the Polish revolt is paid for by the Polish population, rather than, as in the case of Hungary and Czechoslovakia, by the USSR. Both Eastern and Western Europe cry pathetically that they want to become, are, or have been the 'Third Force'; in fact this role has long ago been taken over by the 'Non-Aligned States', most of which are non-European, and by such organisations as OPEC, and Latin-American bodies. It could well be in Europe's best interests to forget her super-power status in the nineteenth century and address herself to the twenty-first century. But this state of reality has yet to dawn on most European politicians whose dreams of power have been formed by Cecil Rhodes and his like.

Naturally, it is not the purpose of this work to compare the problems encountered by the EEC with those of the CMEA; but merely to draw attention to the fact that such problems exist, and that they are, at least in a large measure, the result of the unnatural division of Europe and the pressures exerted by super-powers on their own sphere of influence. But, faced with these difficulties, the European politicians would be better advised to concentrate on bridge-building - difficult though it may be - than on adding to their problems by blindly following the big powers' political struggle. There are some exceptions on both sides of the divide; West Germany has been foremost in expanding its trade patterns with the Eastern Bloc, and Romania has done the same in the West. But West Germany is mostly concerned with trade with East Germany, for obvious reasons; whereas Romania's foreign trade is more an index of its recalcitrant leadership's desire to demonstrate its independence of the Soviet Union than a response to a rational economic need. Indeed, it could probably be proven that in terms of monetary gain, West Germany is losing heavily on its economic 'Drang nach Osten' (as witness the losses on the Polish debt in the period 1981-83), and Romania's economic position has been jeopardised by its extensive trade links with the West.

There could and should be better ways of improving European economies and they have been sabotaged over the last four decades. Those who run European politics have chosen to disregard the natural trade patterns which had existed in Europe for centuries: in those, Eastern Europe exported food and raw materials to Western Europe and bought manufactured goods and high technology in return. These patterns were not very satisfactory, particularly during periods of low grain and raw material prices, but they could have been built upon and improved under the guidance of the ECE. This pattern was the one which has been used by the Russian Empire before the 1917 Revolution, in which a spectacular period of industrial growth and prosperity was attained by Russia on the basis of foreign investment and foreign expertise. While the USSR had been forced into an autarkic economy after 1921 (because of the mutual obduracy of Soviet government and Western bankers), there was no reason why autarky should be extended to the Eastern Bloc after 1945. Some proof of how fruitful East-West economic co-operation could be had been given by the success of the wartime arrangement between the USA and USSR; had it not been for the Cold War co-operation could have continued with mutual benefit.

While the Soviet Union did its best to block East-West trade by refusing to allow the Bloc countries to join the Marshall Aid programme in 1947; mainly according to one author, because:

> Stalin's objections were probably based on his desire to preserve his influence over economic and political development in Eastern Europe and on his personal predilection for the dominance of steel production which would have been threatened by the subsequent proposals for dollar viability ...

the USA was not backward in blocking such trade on its side:

> The American embargo on exports of strategic and technological products, which accounted for approximately 50 per cent of internationally traded products to Eastern Europe, was extended to prevent all recipients of Marshall Aid from trading with Eastern Europe, a policy which was co-ordinated by the establishment of CoCom ... The subsequent slide into cold war, the Berlin blockade and the Korean War meant that by the time of Stalin's death in 1953 the moves towards economic union were sufficiently advanced to prevent the re-establishment of former or potential trade links ...[5]

As a result, Smith maintains that North Eastern and Central Eastern countries were damaged; in particular, Czechoslovakia, which suffered from the high technology embargo and Poland, which had its coal exports undermined by the development of the European Coal and Steel Community. The agricultural policies of the EEC also had a serious effect on the agriculture in some countries of the Eastern Bloc. However, it should not be forgotten that the Western European states had had a large traditional market cut off, with little or no compensation elsewhere. Hence, the policy of isolation, enforced for political reasons, made little sense in economic terms.

But the problems did not end there. For various reasons, which cannot be discussed here, but most of which were connected with Soviet inexperience of trading with socialist states, and with Soviet dislike of the formation of sub-blocs within the Bloc, most trade within the Bloc was conducted on a _Radial_ pattern, that is, between the USSR and each individual country. In the early 1950s, most of the trade from Hungary, Czechoslovakia and Poland was with the USSR; it is estimated to have been between 25 and 30 per cent of their global trade. Over half of Bulgaria's trade and some 75 per cent of Romania's trade was similarly directed. The Soviet Union imported machinery and equipment as well as steel products from Czechoslovakia, Poland and East Germany, and exported raw materials and fossil fuels in return. On the other hand, the trade went in the opposite direction with the less developed countries, like Bulgaria and Romania.

Thus, the accident of political necessity and economic expediency created a situation which was essentially inbred trading; an organisation which has been called by one economist 'a trade diverting customs union'.[6] The result of financial arrangements within the Bloc discourages deals of a competitive nature between the Bloc countries, as well as encouraging them to enter into loss-making deals with hard-currency countries. In the most simplistic terms available to non-economists, the chase for hard-currency deprives the CMEA of valuable potential to improve the economic situation inside the Bloc. Of course, this is not unique to CMEA. A similar situation exists in the EEC, which deprives itself of the benefits of cheap imported goods and food, at the expense of subsidising inefficient home industries. Had this been done in order to maintain full employment (which happens and results in inefficiency in the CMEA), the EEC would at least have justification for such actions. But in the EEC it does not even provide full employment; so it might be argued that the CMEA is in some respects more efficient than the EEC.

In ideological terms, therefore, the CMEA serves the Bloc better than the EEC does Western Europe, particularly as it has, since 1973, suffered a series of severe recessions, resulting in a very high unemployment rate. Politically, the CMEA isolates the Bloc from the West to a large extent, and makes it dependent on the Soviet Union. This has its advantages and disadvantages for all the concerned parties. Economically, however, there seems to be no conclusive answer as to whether the CMEA benefits the USSR, the smaller countries of the Bloc, or the West. Nor is it entirely clear who is the exploiter and who is the exploited within the CMEA. While Smith is inclined to claim that the CMEA does more for the small

economies than for the USSR and that the small
economies benefit from the terms of trade with the
big economy compared with Western European
countries trading with the outside countries[7],
one would be disposed to assume that the balance of
profit and loss is variable and depends on the
circumstances of the period, as well as on the
economic situation outside the CMEA.

What is certain, however, is that whatever
benefit the smaller economies derive from their
association with the big partner, their citizens
feel a sense of grievous exploitation (as witness
the Polish conviction that the shortage of meat is
due to it being sent to the USSR; the Romanian fury
at having to pay more for oil, when the USSR has
exhausted Romania's reserves; and the Czech
annoyance at having to export scarce manufactured
goods to the USSR, to mention but a few instances)
and that the CMEA governments do not lag far behind
in a similar attitude. Thus the economic benefits
which those countries probably derive from the
union are outweighed by political losses; and while
the image of the Soviet Union as the bullying 'Big
Brother' is perhaps more universally disliked than
that of the USA in Western Europe, that analogy is
rather too disturbing to contemplate.

It would probably be worth - had either of the
super-powers a far-seeing leadership which can
count the real cost of domination - for both the
USSR and the USA to estimate whether pulling out of
their own spheres of influence, both economically
and politically, would not have a better effect of
improving their image, and improving the Europeans'
image of themselves. A beaten continent, which
believes (whether justifiably or not) that it is
suffering from oppression, is not a very good
investment for a super-power. On the other hand,
it is questionable whether those same European
nations which were ready for fratricidal wars for
centuries would not again indulge in collective
madness, once the super-powers relaxed their grip.
In the final analysis, therefore, the answer must
be left open: the historian must look at things as
they are, and not as they could be. The real
difficulty is that in the atmosphere of distrust,
prefabricated data and often spurious statistics,
most things are not as they appear to be. Among
those, perhaps the most striking is the difficulty

of enquiring into the bilateral trade patterns in the CMEA.

2. Patterns of Trade within the CMEA

It has already been established that one of the problems in the CMEA is its indeterminate status, in which political factors vie with economic factors for dominance. The second problem is that of its protectionist nature. The third one is due to the protectionist nature of its equivalent in Western Europe, the EEC. But perhaps the most intractable one is that of intra-Bloc trading, for reasons which had been touched upon in the previous section. According to some authorities, the main reason for this was the Korean War, during which the USSR lost interest in integrating the area, and instead insisted on each country producing war materials. In view of this attitude, each Eastern European country developed its own heavy industrial base, duplicating production in other countries, and resulting in a vertical decision-making process.

The difficulties arising out of the arguments between the individual countries may have been instrumental in the calling of the Special Session of the CMEA in 1969; particularly as the post-1968 situation in Czechoslovakia demanded quick action. But there were other problems too. The CMEA's own study mentions as one of the most important ones the shortage of labour; in 1969, after decades of spectacular growth -

> one of the major factors allowing extensive growth - the rise in the number of workers - was almost completely exhausted in the member-countries of the CMEA. This meant that there was a necessity of using more fully intensive factors of development of national economies: technological progress ... particularly in the field of manufacturing plant, machines, better use of the tools, raising of the qualifications of the workers and the use of scientific organisation of labour and production.[8]

In fact, the suggested remedies appear, at least
according to capitalist commentators, to produce a
rapid increase in inflation. The dilemma has been
underlined in 1984, when the 'capacity-utilisation'
was stopping expansion, despite a large level of
unemployment. Like the Eastern Bloc, the West has
found that

> a capacity constraint does not mean absence of
> factories or service facilities with physical
> space for producing more. It means a shortage
> of capacity relevant to current technology and
> market demand and which it is profitable to
> bring into operation at current levels of
> wages and material costs.[9]

Further, Brittan states that 'the alleged crunch is
being brought about by two forces. Manufacturing
output has been growing faster than in previous
recoveries; but capacity has been rising more
slowly thanks to a decade of sluggish capital
spending'. In addition, it is the Federal
Reserve's official view that once the capacity-
utilisation level reaches 82 per cent, inflation
takes off. This provides a 'Catch 22' situation
in Western-type developed economies: high
unemployment, low manufacturing capacity and a
rising inflation combined with high capital outlay
to compensate for previous low capital outlays, are
bound to produce a serious economic crisis, which
would make the recession of the early 1980s a small
hiccup by comparison.

The above comparison makes one wonder whether
the take-off in the Eastern European rate of
inflation in the early 1970s and the subsequent
economic and social crisis did not owe more to the
decisions taken by the CMEA in 1969 to introduce
higher rates of capacity-utilisation and higher
capital spending, than to the rise in oil prices -
which in any case was moderate for some more years
to come. The old chestnut, that the Eastern
European workers have no goods to spend their money
on, has been exploded long ago; they may not spend
on goods in official shops, but they certainly
spend on open markets (whether black or grey). A
surplus of money would certainly not have produced
revolts by Polish workers each time the price of
food was raised; if they had a surplus, such rises
could be absorbed. Indeed, Alan Smith draws

attention to the inflationary patterns in Eastern Europe, and compares them to similar pressures in the UK.[10]

Perhaps it is a pity that neither Mr Samuel Brittan nor the Federal Reserve Board were represented (so far as we know) at the Special Session of the CMEA in 1969; had their advice been available, the countries present may have decided to continue on their previous course of more labour-intensive enterprises, and less capital spending. However, this merely goes to show that Eastern European and Soviet economists feed off the same sources as Western Europe and American ones do: and the difference of implementation is much more due to political pressures than to economic theories. In view of the subsequent events, one wonders if a return to Stalinist economics of autarky in 1970, rather than more than a decade later, would not have been more appropriate than aping the techniques used by 'market economies', and even then with less and less evidence of success. It may well be that the much vaunted technological progress has been the source of more pain than gain for industrial and industrialising countries, and that, like the 'Green Revolution' of the 1950s and 1960s, the sooner it is forgotten the better. Certainly the Poles have developed a new plan, starting in 1982, which has more than a pinch of Stalinism in it: the Three S's campaign (the letters stand for 'Samowystarczalnosc, samopomoc, samofinansowanie') stresses the value of self-help and self-financing. The burden of the debt and the trade boycott by the West have already forced Poland into a retreat from high technology. It could well be that this may be the beginning of economic revival, given a sufficient relaxation in the political climate.

The above information provides sufficient evidence that the economies of the CMEA are not impervious to the same factors that affect the Western economies. Nor are they unaffected by the insistence on following national interest, even within the Bloc. But because the Bloc is, if anything, even more hemmed in by tariffs and regulations than the EEC, and the countries concerned tend to be even more hostile to each other than the members of the EEC, the in-fighting is if not more bitter (can there by anything more bitter than the British-French lamb war?) at least, less conclusively resolved, because of a lack of resolution machinery.

Another complication in the CMEA stems from the fact that, apart from ministers in the Council representing their own national interests, each country has its own national economic bodies whose heads have an interest in retaining their power; in those circumstances even beneficial changes are opposed, and status quo preferred.

It was against the background of such difficulties that the Special Session suggested economic integration and specialisation. Particular stress was put on the development of scientific and technological exchange, co-operation and sharing of documentation. Another important point was the development of the 'Friendship' oil pipeline to ensure the supply of fuel to those countries which did not have it. Further plans included the concentration of large, high-technology projects in specific areas, in order to make them more cost-efficient.[11] Very much in line with current Western economic theories (but out of necessity, because of labour shortages, not because of high labour costs) the CMEA was aiming at very large increases in labour productivity, which was to rise in the five-year period of 1971-75 from four per cent to five per cent. Another important point, which is made by a Western commentator, was that planning was to return to its former, centralised shape, and to play a more important role than financial levers. This was apparently done in view of the Czechoslovak debacle, rather than for economic reasons.[12]

The political rather than the economic importance of the Council was further stressed by the Soviet government's statement that the Twenty-Seventh Session of the CMEA which aimed at 'the development and deepening of socialist integration in the economic sphere will have an important political meaning for the further strengthening of the position of the socialist systems in the world and will (demonstrate) the unity of the CMEA countries'. The Warsaw Pact was equally pleased. 'The strengthening of the economic and military power of the member-states of the Warsaw Pact serves the aim of peace and social progress on a global scale', stated a resume of the meeting of the Political Committee of the Pact held in Prague in January, 1972.[13]

The endorsement of the Complex Programme in 1971 has been accompanied by the establishment of a Committee for Co-operation in Planning Activity in 1972; by the decision that special integration measures would be introduced into each country's planning systems in 1973, by the introduction of an Agreed Plan for Multilateral Integration Measures in 1975 and, perhaps most importantly, by the establishment of the International Investment Bank in 1970, whose operation was mainly concerned with promoting joint planning measures, and improving long-term credit facilities for those countries which wished to follow the specialisation in industry agreed in the Complex Plan. The usefulness of the Bank must be obvious to all member-states of the CMEA, because Romania which refused to join in 1970, finally applied for membership in 1971.[14]

There is no doubt that the USSR finances most, if not all, of the capital expenditure of the Bloc, particularly since the beginning of the debt crisis. It is also responsible for the debts incurred by several countries (most notably Poland) with the Western banks or governments. On the other hand, there is also overwhelming evidence that the USSR is the major influence and the major trading partner in the Bloc, despite (or perhaps because of) the introduction of integrational measures at the beginning of the 1970s. If one doubts the conclusions of Western economists, one need only look at the detailed account of intra-Bloc trade provided by the joint CMEA study: this makes it plain that from between half and three-quarters of the trade in the 1970-75 period was of a _radial_ nature; i.e. between the Soviet Union and one country, and that the agreements on specialisation seemed to concentrate on the two areas of utmost importance: on the one hand, the export of fossil fuels from the USSR to all Eastern European countries, on the other, the development of machinery, vehicles and chemical plant, as well as computers to provide the backbone of new or renewed Soviet industries.[15]

Discussing the same subject, one Western economist estimated, on the basis of figures issued by the CMEA, that more than a half of the trade was still, in 1975, of a _radial_ kind:

In 1975, this share, calculated as a percentage of the total trade of individual countries which can be subject to a downward bias, ranged from 53.9% in Bulgaria to 28.1% in Poland and 19.4% in Rumania ... Calculated as a percentage of the total intra-bloc trade it ranged from 74% in Bulgaria to 47.9% in Rumania, with the remaining four countries having their share of between 50% and 57%. It seems, therefore, that the "radial" pattern, which was established during the late 1940s and the early 1950s, is still very much in evidence, although its relative importance differs from one member country to another. In comparison with the trade of East European countries with the USSR their trade with any other individual COMECON country is small. If the volume of trade may be accepted as a rough indicator of economic integration, COMECON integration is still very much simply a dependence of individual member countries on trade with their big neighbours which takes place even in the absence of any integration measures and any special institutions. The links are, however, particularly strong because of the special political relationship between the Soviet Union and Eastern Europe. Without closer links among East European countries, it is, however, difficult to talk about the integration of the bloc as a whole.[16]

The subsequent developments, following the oil crisis, the debt problems and the Western recession, only served to strengthen the dependence of East European countries on the USSR. This was made even worse by the trade boycott imposed on the USSR after the Afghanistan invasion and on Poland and USSR after the outlawing of Solidarity. Other measures, such as the ban on the export of high technology, and the clamp-down on various East European trade missions, often done in the guise of anti-spy operations, completed the bleak picture. If Eastern European countries had been on the road to less dependence on the Soviet Union at the beginning of the 1970s, that prospect was almost completely out of the picture at the end of the decade. The oil crisis, must, therefore, be counted among the most important events in Eastern European history.

3. The Results of the Oil Crisis

The oil crisis, or rather, to give it an exact definition, the rises in the price of crude oil following the Israeli-Egyptian War of 1973, engineered by OPEC, for reasons which have not yet been made exactly clear (but which had much to do with OPEC's grievances about the low prices enforced by the Western oil companies on the producers over a long period of time) had a dual effect on the CMEA countries. On the one hand, these countries - or some of them - were net fuel exporters, which made their exports more valuable. Therefore, unlike the EEC, the CMEA could expect some gain. The dramatic difference in the position of both blocs in this respect is best shown in figures:

> COMECON, seen as a uniform area, is autarchic with respect to its energy supply. Contrary to the EEC which had to import almost 60% ... of its energy consumption from third countries in 1975, COMECON has always been able in recent years to achieve an export surplus of about 6% of its energy consumption ... the result for 1975 is a net export of 100 million tons SCE* which corresponds to about one third of the energy consumption of the Federal Republic of Germany ...; these and the following data do not include primary power. Net exporters, however, are only the Soviet Union and Poland. All other European COMECON countries have depended increasingly on energy imports in recent years. In these five countries, the share of such imports in overall domestic consumption ... increased from 20% to 30% between 1970 and 1975.[17]

The Comecon is further fortunate in its use of energy resources. Unlike the other areas in the world (with one exception) the area uses a 'mix' of fuels which is much more suited to its reserves.

---

* Standard Coal Equivalent

As one oil expert stated not many years ago: 'Most of you will not need to be told that oil-import dependency has grown rapidly in Eastern Europe ... and you might assume that this has brought them into approximately the same "mix" of primary energy usage as other parts of the world, especially industrial counterparts'. In fact, a survey comparing the CMEA countries with all the other world regions in the BP Statistical Review of the World Oil Industry for 1978, in the use of oil and natural gas shows that this is not so. 'On both counts, Eastern Europe is seen to have a lower oil or oil and gas content in its use of total energy than any main region except China. This is remarkable in view of the relative lack of industrialisation in developing areas who neverthe-less have a more "modern" energy mix than one of the world's major industrial areas'.[18]

According to Scanlan, two factors emerge; firstly that the USSR, Hungary, Bulgaria and Romania are roughly similar in their energy consumption; oil and natural gas together comprise at least 50 per cent of their total energy usage. This is against the OECD regions which use about 70 per cent of oil and natural gas, but, more interestingly, compared with the so-called 'northern' three, Poland, GDR and Czechoslovakia, one finds that here the total use of oil and natural gas is one third of their energy use, and oil only a quarter. The rest of the energy use is accounted for by the use of non-fossil fuels (hydroelectric and nuclear) which amount to about three per cent of the total and by coal and lignite consumption.[19]

While it is perhaps natural that a commentator from a major Western oil company should find Eastern European energy policy obsolete (however beneficial this turned out to be in the long run), the same view about the attractiveness of oil as against coal was being widely expressed in Eastern Europe, particularly in Poland, even after 1973. One major article on the virtues of crude oil, published in 1974, stated the following:

> The economic superiority of oil is quite obvious. It is a universal fuel, with a calorific value 1.5 higher than that of better quality coal. It is more efficient and much cheaper to transport. This is why increasing

use of liquid fuels has helped lower
production costs in industry and agriculture.
Countries that employ more efficient and more
economical raw materials can produce more
cheaply, and thus achieve a faster rate
of growth of national income, than countries
that base their production on less efficient
materials, which mean more expensive
industrial production.

Indeed, as the author noted, the use of oil and
natural gas has risen sharply in Poland since 1968.
The superiority of oil also meant that 'coal has
also lost its earlier importance as a raw material
in the chemical industry. It has been replaced
largely by oil and partly by natural gas, which are
indispensable for modern chemical synthetics ...',
some of which cannot be made from coal at all.[20]
A few months later, another commentator saw
things rather differently. In view of the energy
crisis the demand for hard coal has increased,
hence it was worth looking at Polish coal
production with reference to domestic economy, and
its value on the export market.

Coal is at once the most important source of
energy in Poland and its main export. Thanks
to coal, which provides 70% of our primary
energy, Poland is (apart from the Soviet
Union) the country least dependent in both
Eastern and Western Europe on imports of fuel.
... We have sufficient hard and brown coal
resources to last us for at least three
hundred years. It seems pointless to discuss
today whether we were right in not following
the example of such countries as France or
Holland, which in general gave up coal in
favour of oil and its products. As our most
important export, hard coal made up 9.8% of
our total export value in 1973. ... In
previous years, the part played by coal in
Polish export was even bigger.[21]

After the eulogy, came the usual monetarist
warning: while it was difficult to estimate the
cost of mining Polish coal, because of the
unrealistic rate of exchange and fluctuations of
foreign currency and prices, Polish mining must be
made more productive, and the increased amount of

coal to be mined in the future two decades must be accomplished without increasing the work-force. While the writer of the article praising oil against coal may have been following one fashion - modernisation - the second writer seems to have been reading Milton Friedman. Both were wrong: the cost of miners' disturbances in 1976, not to speak of 1980-82, which were exacerbated by the increased production norms, must have been much higher in real terms (apart from social and political terms) than the lower cost of production. Like the British miners' strike in the spring and summer of 1984, the government was playing coal mining off against the oil gambit, hoping to squeeze the miners into accepting lower wages and higher productivity. In both cases, the gambit misfired; which shows that like the Conservative British government, the Polish government (and it may be added other CMEA governments) have little idea about efficiency in <u>real terms</u>, and are susceptible to current fashions among economists. At the very least, a Conservative government may be excused on the grounds of following ideological dicta; the Socialist Bloc governments have no such excuses.

However, in 1974 and 1975 these events were still in the future. In the meantime, the oil price rise benefited the net exporters. Smith notes that:

> The initial net impact of the 1973 increases in world energy prices on the terms of trade was a considerable boost to the USSR as a substantial exporter of oil and oil products; was approximately neutral to Romania ... and to Poland (whose coal exports increased in value); but was a severe disadvantage to Czechoslovakia, Hungary, the GDR and Bulgaria. By the end of the decade, the collapse of Polish coal production and Romanian oil output and the failure of domestic energy output to meet plan targets, resulted in those countries requiring substantial energy imports, and therefore being considerably disadvantaged by the second round of world oil price increases in 1979.[22]

The full impact of the price rises has given us a vast literature on the subject, with very little conclusive evidence. The evidence is difficult to establish because of the confusion of the whole issue. The oil crisis generated a vast recession in the non-Socialist countries, accompanied by massive inflation. The 'stagflation' which is still in evidence in 1984, was exacerbated by a doubling and trebling of interest rates. Those countries of the Socialist Bloc which had contracted large Western debts, were the first to be exposed to the blows. Their debts were said to be the vastest ever incurred; but it was only when the Latin American debt crisis broke out in the early 1980s that they were seen in true perspective. Latin American debt turned out to be between ten and twenty times higher than the Eastern European debt, (depending on the calculation); and, unlike the latter, the Latin Americans had no super-power as a guarantor. In hindsight, the Eastern European, particularly Polish debt was as safe as any debt could ever be; yet the repercussions of this debt were to prove far more serious than anything that had yet happened to Latin American debtors.

This makes one wonder whether the existence of the debt was not being used for political purposes by some of the creditor governments; and, while some of them have admitted as much (i.e. in the linking of 'human rights' issues to credits by the US Administration), the whole extent of the pressure and its purely political nature have yet to be explored in depth. Another question which may well be seriously asked is whether the clamour about the Eastern European debt did not provoke the Latin American crisis; crying wolf can have unexpected results in other areas; and, if this were so, whether, in addition to creating extremely difficult problems for the population in Eastern Europe, the banking institutions and government bodies did not produce a monster of their own making: a Latin American default, bringing about the collapse of the global banking system. It is early days yet to discuss such a probability, and this is not within the scope of this work. However, it is being pointed out that the political and economic balance is so finely tuned globally that one small deviance can produce an avalanche in other areas.

Which brings us back to what actually happened in the CMEA in the fateful decade of the 1970s. It

has already been pointed out that the Bloc as a
whole had more to gain than to lose by the rise in
oil prices: higher hard-currency exports from the
USSR and Poland more than compensated for the fuel
shortage in the non-producing countries. A well-
known economist has expressed his views in the
following way: firstly, that both the USSR and
Poland benefited by the export of fuel, and the
Soviet Union benefited to a great extent by the
spectacular rise in gold prices. Secondly, though
the exhaustion of labour reserves may provide part
of the answer for poor economic performance, in the
Eastern European case this does not apply evenly;
thus, while Poland, Bulgaria and Romania still had
surplus labour force in the 1970s, Bulgaria's
performance has been good, while that of Poland and
Romania - very bad. Thirdly, a reason often cited
has been:

> The heavy defence burden, the irrational price
> system, the extraordinarily long lead times in
> investment, the unpopularity of collectivised
> agriculture, the unwieldy because over-
> centralised administration of everything ...
> But all these drawbacks have plagued the
> system since its beginning, and it has
> performed excellently despite them in the
> past. ... Nothing indicates that any of
> these drawbacks have grown worse, quite the
> contrary.

Of other drawbacks, this economist accepts that the
lack of incentives is serious - but in his opinion,
much less serious than it used to be; that the
extractive industry, including agriculture is
showing diminishing returns; and, perhaps more
importantly, that these countries have reached
their minimum technological lag. None of these
satisfies the writer as a complete answer - both
cumulatively and separately - to the economic
crises in some of the East European countries
following the 1973 oil price explosion.[23]
    Instead of finding the answer, Wiles prefers
to discuss the 'imponderables', and comes to the,
not unexpected, conclusion, that the problem is the
general dissatisfaction of the population, which
will not take any more <u>diktats</u> from above. He
suggests 'mercatisation' of the economies, allowing
more democracy and free criticism. This, even

though he himself admits that a market economy is not necessarily always a good thing, and despite the fact that it was during a strong liberalisation of the CMEA economies that the crisis actually occurred.

We can make the following hypotheses about the crisis or the series of crises in the 1970s. First of all, it has been stated that revolutions do not happen during hard times, but in times of relaxation (while this theory can only apply to the Great French Revolution with precision, it also has some relation to the situation in Eastern Europe in the 1970s). Secondly, a mixed economy is very difficult to sustain for a very long period of time; maintaining a mixed economy in a centrally-planned system probably means having a mixture of the worst elements of both. Thirdly, the crises did not occur primarily as a result of oil prices, but as a result of rising interest rates which the banks began to charge because of the rise in oil prices. This is a cause and effect problem which seems to have been neglected in the West. Fourthly, and even more importantly, the trade barriers, boycotts and exclusions which the West imposed on the CMEA in the 1970s exacerbated the problem of the debt; if this could not be seen directly in the evidence emanating from the CMEA (for political reasons this has been under-emphasised in public, though has often surfaced in private), it can be clearly seen in the Latin American debt problem: lack of exports to the creditor countries means that the debt is defaulted upon. These barriers may or may not have been applied in the guise of political reprisals; but they appear more like desperate efforts by the West to retain its own markets for its own products in the face of the rising recession. And finally, and most importantly, the biggest problem has been created by the recession itself: lack of purchasing power due to the unemployment in the West, producing more unemployment and less purchasing power meant that the Western economies have had a low or even zero growth rate. While the volume of trade between the Eastern and Western Blocs has never been very substantial, it cannot be forgotten, that with the exception of Soviet gold sales, _all_ hard-currency earnings accruing to the CMEA come from exporting to the West. Hence, even a reduction of ten per cent would imply a corresponding reduction in debt-repayment.[24]

We have no way of knowing whether the debt crisis was engineered in some fashion possibly through co-operation between some bodies in the West and the East, which had an interest in keeping up tensions within and between the Blocs. But a look at another crisis in the past may give us insight into why, what has been a sensible price rise in oil, has degenerated into a global crisis. The nearest comparison can be made with the Wall Street crash in 1929. As an eminent economist sums it up:

The great stock market crash can be much more readily explained than the depression that followed it. And among the problems involved in assessing the causes of depression, none is more intractable than the responsibility to be assigned to the stock market crash. Economics still does not allow final answers on these matters. But, as usual, something can be said. As already so often emphasised, the collapse in the stock market in the autumn of 1929 was implicit in the speculation that went before. The only question concerning that speculation was how long it would last.

But, he continues, we do not know why the speculation was so great, and to say that credit was easy, is no answer at all.

On numerous occasions before and since credit has been easy, and there has been no speculation whatever. Furthermore, much of the 1928 and 1929 speculation occurred on money borrowed at interest rates which for years before, and in any period since, would have been considered exceptionally astringent. Money, by the ordinary tests, was tight in the late twenties.[25]

Galbraith maintains that the cause of the speculation may have been a relatively long period of prosperity, and a surplus of money, coincidental with the mood of the country's leaders. But he denies that the recession was inevitable, and suggests that the exact cause of this recession has still to be discovered. But as there was a mood for speculation earlier, so now:

> A great many people have always felt that a depression was inevitable in the thirties. There had been (at least) seven good years; now by occult or biblical law of compensation there would have to be seven bad ones.

This, and other theories, Galbraith dismisses as nonsense. In his opinion, there was no need to 'rest' the economy; the economy was in good shape and there was demand for its goods on the market. However, there was a considerable drop in consumption in the summer of 1929, which, he suggests, may have been caused by high interest rates. This affected only the purchase of houses in the first place; but housing is an important economic indicator. The more rational explanation, Galbraith thinks, is that the US had at that time suffered a bad income distribution (five per cent of the population received some one-third of personal income); a bad corporate structure, particularly within the newly-formed holding companies and investment trusts; a weak banking structure, where one failure led to a domino-effect; and a dubious state of foreign balance. United States have been making large loans particularly to Germany and Central and South America. For various reasons, as those countries could not pay back (as their gold reserves fell), they went into default and American exports fell correspondingly. Thus, the US lost on both counts; non-payment of debts, lack of servicing of debts and a reduction in exports all contributed to the recession. Finally, the state of economic intelligence was so poor that:

> In the months and years following the stock market crash, the burden of reputable economic advice was invariably on the side of measures that would make things worse. In November 1929, Mr Hoover announced a cut in taxes; in the great non-business conferences that followed he asked business firms to keep up their capital investment and to maintain wages. Both of these measures were on the side of increasing spendable income, though unfortunately they were largely without

effect. The tax reductions were negligible except in the higher income brackets ... investment outlays and wages were not reduced until circumstances would in any case have brought their reduction.

The answer, said both the Republicans and the Democrats, was a balanced budget, for fear of inflation.[26]

No one needs to be reminded that the Great Crash put the world economy at risk for a long time, nor that it led to the Second World War. But, it might be argued, the Wall Street Crash cannot be repeated, because of the regulations introduced after 1929. However, history never repeats itself exactly, though there is cyclical similarity in many events. And, if one substituted the Oil Price Crisis for the Wall Street Crash, and Eastern Europe for Germany, one could draw almost remarkable parallels of the crisis in the 1970s with that of the 1930s. One even has the rise of one military dictatorship in Eastern Europe to make the parallel still more uncanny.

It is not known who started the crash, though Galbraith states that:

> In the early days of the crash, it was widely believed that Jesse L Livermore, a Bostonian with a large and unquestionably exaggerated reputation for bear operations, was heading a syndicate that was driving the market down. So persistent did these rumours become, that Livermore, whom few had thought sensitive to public opinion, issued a formal denial that he was involved in any deflationary plot.[27]

Similarly, no one knows why the prices were driven up by OPEC in 1973, though by 1979 the falling demand, because of the recession the first rise caused, was probably necessary. But, like the Great Crash, these price rises, <u>by themselves</u>, would not have caused the recession. It was a combination of high debts to the USA, high interest rates and reduced demand (which created unemployment or was created by the unemployment) which produced the recession; as in the 1930s, the recession was world-wide; though it affected the Eastern Bloc less than the West - at least as far as the unemployment and inflation goes; partly because of the still autarkic nature of the system, but partly also because of the vast Soviet gold reserves. The Soviet Union alone has been able to protect her sphere of influence from the worst effect of the recession, even if the Eastern Europeans were forced to cut their living standards.

But the cut in the living standards undermined the political concensus (or at least a lack of strong opposition) of the post-Stalinist govern- ments. This affected particularly Poland, which had the largest Western debt in the Bloc. But perhaps if the Polish shipyard workers in 1980 had been able to read what a Polish politician - a strong anti-Communist - had written in 1932, during the worst depression in the countryside, they might have thought twice about their actions. These are his words:

> Despite best intentions and the pressure of bailiffs, many villagers stopped paying taxes. ... The countryside eats badly. Even the better-off farmers do not use sugar. They also save on salt, which is often their only seasoning. They cut matches into sections, use flints to start the fire, carry cinders from one end of the village to another as a matter of course. At night, the village is dark, only in some windows is there a weak tallow candle. ... Tuberculosis has spread mercilessly, taking many victims, particularly young ones. The population goes without shoes ..., without linen, wearing out old rags, which are remnants from better times. Schools are empty, and the churches are beginning to empty. ... There are no new books in the villages, newspapers have become a rarity.[28]

The shipyard workers are predominantly of peasant origin; many of them are worker-peasants; since memories of times like these do not fade quickly, it would have taken either a lot of provocation or a lot of encouragement, to start the Solidarity inspired strike. Part of the provocation was, of course, a fear that the 1930s could be back, as the government raised basic food prices to an extremely high level. The other factors will be discussed in the following chapter.

4. The Oil Crisis in Global Perspective

The effects of the oil crisis in the Eastern Bloc were so manifold that a full literature will probably take many years to compile. They affected each country differently, but their overall effect has already been assessed earlier: the crisis made the smaller countries more dependent on the USSR both militarily and economically; it made the population poorer and less in control of its own living standards; and it produced East-West tensions of a grade not known since the days of the Cold War. Some countries, such as Poland and Romania, suffered more than others, though for different reasons and in a different manner. Others, such as Czechoslovakia and East Germany had some problems, but not too acute. Yet in others, such as Hungary, the crisis diminished the prosperity but not sufficiently to produce a serious crisis. In the underdeveloped Bulgaria, the crisis actually coincided with economic and technological growth.

But it would be a mistake to refer to East-West consequences alone, because the results were widespread. Thus, the Iranian crisis of 1979, when the Shah was deposed, was a direct consequence of the price rises of oil; the consequence of this was the American hostage crisis, which provoked the Soviet Union to invade Afghanistan. The consequence of this was the Olympic boycott in 1980, and the breakdown of economic relations (such as the ban on grain sales by the US to the USSR) between the super-powers. Other consequences, such as the default (or de facto default) of many Central and Latin American countries; the increased anti-Communist stance of the Reagan Administration which owes much to Latin American insolvency; the increased guerilla activity, which promotes US intervention and increases the US budget deficit; the resultant Soviet-US tension in the American sphere of influence, which raises defence budgets of both super-powers, are but some of the consequences.

It is probably wishful thinking to talk of the 'Eastern European economic crisis' as a phenomenon on its own; Wiles diagnoses it differently, looking at the 'British disease', as compared to the 'Polish disease':

There are of course plausible and substantial orthodox causes as well: "stop-go" and the international position of sterling, and now monetarism in high places. I do not seek to decry any of the "orthodox" explanations, merely to reduce their weight in the total aetiology. Note that such explanations differ strikingly between Eastern European Communism and advanced capitalism, while "imponderables" have a <u>striking similarity</u>. ... Will the Polish Disease go away again, like influenza, or is it here to stay, like rheumatism? Prediction is a hazardous game. Two good Soviet harvests running; a 25% fall in the relative price of oil; the adoption of the Hungarian system by Czechoslovakia ...; the success of the SALT talks - each of these might make the scene look very different for some countries. But not for all, and for how long? My impression is that these authors, including myself, have not diagnosed the flu.[29]

It is a wise author who does not make predictions; an even wiser one would look, if not to the causes which, unlike flu, are not so easy to diagnose, but to comparisons. The comparison is not between one Eastern and one Western European country or between one harvest and another. A historian will observe very carefully major clashes between large powers; major economic catastrophes; and effects of such events on a global as well as time-scale. And a wise historian will not make predictions either; but he will wonder whether cause and effect could not be put together by the world's politicians, particularly if the crises are only separated by barely a generation or two. Some politicians do not study history at all; others study it to bad effect; but there is at least one major politician in office in 1984 whose father is said to have been ruined by the Great Crash in Wall Street. Maybe historical messages could be addressed to the right quarters, instead of being sterilely discussed by academics, who will later say: 'I told you so!'.

CHAPTER SIX: FOOTNOTES

1 Dennis Swann: The Economics of the Common Market, p. 15.
2 Analysed by Swann in The Economics, Ch. 1.
3 Wspolnota Socjalistyczna, p. 17 emphasis in text.
4 Wspolnota Socjalistyczna, pp. 35-36.
5 Alan H. Smith: The Planned Economies of Eastern Europe, pp. 149-150.
6 For a detailed analysis of the trading and financial patterns, see: Smith: The Planned Economies, pp. 155-163.
7 See Smith: The Planned Economies, pp. 167-173.
8 Wspolnota Socjalistyczna, p. 43.
9 Samuel Brittan: The Coming Capacity Crunch, Financial Times, 5 July 1984.
10 See Smith: The Planned Economies, Ch. 7: 'Wage Pressures and Open Inflation in Eastern Europe'.
11 See: Wspolnota Socjalistyczna: pp. 46-50 and pp. 66-71.
12 Smith: The Planned Economies, p. 193.
13 Wspolnota Socjalistyczna, p. 56 and p. 57.
14 Wspolnota Socjalistyczna, p. 220.
15 See: Wspolnota Socjalistyczna, pp. 84-106.
16 Z. M. Fallenbuchl: The Commodity Composition of Intra-Comecon Trade and the Industrial Structure of the Member Countries; NATO Colloquium 1977, pp. 104-105, emphasis added.
17 J. Bethkenhagen: Joint Projects and their Influence on Future Comecon Energy Autarchy Ambitions, NATO Colloquium 1977, p. 37.
18 Tony Scanlan: The Effects of Energy Development on East European Economic Prospects, NATO Colloquium 1977, p. 222.
19 Scanlan: The Effects of Energy, pp. 222-224.
20 A. Gladzicka: Crude Oil in the Polish Economy in the Years 1968-1971, Przeglad Zachodniopomorski, No. 2, 1974; as reproduced by RFE Research, Polish Press Survey, 20 February 1975.
21 J. Danielewski: Polish Coal on Foreign Markets, Sprawy Miedzynarodowe, October 1974, as reproduced by RFE Research, Polish Press Survey, 20 February 1975.
22 Smith: The Planned Economies, p. 197.

23   Peter Wiles: <u>Zero Growth and International Nature of the Polish Disease</u>, pp. 7-17. Drewnowski: <u>Crisis in the Eastern European Economy</u>.

24   According to <u>Wspolnota Socjalistyczna</u>, in the 1970s the Eastern European trade with capitalist countries was 23.7 per cent of all trade. This accounted for imports and exports, see Table, p. 251.

25   J. K. Galbraith: <u>The Great Crash 1929</u>, pp. 186-187.

26   Galbraith: <u>The Great Crash 1929</u>, pp. 198-201.

27   Galbraith: <u>The Great Crash 1929</u>, pp. 155-156.

28   Quoted from W. Witos: <u>Essays and Speeches</u>, see: O. A. Narkiewicz <u>The Green Flag</u>, p. 223.

29   Wiles: <u>Zero Growth</u>, Drewnowski: <u>The Crisis in the Eastern European Economy</u>, p. 16, emphasis added.

Chapter Seven

THE AFTERMATH OF THE RECESSION

---

1. The Birth of Solidarity

We have discussed some of the circumstances which
led to the setting up of Solidarity; as well as
the initial effects its creation has had on the
country and the government. The title of this
section has been borrowed from a book entitled
The Birth of Solidarity; the Gdansk Negotiations
1980, which contains a full record of the
negotiations in Gdansk to allow the setting up of
the trade union.[1] The borrowed title has been
used here on purpose to illustrate some of the most
amazing characteristics of the early days of the
movement: firstly, its full and enthusiastic
reportage by the Western media, and the subsequent
wave of sympathy for the 'brave Poles'; secondly,
the easy access which the media had to the
negotiations throughout the first period; and
thirdly, the Polish party's and government's
initial passivity, and at times, even positive
attitudes towards Solidarity, coupled with Soviet
passivity in the face of what could constitute a
major threat for the Bloc.
    One cannot comment on the first phenomenon;
after all, the Prague Spring did receive a large
amount of publicity in the West, though not to the
same extent as the Polish events. This could be
accounted for by the presence in the West of very
many, and very highly distinguished scholars, many
of whom had to leave Poland in 1968; on the other
hand it could be accounted for by the disappoint-
ment in the collapse of the Czechs. The Poles are
known to fight on; a similar wave of sympathy went
out to the Warsaw insurgents in 1944, without the

slightest hint of any help, till they were almost completely eliminated by the Nazi troops.[2] Sympathy was shown to the Poles after the two nineteenth century uprisings; though similarly, no efforts were made to help them in their mortal struggle. But fighting on to the end may not be in the best interests of the nation; without adopting the attitude of one writer categorically asserting that he considers 'the events of August-September 1980 to be the greatest Polish lunacy since the 1863 Uprising', one must agree that it ranked high on the list of Polish heroic efforts in a good, but lost cause. This writer may admire the spirit which creates heroic fighters but deplores the reality of the situation. In 1830, 1863, 1944 the best and noblest of Polish instincts have risen to the fore and were brutally extinguished. In 1980, the situation was rather different; there was serious doubt among the most patriotic members of society about the validity of the exercise - one such example will be mentioned later - and while nobody disputes the heroism of the participants, one has some doubts about their political consciousness and the final aim of the enterprise.[3]

The second factor: that of accessibility to the Western media is more unusual; the full exposure of the meetings of the union members and of the meetings with government representatives; the humiliation of senior ministers in front of the cameras; the ostentatious wreath-laying ceremonies by senior party members in front of the monument to the victims of the 1971 violence ordered by the government, the apparently complete victory of the strikers - again in front of the television cameras - are more difficult to explain. Western journalists in Poland have for a long time had quite a good access to many events, but hardly to such events as were publicised in 1980. Did this mean the breakdown of the party and government or did it mean that the party was biding its time, till such time as it had gathered strength to combat the strikers, or till the Soviet troops took over? Or, was the party completely divided within itself and unable to decide on the course to take? All these and a few other causes are cited by commentators; Sanford suggests that:[4]

a. the party had lost its capacity to rule, but
b. that it had a solid backing in the strength of the police and the army, and
c. that it was biding its time in order to avoid the last resort, that of physical coercion.

and he is probably right. But this ignores the basic underlying factor: the party and the government were passive, and their passivity was covertly approved by the Soviet government and party. The strongest factor in this passivity must have been, inevitably, Brezhnev's long illness and the Kremlin's preoccupation with its other problems - one of them being Afghanistan.

The events were accessible, because the authorities were passive, and not because some special dispensation had been given by one or the other of the sides in the conflict. The authorities were passive not because they were unable to rule, but because Moscow was otherwise occupied and the Poles were uncertain what to do. And the Poles were uncertain about what to do because the supposedly 'monolithic' party was not a party at all, but merely a <u>congeries</u> of warring factions. There has been no authentic, classical Communism in Poland since Stalin exterminated the CP in the 1930s and this event was followed in the 1940s by the building up of a completely artificial body, uniting ex-socialists, ex-populists, and newly created communists in the PUWP.[5] The various factions in the PUWP and their in-fighting are amply described in many works, the most recent, contemporary in-fighting by Sanford, but these are merely the tips of the iceberg.

Unlike the Communist parties, ruling or non-ruling, the PUWP's in-fighting had nothing or little to do with ideology or policy; the party believes in neither - it has everything to do with power-holding. Without going into the history of leadership changes from 1956 onwards, which is the most dramatic manifestation of the quest for power, one need only to look at some lesser known episodes in the history of the recent party animosities. Perhaps the most interesting one was the struggle between Gomulka and General Moczar (a title owing more to secret police activities than to military prowess) which has been the subject of vitriolic, but justified, attacks in the Polish emigre press.

Discussing the quarrel between Moczar and Gomulka, following the 1968 events, a writer wonders why Moczar was allowed to retain some posts, and was even promoted to important bodies, despite his anti-Gomulka behaviour. The reason is that Gomulka

> knows full-well that Moczar has ... strong support in Moscow. His fight of several years' duration with the 'Pulawy-Jewish' fraction of PUWP was very favourably viewed by the Russians. The anti-Jewish trend ... of communism began in Moscow, not in Warsaw ... it is also from Moscow that other, less well known, impulses come. The Soviet party, or its bureaucracy, is no less quarrelsome and broken up than the Polish party. This is unavoidable in a situation when fractional in-fighting in parties replaces the exchange of ideas and views in the public life of communist countries. Part of the bureaucracy in the Soviet party is openly favourable to Moczar. This is the part which is dissatisfied with the centrist policies of Brezhnev; just as Moczar is dissatisfied with the centrist policies of Gomulka. These are mostly certain influential military circles, which have recently grown stronger and naturally, the security police service. ... Gomulka must take into account such links which Moczar has with the Russians. ... But the most important (factor) is the situation in the party. Gomulka knows full well that Moczar has in the last few years won over the majority of the young party bureaucrats. ... Moreover, he alone, apart from Gomulka, has his own conspiratorial network, infiltrating the majority of party organisations and many state organisations, and being served by the Security Police.

The writer further goes on to say that, despite everything that happened, Gomulka still considers Moczar important because he had created him himself; that Moczar played an important part in discrediting Gomulka's enemies, but even more cogently, because of the problem of succession:

Gomulka feels that he will have to give up his leading role in the party soon; the fight for succession is raging, and apart from Gomulka's favourites, there is also 'Gierek, who has lost ground, because of having sided with Moczar'. According to the writer's view, struggle against Moczar (or his supporters, like Gierek) is impossible; Moczar's men are everywhere, and when sacked, another Moczar man has to be appointed:

> This is the essence of the problem. Gomulka developed the party on the basis of eliminating the best (people) and promoting the worst, stupidest, most opportunistic (people). The ruling elite which has been selected from among the young peasant membership which flooded the party, was selected strictly according to the above principle. Can this elite go in any other direction than that proposed by Moczar?[6]

Despite the hostile tone, the article contains several statements which have since been proven. In the first place, Gierek, whom Gomulka opposed, and Moczar proposed, did become the next leader. Secondly, there was an obvious dearth of able people in the party in the 1970s, which was part of the reason for the recurring crises. Thirdly, the military and security forces did become much stronger, and Gierek's deposition was followed by the leadership of Kania, head of security, and then by Jaruzelski, an army general. The 'immobilisme' of the last Brezhnev period did produce splits in the CPSU, strengthening the armed services and the security forces; and resulted in the accession to the top posts of a former head of security, Andropov. His death brought to power a figurehead, Chernenko, who is clearly being used by the defence lobby for its own purposes, and who will not last very long, if his health and age are taken into account. Will the next Soviet leader be a top military man? Only time can tell, but the hypotheses put by a writer in the late 1960s clearly had more than a grain of truth in them.

There is little need to discuss the struggle within the Polish party both during and after the Gomulka period. This struggle began to subside slightly as Gierek's 'dash for growth' with the help of foreign capital began to work in the early

1970s, and ensured a level of prosperity which the
country has not experienced hitherto. The oil
crisis began to bite slowly, but surely. The first
warning came in 1976, the crash came in 1980.
Because of the quarrels and because of the
elimination of able people from among the 'peasant
communist elite', the dissidents grew in strength,
and attracted those who had been pushed out by the
Establishment. The movement of dissidence was
strengthened by the able, the party (and
government) were almost completely run by the
'opportunistic' elements. It is in this phenomenon
that one must seek the 'birth of Solidarity', not
in the growing economic crisis. The economic
crisis, while serious, could have been avoided had
there been able leadership. While Gierek had been a
good provincial boss, his complete lack of
charisma, his long and boring speeches on
television, and his associates' low reputation, did
little to help on a national level. The crisis did
not occur because of economic problems (grave
though these were); nor did it occur because the
elite lived too well (though it did); it occurred
because there was no cohesive ruling body, whose
actions could manage the country. There was no
'party' as such, just a large number of youngish
people, brought in to support the leader, rewarded
for passivity, and ideologically illiterate.

It was at this juncture that the country
suddenly and apparently miraculously received a new
leader; one whose ideology was very strong, and
more importantly, in keeping with the ideology of
the nation. This leader was the newly elected
Polish Pope. Historians in future years may yet
find out why the clearly able, but not generally
known, Polish cardinal was elected. Whatever the
reasons were, the results were startling. The
Polish faith in the miracle of independence, not
only of the party but of a much older enemy: the
Russians, grew apace. Few commentators doubt that
it was the Pope's election which sparked off the
Solidarity movement, though it is certain that
the Pope did little more than provide tacit support
for the nation and limited open support for 'human
rights'. Nobody could blame Pope John Paul II for
overdoing his support for Solidarity, and the
Polish Church itself was and still is divided on
the issue.

Much has been said about the strong
Catholicism of the Poles; what is generally
neglected is the fact that it is the countryside
which is Catholic, and tends to believe literally
in miracles, whereas the city population had, for a
long time, been 'mission territory', rather on the
lines of the French urban working-class population.
But in the 1970s both the party and the urban
working class were closely tied to the countryside.
It has already been seen above that the party was
'flooded' with peasant youth; in the cities
Solidarity found its supporters among recent
migrants from the country areas.

Although there was some slowing in the
demographic trend of migration from the farms
to the urban centers in the 1970s, close
familial ties between city dwellers and
country folk remained. It was still true by
the late 1970s that a high percentage of
industrial workers were no more than one
generation removed from the farm. This factor
might help to explain the political cohesion
of the two 'Solidarity' groups, urban and
rural, that emerged in 1980. ... Two
additional factors strongly favoured a
consolidated movement: the Roman Catholic
Church and Polish nationalism. These
traditional forces provided a moral and
emotional momentum toward political cohesion
that gave the movement essential strength.
The Church, speaking in the name of the
nation, has been an important (if calculating)
protector of the dissident intellectuals and
striking workers since 1975-76. Pope John
Paul II's visit to Poland in the summer of
1979 was an event of religious and national
importance, displaying the unity of the nation
in the face of a grudgingly tolerant PUWP.
While it is interesting that the Church showed
a moment of hesitation upon the outbreak of
the strikes in August 1980 ..., clearly the
authority of the Church - unmistakably
symbolized by Lech Walesa's signing of the
August 31 agreement with the souvenir pen from
the pope's visit - gave the fledgling
Solidarity organization a moral legitimacy
that magnified its power and cohesion
substantially. The blending of religious and

national symbols was magnificently demonstrated at the first Solidarity Congress, held in early September 1981: both a crucifix and an emblem of the Polish eagle adorned the podium, and the delegates opened the congress with the singing of the national anthem and a religious hymn.

The Church's initial hesitation was, according to the authors, quite serious:

Cardinal Stefan Wyszynski's first public utterance on the subject of strikes was in a sermon at Jasna Gora on August 15, 1980 - six weeks after the first protest strikes. While acknowledging the rightful grievances of the workers, the Primate cautioned moderation. Subsequently Church spokesmen showed their sympathy for the strikers, but also called for calm and for honest work.[7]

It is clear from the above, and from many other accounts, that the Church was not the main factor in the founding of Solidarity, rather a bystander, drawn unwillingly into the fray. The main reason for this may not have been, as has since been claimed, the Church's satisfaction with the status quo, or its fear of the consequences; it is much more likely that the Church distrusted the intellectuals who were undoubtedly manipulating the Solidarity movement from behind the scenes. Jacek Kuron and Adam Michnik, both Marxists, and both founders of KOR, and non-believers, were not the Church's favourite sons. Having only just attained great importance through the massive transfer of population from the countryside to the cities, and through the election of Pope John Paul II, the Church was unwilling to jeopardise this for the sake of an ideology only held by a few Marxist intellectuals. The Catholicism and nationalism which sustained Solidarity were but tools used by a few to mobilise the masses. As an old-established and wise institution, the Church understood this better than the nation or foreign observers.
However, willy-nilly, the Pope became the symbol of the struggle, and Solidarity embodied religion and nationalism in its ideology, even though its statutes stated a more liberal view:

'We are not - and have no wish to be - either a religious or an anti-religious organization, but only a union organization which is pluralist in the strictest sense of the term'.[8] The Pope was probably less struck by this non-religious article, than by the Marxist revolutionary viewpoint expressed by Kuron:

> Our society has already - for the first time in 35 years - organized itself without depending on the government authorities, thus providing democracy with a measure of real insurance. The central authorities are helpless in the face of organized society. They now are deprived of a social base, for they can no longer count on and appeal to the support of any social groups. They can only resort to the use of armed force; and under the present conditions, it would be that of an alien power.[9]

Any religious organisation, but most particularly the Polish Church would, rightly, be suspicious of such a blatantly Leninist tactical approach, combined with Trotskyite ideology. But it could do little to stop the movement; to abandon the nation in time of its greatest need was impossible; to go along with it would be unwise, for behind the scenes lurked the spectre of neo-Marxism. It has been asked what would have happened had the Church not supported the movement; would it have taken off at all? In fact, a different question should be asked: What would have happened had the Church supported the movement wholeheartedly? If that had been the case, there is little doubt that an armed uprising may have occurred, with consequences which do not bear thinking about. The Church's caution, hesitation and backpedalling may have saved the situation once again, and it could have been its reward to have a former pupil of a smart Jesuit school named to the top Polish post. But the nation owes it much more than the Establishment; because the fate of Hungary in 1956 has been only narrowly avoided.

This attitude could not stop <u>Solidarity</u> from making the most capital out of a Polish Pope, and without doubt it helped to raise the population's expectations. Eyewitnesses who have no love for the Polish party stressed that little short of a miracle was expected in pro-<u>Solidarity</u> circles during its heyday; though no one was quite sure what kind of a miracle there would be. Doubtless the expectation was that the Soviet Union would collapse under the impact of <u>Solidarity</u>, or that the West would start a war on its behalf. This expectation has been expressed clearly in 1969:

> The national question will undermine the Soviet state and the whole Eastern Bloc. The change will be accelerated by many other economic, technological and international factors. ... The (Moczar) episode is the forerunner of a very important change in Poland and in the whole communist world.[10]

The 'Riga syndrome' was obviously as alive in 1980 as it had been in 1918. The Pope was made an unwilling instrument of other interests. The nation had been tricked. But the party and the government had hastened their own downfall through their irresponsible economic policies. For it was the economic crisis which was the most important factor in the birth of the <u>Solidarity</u>.

2. <u>Crossing the Rubicon</u>

It is always difficult, when discussing Polish events, to avoid falling into the trap of slipping from the sublime to the ridiculous. What one commentator describes as 'crossing the Rubicon' appears to another as an expression of the 'politics of the stomach'. No doubt both authors are right in some respects. But the truth is somewhere in-between, and the reality of the problem was that the Polish revolution was sparked off by an external factor: the banking crisis in the West. As the first commentator rightly states:

> the trap in which Poland found itself, in December 1981, was one that had been sprung in the previous April. In that month, the Polish Government came to a preliminary agreement with the western banks with which Poland had debts outstanding, to reschedule the repayments, amounting to some $2.4 billion, that were due during the rest of that year. This tentative agreement specified that by the

end of 1981 Poland was to pay at least $500 million of the interest due on the loans. The compact with the banks gave the country some much needed breathing space in which to attempt to break out of the economic quagmire, and a start was made with the introduction of rationing for essential consumer articles. Nevertheless, production slowed down inexorably. By the end of the summer food supplies from the countryside were down by one third to a half of what they had been in the previous year; farmers simply withheld deliveries, unwilling to accept any more worthless money from the state purchasing agencies than they were obliged to take. Exports to the West fell from $5.6 billion in the first nine months of 1980 to $4.2 billion in the corresponding period of 1981. Over the same period imports were forced down from $6.15 billion to $4.8 billion. There was simply not enough revenue to cover essential imports of food, medicines, fuel, raw materials and spare parts. The breathing space was clearly insufficient.[11]

By mid-summer the food supply situation became very difficult and the workers occupied the Lenin Shipyard at Gdansk, but strikes on a large scale had already started earlier, with the raising of food prices in July. On 16 August 1980, the first Inter-Factory Strike Committee was formed in Gdansk. Several government and party reshuffles at the top, and attempts to negotiate with the strikers, were eventually followed by Gierek's deposition on 6 September 1980. Stanislaw Kania took over the post of First Secretary, though he lasted only a few months. The Solidarity negotiations went on and the real crisis was postponed till 1981.

To quote Toporowski further:

At the beginning of December (1981), the Polish government again approached the banks, offering to pay $150 million of the $500 million agreed for 1981, but seeking a period of grace for the remainder of the sum. The banks ... refused even to discuss the matter. In so doing, they sealed Poland's fate. It was obvious that General Jaruzelski would have

only one option left open to him. This was to
have recourse to the Soviet Union for
assistance. It was also obvious that the
Soviet Union would demand its pound of flesh
in return.

The banks apparently had no choice but to refuse;
for nearly eighteen months Poland was in a state of
political paralysis. Reforms were not carried out,
because the Solidarity conference at its first
national meeting in September and October

approved two mutually contradictory sets of
reform proposals. One was a demand for the
immediate dismantling of all state controls
over the economy, and their replacement by the
unrestricted operation of market forces. ...
The other set of reforms demanded a wide range
of state controls over the economy to ensure
the maintenance of full employment, present
living standards, and real wages.[12]

The banks were also split among themselves;
there were 501 Western banks holding the Polish
debt, and since Poland stopped making scheduled
payments at the end of 1980, many banks vetoed any
agreement over the rescheduling of the debt. The
only bank in which Polish debts played a
significant role in its assets was 'the West German
trades unions' bank. ... Because of the trades
unions' links with the German Social Democratic
Party, this bank was persuaded to lend heavily to
Poland for political reasons'. But the American
banks in particular 'were very keen on inflicting
the hardest possible conditions on Poland, in
accordance with the orthodoxy of bankers and
economists nowadays that severe financial
purgatives must be A Good Thing in principle for an
economy that is suffering a crisis'. On the other
hand, Solidarity played into the hands of the
hardliners (both Western bankers and Polish party
ones) by taking little note of the economic crisis.
At a meeting of its National Council on 3 December
1981, and the subsequent one held in Gdansk, 'the
National Council called for a vote of no confidence
in the Government, and its replacement by a
"provisional" government, to include Solidarity
representatives, which would organise free
elections.'[13] As Solidarity was playing with

the idea of overthrowing the government, and the party hardliners were considering asking for the intervention of 'fraternal troops' à la Czechoslovakia, Polish economy took a further downward plunge. Food exports dropped by half at the end of 1981; domestic consumers were deprived; coal, copper and other exports all but stopped, and the collapse of the exports brought about the collapse of imports. This

> strangled the country's industrial production. In the folly of the investment cycle in the 1970s and Poland's honeymoon with western technology, large sectors of Polish industry became dependent upon spare parts and raw materials which could only be purchased from the West. Cut off from these imports, industrial production collapsed, reinforcing the decline in exports. This downward spiral, which has been dragging the Polish economy down since 1979, accelerated last year, and there are fears that national income may have dropped by a staggering 15 to 18 per cent compared with a decline of four per cent in 1980 and of two per cent in 1979. In the early days of December then, Poland was a crisis awaiting a <u>denouement</u>. When it finally came, it was precipitated not by Moscow, Washington or the Vatican, but by the western banks themselves.[14]

Perhaps a further irony lies in the fact that just before his deposition in early September, 1980, Gierek was on the eve of a visit to France, where he was hopeful of getting further credits - and that he would probably have been successful. Nor was the Jaruzelski take-over in December, 1981, unavoidable, had the banks relented and allowed Poland to reschedule in an orderly manner. While the banks never openly advocated a military dictatorship in Poland in 1981, they did do so in 1926, when the Polish debt mounted and Pilsudski stepped in with his brand of 'cleansing' politics. General Jaruzelski is following a well-worn path of imposing discipline on the unruly patient; but while this type of remedy is well known in Latin America (with well-known consequences), it has hardly ever worked in Europe.

189

3. Crisis Management in Poland

In the November, 1981, issue of The Tablet, an editorial entitled Poland's political void, stated that appointing General Jaruzelski as head of the Party in addition to his posts of Prime Minister and Minister of Defence was a clever move. 'The Poles love their Army and the patriotic glamour of the armed forces attaches a fortiori to the top man in uniform'.[15] If The Tablet was expressing the Vatican's line - and this is not likely - it misunderstood the Polish attitudes to the People's Army completely. Poland has a political void; it has been deprived of a normal political life since 1926 (not counting the brief period of 1945-48) when a succession of political blocs of one kind or another dictated policies. The People's Army is as unloved as previous instruments of the government's oppression. This does not exclude admiration for brave and gallant soldiers, but does not cover the top brass or the politicised officer corps.

But deprived of a political life, the Poles have transferred it to religion. After the Jaruzelski coup, the population prayed for a miracle even harder than before. That miracle almost eluded it, when an attempted assassination of the Pope misfired on May 13 1981. The attempt gave rise to the belief in some circles that the Soviet Union engineered the assassination, via Bulgarian go-betweens, in order to deprive the Poles of leadership. This belief has been described as absurd by the ex-CIA operative, reviewing some books on the assassination attempt.[16] Hood concludes that the assassin, Agca, was a psychopathic free-lance terrorist, who had killed on impulse before and who was (literally) killing time, waiting for another assignment.

We have already mentioned above that the Polish Church was not very happy about Solidarity; and the line taken by The Tablet; whether coming from the Vatican or not, seems to confirm this. A stable situation in a Communist Poland would seem preferable to the Church to a revolution. The previous Primate, Cardinal Wyszynski, whose death in 1981 deepened the crisis, made this clear in a sermon:

We teach that it is proper to render unto Caesar the things that are Caesar's and to God that which is God's. But when Caesar seats himself on the altar, we respond curtly: he may not.[17]

Moreover, the Church did not trust the intellectuals at any time, even Catholic intellectuals. Wyszynski's 'advocacy of a people's Catholicism was based on the premise that ordinary working people were more reliable supporters of the Church than were Catholic intellectuals. He felt that because the Catholic deputies to parliament from the 'Znak' group functioned with the regime's consent, they had a vested interest in pressing the Church into concessions and compromises'. The Church, he told the intellectuals at one point, does not need politicians, only confessors and defenders. It was the Marxist intellectuals, like Adam Michnik, who chose the Church as the most likely ally. Michnik, an atheist and a target of anti-Zionist propaganda in 1968, decided in the 1970s that the Church was the only anti-totalitarian force in Poland, capable of opposing the regime. In August, 1980, Wyszynski still spoke out against the strikes; and, though towards the end of his life he kept in touch with Walesa, he is said to have done so merely to counsel moderation and to mediate between the union and the government.

Wyszynski's successor, Cardinal Glemp, is less of an intellectual force than Wyszynski. He found it more difficult to assign <u>Solidarity</u> its proper place in the political hierarchy. But he did not hesitate to stress the Church's essential neutrality in the conflict:

For the church, the emergence of Solidarity as a power which has moved to the forefront of society, came as a big surprise, but acceptance of Solidarity as a free trade union movement did not confront us with any problem. ... The church is supporting Solidarity not as an ally but as a defender of human rights in the spirit of the Gospel. ... The Church will counsel moderation and restraint in any conflict situation.[18]

Many more sermons since have underlined the Church's role as a mediator not as a political partner of anyone in Poland.

Deprived of political independence, and of the support of the Church, what is left for the movement? The crossing of the Rubicon - and this was done both by <u>Solidarity</u> and by Jaruzelski in 1981 - has left it with few choices. At the time of writing this chapter (13 July 1984) Jacek Kuron, Adam Michnik and two other leaders are on trial for an attempt to overthrow the state. According to a statement by the Polish Ambassador in London, they will get light sentences, and the rest of <u>Solidarity</u> prisoners will be amnestied on the anniversary of independence on the 22 July.[19] In Stalinist terms, the government of General Jaruzelski is a mild one; but the euphoria of the <u>Solidarity</u> days has not been forgotten. It is difficult to adjust to the dictatorship, and there is little hope of progress towards political liberalism. On the other hand, the debt is being paid off, and summer holidays have come. Will the Poles respond like the Czechs in 1969? This seems likely, particularly in view of the fact that the expected miracle did not happen; the Church has lost some standing, and the West is only remembered because all the chickens and pigs had to be slaughtered when American feedstocks were stopped by boycott. An acute shortage of meat and undermining of confidence may work the miracle of restoring the Polish economy, where the 'politics of the stomach' disrupted it.

4. Eastern Europe's Response to the Crisis

During the Hungarian and Polish revolts in 1956, and the Czech Spring in 1968, there was strong support for the movement in some countries of the Bloc. The Poles and the Hungarians provided support and asylum for each other, Yugoslavia supported both countries (though not totally, as witness the handing over of Imre Nagy); in 1968, the Czechs found Romania to be their unlikely ally, when it refused to send the troops in with the Warsaw Pact troops.

But the <u>Solidarity</u> movement, while it found some support mostly among workers' groups in the USSR does not seem to have generated any large movement of dissent in the Bloc, nor is there evidence of any particular country speaking up for the Poles. On the contrary, most countries of the Bloc, and apparently the populations, remained at best neutral, at worst openly hostile. This phenomenon would be strange were it not for several new factors, which did not exist in the previous revolts.

The first factor is probably the rising standard of living in the Bloc, and the continuing 'embourgeoisement' of the population. This is testified to by some economists, while it is denied by others. But the absence of sympathy movements seems to confirm the former's conclusions. As one author noted:

> In the 1970s there was a substantial improvement in living conditions throughout East Europe. One sign of this development was the increase of <u>per capita</u> net material product in each country. A good deal of the expansion in livestock herds and meat production was fuelled by imports of Western feed grain. ... Nominal wages increased from an annual growth rate of 1.8 per cent in Bulgaria to 10.3 per cent in Poland during the 1976-77 period. As food - the largest item in family budgets - was subsidised, the increases in real income were proportionate, especially in Poland. Although domestic output of consumer durables output, including cars and housing, did not expand at the same rate as disposable income, some expansion in imports of high quality foreign consumer durables furthered the perception that living conditions were improving. ... It is my impression that this visible improvement in consumption was the critical element of a social contract between governments and citizens throughout Eastern Europe. Never spelled out by rulers or ruled, the social contract was and remains a tacit and ill-defined understanding. In return for increased material benefits, and in some countries greater professionalism in planning and management, East Europeans tolerated low participation in economic and political decision-making, rigid and highly centralised

193

political and economic systems, and the denial of many basic civil rights.[20]

According to this author, it was the Gierek regime's inability to deliver the goods at the end of the 1970s which undermined the 'social contract' in Poland. As a result, the governments in Hungary and East Germany modified their methods, to allow for a greater degree of pluralisation in management.

In Eastern Europe, wider participation - not Western-style civic participation, but increasing technical professionalism and decentralisation of decision-making in agriculture and industry - is increasingly becoming an element of the revised social contract.[21]

Hardt's further conclusions are that while the Soviet Union would be able to quell any uprisings in the Eastern Bloc by military means, 'resort to that ultimate weapon in intra-CMEA affairs has been expensive, crude and often counterproductive. By contrast, energy policy provides the USSR with a more effective and flexible mechanism of control ...'.
He contends that the Soviet Union uses the energy policy for two reasons:

Besides the vital role of maintaining control over Eastern Europe, the Soviet Union is also interested in fostering the overall economic health and political stability of the region. Economic well-being is essential for maintaining East Europe's substantial contributions to the Soviet economy. Political stability is not only important to the retention and viability of the political systems that conform to Soviet desiderata, but also to the economic incentives that affect the productivity of the East European systems.[22]

But, try as he might, he fails to detect any danger of further revolutionary movements in the Bloc, though he does forecast a default by Poland and/or Romania. So far, by 1984, this has not happened either. Economic considerations apart,

the only really serious political consequence of
the Polish crisis was the crisis of West European-
US relations, caused by the ban on technology
transfer and the gas pipeline row. This, in turn,
led to a crisis within NATO, which provoked some
NATO countries to refuse their share of 'theatre'
missiles intended for the Eastern Bloc in case of
war.

While these Western crises may be only a
hiccup, it does seem that the Polish revolution
only succeeded in hurting the Poles themselves, and
the relations within the Western Alliance. Maybe
this was a case of an American intervention on
behalf of the Poles being as unproductive, as
Soviet intervention used to be on behalf of
'fraternal' parties. At the time of writing this,
the case must be left open.

CHAPTER SEVEN: FOOTNOTES

1   The book has been translated into English and introduced by A. Kemp-Welsh, and published by Macmillan's in conjunction with St. Antony's College, Oxford, in 1983.
2   On this, and the disillusionment which followed see: J. K. M. Hanson: <u>The Civilian Population and the Warsaw Uprising of 1944</u>, Chs. 3.7 and 4.3.
3   The quotation about 'lunacy' comes from Sanford: <u>Polish Communism</u>, p. 8.
4   Sanford: <u>Polish Communism</u>, pp. 8-9.
5   For the account of the above, see: O. A. Narkiewicz, <u>The Green Flag</u>, Chs. 10 & 11; Dziewanowski: <u>The Communist Party of Poland</u>, Parts 3 & 4.
6   Apolinary Kaminski: <u>Gomulka i Moczar, Kultura</u>, No. 9/264, 1969, pp. 74-78.
7   D. W. Paul and M. D. Simon: <u>Poland Today and Czechoslovakia 1968</u>; <u>Problems of Communism</u> September-October, 1981, pp. 32-33 and footnote 30.
8   <u>Polityka</u>, 15 November 1980, quoted by Paul & Simon: <u>Poland Today</u>, p. 36.
9   Jacek Kuron: <u>What Next in Poland?</u>, <u>Dissent</u>, Winter 1981, p. 35; also see: Paul & Simon: <u>Poland Today</u>, pp. 35-36.
10 Kaminski: <u>Gomulka i Moczar</u>, p. 78.
11 Jan Toporowski: <u>The Polish Coup; 2. Crossing the Rubicon</u>, <u>The Tablet</u>, 6 February 1982, p. 124. The phrase 'politics of the stomach' is used by Sandford: <u>Polish Communism</u>, p. 18.
12 <u>The Polish Coup; 2.</u>, pp. 124-125, and <u>The Polish Coup; 1.</u>, Politics versus economics: <u>The Tablet</u>, 23 January 1982, pp. 76-77.
13 Toporowski: <u>The Polish Coup; 2.</u>, pp. 124-125.
14 Toporowski: <u>The Polish Coup; 1.</u>, p. 78.
15 7 November 1981, p. 1087.
16 See: William Hood: <u>Unlikely Conspiracy</u>; <u>Problems of Communism</u>, March-April, 1984, pp. 67-70.
17 A sermon delivered in June, 1953, quoted in: Jan Nowak: <u>The Church in Poland</u>; <u>Problems of Communism</u>, January-February, 1982, p. 7.
18 Nowak: <u>The Church</u>; pp. 11-14.

19 Informal statement by the Polish Ambassador on 15 June 1984. In fact, an amnesty followed in July, and by mid-August, almost all the political detainees were freed, including Kuron and Michnik.
20 John Hardt: Implications of the CMEA Five Year Plans for East-West Economic Relations, NATO Colloquium 1982, pp. 282-283.
21 Hardt: Implications; pp. 283-284.
22 Hardt: Implications; pp. 284-285.

Chapter Eight

INTRA-BLOC AND INTERNATIONAL RELATIONS

1. A Mechanism to Obtain Compliance

The perception of Soviet policy, both within the
Bloc and outside have been seen by many observers
as an attempt at the preservation of its hegemony
within, and maintenance of a balance of power
outside the Bloc. This has been summed up rather
simplistically in the above phrase; that the
maximum Soviet effort is expended on evolving
mechanisms to obtain or retain compliance. In
fact, a brief glance at the global situation will
show that a mechanistic approach to foreign policy
which this phrase implies will prove sterile.
    It is not the intention of this chapter to
expound the multiplicity of interests or the
complicated network of alliances in the world in
the last two decades. Nor is it possible to
analyse the system which keeps the world going;
even if at times it appears to be going haltingly.
But one must observe several basic facts: the first
one is that whatever the weight of the minor blocs,
such as the EEC, the Third or Non-Aligned World, or
the Latin American bloc (by minor I do not mean in
the sense of small area or small population, but in
terms of military power, political influence and
economic development), the world has been dominated
by two super-powers since the Second World War, and
that both of these powers are pressed by manifold
interests, both internal and external, which all
but undermine such mechanisms as soon as they
appear to be in place.
    The USSR does not lag behind the USA in its
power drives; at times it appears to be ahead, as
in the period of detente, which culminated in the

invasion of Afghanistan; at times, it is the USA which predominates, as in the case of the Reagan Administration's policy in Central America. Perhaps the essence of internal pressures in the US is best exemplified by a cartoon published in 1980, showing President Carter in the middle, with Edmond Muskie on his right and Zbigniew Brzezinski on his left side, in a dominating position. Carter is saying: 'I just hope nobody thinks you Poles are holding me hostage'.[1] Carter's policy failed in Iran externally, and in the US internally: in Iran his intention to liberalise ended in the hostage crisis; this was followed by the Soviet invasion of Afghanistan, by the grain embargo, and the American farmers' rejection of Carter's policy. In the meantime, the Polish crisis was growing though it was still a few more months till <u>Solidarity</u> would be founded.

At the same time as Carter was experiencing the worst crisis of his period, which led to his fall in the election; the USSR was in a similar situation. It has been attempting to ensure its security from US intervention for several decades and had been about to have the SALT II Treaty ratified just before the invasion happened. The Soviet Union had plenty of reasons to wish to improve its relations with the other super-power. For many years it has been afraid of the real or imagined threat to itself and the Eastern Bloc. There is some reason to believe that it may have been right to be afraid. According to a former senior CIA official, the Agency had been working for many years to destabilise Eastern Europe. He alleged that in 1956, the CIA was training large numbers of East European volunteers for para-military operations to liberate their countries from the Russians. He stated that 'units of Poles, Czechoslovaks, Hungarians and other East European nationalities had been undergoing military training at a secret CIA base in West Germany from the early 1950s'. The uprisings have been pre-empted by the publication of Khrushchev's secret speech in New York, which precipitated the revolutions in Poland and Hungary before the secret armies were ready.[2] This interesting revelation may be put against the complaint made by Lech Walesa that the Gdansk strike occurred too early; did he mean to say that other preparations were being made in 1980, which had not been completed before the Lenin Shipyard workers went on strike?

Yet, despite Czechoslovakia in 1968, and the subsequent crisis, the early 1970s began with good auguries for the relations between USSR and USA. The war in Vietnam had exhausted American patience and treasury; the Sino-Soviet conflict was getting worse, not better; the Brezhnev leadership had consolidated its power. Times were right for a rapprochement between the super-powers; and a rapprochement was engineered mainly through the efforts of the modern would-be Machiavelli: Henry Kissinger. This led to the signing of the Final Act of the CSCE in Helsinki in 1975; to the end of the Vietnam War and to the renewed discussions on the limitation of nuclear arms between the super-powers.

More importantly, perhaps, the Czechoslovak tragedy led to the development of a new trend in the non-Communist world: the Eurocommunist parties. The parties which adopted this trend, opted for a new independence of the CPSU and some of them (like the PCI) were prepared to retain American troops on their soil, in return for the security NATO gave them. An ideological defeat for the Brezhnev Doctrine, Eurocommunism was initially welcomed by the Americans, till Kissinger began to suspect that it was covertly supported by the USSR, for its own reasons.

Thirdly, the 1973 oil price crisis made the super-powers more wary of engaging each other in a war of words; the small Arab states have just shown the rest of the world how determination could break down world order. In addition, in the early 1970s the USA was dependent on its oil on the Middle East; whereas the USSR still had ample reserves. A war could develop over the possession of the massive oil reserves in the Middle East; a prospect which the USA, still suffering from the Vietnam Syndrome, did not relish.

On the Soviet side, the perception was that of American encirclement, summed up in the hypothetical reasoning of the Soviet Ministry of Defence:

> In the past five years, the enemy had added more than 3,000 nuclear warheads to its inter-continental missile force. It has added alarming new technology to its major weapons

systems so they are now vastly more accurate,
more lethal and easier to defend than they
were just a few years ago. The enemy is
building a new missile-bearing submarine force
that may be impossible to detect at the
bottoms of the world's oceans. They are
considering construction ... of a new system
of mobile, concealed, land-based missiles.
They have developed technology enabling them
to deploy an entirely new kind of inter-
continental weapon - one virtually immune to
existing defences or detection. The enemy is
giving its conventional forces impressive new
weaponry, some of it still beyond this
country's ability to duplicate. Moreover, the
enemy's allies are modernising their forces in
potentially crucial areas. The other side now
had deployed 2,000 new tanks in Central
Europe ...

This assessment of Soviet military alarm was given
in 1977, after President Carter was elected to
power, with the comment that this was Carter's
major problem.[3]

Carter's presidency aroused great hopes all
over the world that change was on the way.

His speech in Indiana on Sunday night should
make this clearer than ever. It reveals a
view of the world, and of America's place in
it, that is in many important respects
different from that of Dr Kissinger and
previous Administrations. ... The new policy
does not appear to be based on any gullibility
about Soviet intentions, or any willingness
unilaterally to weaken the West. ... What he
is saying first, is that American power, to be
effective, must derive not only from military
and economic strength but also from moral
values. ... Secondly, he is saying that
rivalry with the Soviet Union is not the be
all and end all of policy, that it does not
dictate the response to every situation,
justify any alliance, and sanction the use of
means that are inconsistent with American
values. ... In the good American tradition,
he believes that virtue will triumph, that in
the long run the good guys will beat the bad
guys. His concern for human rights is,

therefore, not just the moral icing on the cake, but an essential part of the recipe.[4]

It was Carter's misfortune that the Iranian crisis led to Soviet invasion of Afghanistan, and the American hostage crisis. 'One of the first measures President Carter took to protest at the Soviet invasion of Afghanistan was to ask Congress to postpone consideration at the Salt Treaty', reported Lawrence Freedman in January, 1980. The SALT Treaty had little chance of getting through the American Senate and the Soviet government was apprehensive about NATO's decision to 'modernise' the long-range theatre nuclear forces in Europe. In view of various other additional problems, Freedman doubted if the SALT negotiations would have succeeded in any case, but, he added:

> While Salt may have few mourners ... its loss is not without problems. With all other arms control negotiations hopelessly bogged down there appears to be no credible alternative to sustained arms competition nor an available means for reviving super-power detente.[5]

Few commentators can feel as pleased as Professor Freedman at seeing his conjectures come true with a vengeance.

Not only did the Carter Administration suspend arms negotiations, but in its helpless fury about the Iranian crisis, it dropped its high moral attitudes of the early days. In April, 1980, the Administration issued an ultimatum to its European allies about anti-Iranian sanctions:

> President Carter took the unprecedented step yesterday of putting public pressure on his European allies by giving them what was seen as an ultimatum in a television interview. He said he had given Britain, West Germany, France and Italy a specific date by which he expects them to join the US in full-scale sanctions against Iran to secure the release of the American hostages. Otherwise he would be forced to take stronger action.[6]

One gathers that Brandon is not complaining about the pressure, as much as about the fact that it was so open; the Nixon Administration was much more covert about pressurising NATO to support its policies. But this is sufficient to illustrate several points, or perhaps one specific and salient point: <u>detente</u>, and all other international relations on the global scale depended on one set of relations only: relations between the USSR and the USA.

Both the super-powers have a 'mechanism to obtain compliance' which they use or attempt to use as they see fit, irrespective of who is in power. However, this mechanism often proves to be useless, as it was in the case of Ayatollah Khomeini's behaviour or in the refusal of Western Europeans to follow the US sanctions. Similar problems occur with the Soviet mechanism. It proved of very little use in outlawing <u>Solidarity</u> in Poland, and it had no use in pressurising Romania to follow certain Soviet policies.

It is the intention of this chapter to demonstrate that the existence of such 'mechanisms' undermines international relations to the point where they virtually grind to a halt. Because each super-power considers that it can bend its allies to its will, and because it is often unsuccessful, the mechanism misfires, and provides a distorted mirror image: the unfamiliar is seen in place of the familiar. This seems to be the main problem in discussing relations between the CMEA members, and their relations with the non-Socialist world. It also makes model-building difficult, if not impossible. Models can only be constructed on the basis of probabilities; but a distorted mirror produces thousands of probabilities, many of them new and unexpected. Hence, the position depends on the time, place, contenders and external circumstances, and on the infinite probability of change. In the circumstances, all one can hope to do is to analyse specific cases of relations and attempt to define bilateral relations between the Eastern Bloc countries and the Eastern Bloc with Western countries.

2.   Relations within the Eastern European Bloc

Historically speaking relations between countries in Central, Eastern and South-Eastern Europe have never been good, though at times they deteriorated more than ever. The Soviet domination of the Bloc has had one good effect: it stopped local wars between small countries. On the other hand, it did not stop the quarrels arising out of traditional enmity or conflict of interests. The domination exerted by the USSR is either economic or military in nature; the political domination (which seems to be the main subject of many books on the Bloc) is implicit in the political systems of the countries and is hardly ever used explicitly, except in the case of countries outside the Bloc. Thus, as one military expert tells us: 'The Warsaw Pact's primary purpose is to contain a turbulent and eruptive group of countries under Moscow's influence. Consequently, the central uses of the Warsaw Pact are internal; to contain, to police and to maintain stability'. After Stalin's death, Krushchev asserted that Stalin misunderstood the nature of dissent in Eastern Europe, and that his tactics towards Tito had misfired: Khrushchev then told the assembly at the Kremlin that

> we have dearly paid for this "shaking of the little finger" ... But no matter how much or how little Stalin shook, not only his little finger but everything else that he could shake, Tito did not fall. Why? The reason was that in this case of disagreement with the Yugoslav comrades, Tito had behind him a state and people who had gone through a severe school of fighting for liberty and independence, a people which gave support to its leaders.

Kolkowicz believes that Khrushchev attempted to relax the policing of the Bloc, but this failed during the Polish crisis in October, 1956:

> Eight months later Khrushchev himself shook his "little finger" at the Polish Communist Party leaders in Warsaw with minimal results. Several weeks later the Soviet leaders abandoned their past methods and suppressed the Hungarian uprising with the Red Army. In the intervening years the Soviet leaders, far from having stabilized the East European political situation, faced new sources of dissent and opposition. The Albanians left the Warsaw Pact; the Romanians continued to oppose Soviet authority in Eastern Europe; the

Czechs embarked upon a policy of radical internal reforms at home, and profound changes in their external relations. These developments suggest that Soviet policy towards Eastern Europe has suffered since the death of Stalin from a form of dualism: on the one hand, the Soviets sought a policy of "decompression" in Eastern Europe, or, more properly, a policy of managed change in the Stalinoid political and social processes in the former satellites; on the other hand, they continued to insist that such change must be evolutionary, rather than revolutionary, and that changes must take place within the framework of the unity of the socialist camp under Soviet domination. Since 1960 the Warsaw Pact has become the main mechanism of such managed change in Eastern Europe.[8]

All authorities agree that the dominant factor in the intra-Bloc relations is dependent on Soviet policies. These opinions are not confined to Western commentators; they are also expressed - in somewhat different forms - by Eastern Bloc commentators. However, there is also agreement - both in the West and in the East - that Soviet policies, while consistent in one area: that of retaining influence within the Bloc by whatever means may prove most efficacious, alter with the changes in leadership, with internal and external variations and with the passage of time. Thus, it is dangerous to go by precedents. In 1980-81, the Western commentators believed fervently that the USSR and Warsaw Pact troops would invade Poland - using the Czech precedent. In fact, a mixture of deception, persuasion and coercion was used to ensure a return of a loyal regime, even if under a military leader. It is certain that the Soviet commander of the Warsaw Pact cleared General Jaruzelski for the post of dictator, in a way in which no Czechoslovak party leader could have been cleared by the CPSU. This may, or may not, mean that the military are in the ascendant in the Soviet Union. But far more likely, it means that the military leaders are to be trusted more than the political leaders, and that the Warsaw Pact alliance has a firmer grip on the Bloc than either the CPSU or the CMEA. Hesitations about choosing political leaders were well illustrated in

Czechoslovakia in 1968-9, when party leadership was not consolidated till a year after the invasion - the reason being that no single Czechoslovak leader was felt to be trustworthy enough after the Prague Spring. Similar problems arose in Poland after the deposition of Gierek; Kania was entrusted with the top post for a brief period only, and was soon replaced by Jaruzelski. This was as much an index of Kania's mediocrity, as of his dubious loyalty to the Bloc. It was even rumoured that Kania was too sympathetic to the Solidarity movement to be trusted, and certainly some of his actions seem to confirm this.

It has already been shown earlier on in this work that the CMEA relations are in general of a radial nature; the USSR being the main trading partner on a bilateral basis. The relations between parties work in a roughly similar manner; this will be discussed later on in this chapter. But the cement which binds the Bloc together is, without doubt, the Warsaw Pact. This is proven, despite the fact that the treaty is disliked by the smaller nations as much as the CMEA. The reasons for the dislike were spelled out by Kolkowicz in the following manner: the Eastern European attitudes towards the Warsaw Pact are negative because: 1. Eastern European countries have to maintain a very high expenditure on their defence establishments, when the period of detente had eroded the sense of threat (needless to say, this was written before the advent of the Reagan Administration); 2. The division of labour which the USSR requires, forces most Eastern Europeans to maintain very large conventional forces, which drain the industrial resources and do not correspond to the real defence needs of these countries. A Czech official maintained in 1968 that about 70 per cent of the defence budget was used for 'general needs' while only 30 per cent was invested in new technology, facilities and reserves. It is estimated that in the West, more than half of the military budgets is used for modernisation, by comparison; 3. Eastern Europe has to conform to a unitary strategic doctrine which does not necessarily comply with national defence needs. This has been expressed by one, unnamed participant in a Warsaw Pact conference in the following terms: 'Thus the relations of the two sovereign countries, one a big one and the

other a small one, must be precisely defined in all
respects. Otherwise, the feeling of wrongdoing
will persist. This problem is very sensitive in
the military sector'; 4. The USSR has a monopoly
over command in the Warsaw Pact. Only token
participation is allowed to the minor partners.
There is a vertical command structure within the
Pact, which means that the military maintain links
outside the normal governmental and party channels.
In addition, the Soviet command retains a hegemony,
in a way described by a senior Czech party member
and general in July, 1968:

> So far the situation is that this command is
> formed by marshals, generals, and officers of
> the Soviet Army and that the other members'
> armies have only their representatives in this
> joint command. These representatives,
> however, so far have held no responsibilities
> or functions to co-decide, but rather played
> the role of a liaison organ.[9]

Further, it is noted that: 5. The Warsaw Pact is
being used by the Soviet Union for internal
political aims. Some Eastern European leaders have
resisted this strongly; particularly so in the case
of Romania's Ceausescu, who refused to allow
Romanian troops to take part in the Czech invasion,
and has since refused to take part in Warsaw Pact
manoeuvres.

On the other side of the argument, it must be
noted that the USSR probably had no intention of
creating the Warsaw Pact in the first place; that
it was a hasty reaction to West Germany's entry
into NATO, and that while NATO had little
hesitation in entrusting some command posts to non-
Americans (particularly if they had good anti-
Communist credentials), they have kept the control
of the nuclear forces under tight American command;
in the case of the 'modernised' weapons, the
Pershing and the Cruise, there is no military - and
apparently little political - control over their
use by the Americans on European soil against the
Soviet Bloc. One doubts that this arrangement is
any more democratic than the Warsaw Pact
arrangement, particularly since the parliaments in
several NATO countries were against the American
control or the placement of the weapons; and at
least two major opposition parties (the German

Social Democrats and the British Labour Party) have opposed the weapons in principle.

Democratic the Warsaw Pact may not be, but as Kolkowicz rightly states, the Eastern European leaders may not want to change the established relations within the Bloc, while seeking greater independence from Moscow; this is partly because they have realised that they cannot rely on Western help in the event of anti-Soviet actions; partly because they fear a rearmed Germany; and perhaps most importantly, because they have to rely on the Soviet nuclear umbrella in case of a nuclear conflict between the two super-powers. These reasons are as valid in 1984 as they were in 1969, when the essay was written. However,

> the events in Czechoslovakia and Eastern Europe seem to indicate that despite the inherent obsolescence of the Warsaw Pact as an effective externally-oriented military instrument, the Pact will continue to be kept alive and to serve Soviet policy interests. However, the utility and viability of the Pact has undergone a profound metamorphosis as a result of the Czech crisis. While at a first glance it would seem that the unity and internal cohesiveness of the Pact were strengthened as a result of recent events, it is more realistic to examine some of the fissures and cracks in the Pact structure. For, in reality, the latent divisions within the Pact have become even more polarized, with East Germany, Poland and Bulgaria showing their strong adherence to the Pact, and with Rumania, Czechoslovakia and Hungary indicating, explicitly or implicitly, their strong misgivings about its utility.[10]

This judgement seems correct, though some members of the Pact have switched their attitudes somewhat since. But there is also an erroneous hypothesis: the Warsaw Pact troops have been used to quell disorder within the Bloc, but this does not prove that they could not be used with the same success outside the Bloc. The Soviet troops were first used against the Krondstadt revolt and later against the peasants during the collectivisation drive. This did not make them less effective in the Second World War. The Polish troops have proved their loyalty to the government in 1970, during the riots, and again in 1980-81 periods, by being the main support of the regime; and ensuring that no armed intervention on a large scale was necessary. It would be foolish to delude oneself with the belief that in the case of international conflict, any of the Warsaw Pact troops would defect on a large scale. The best proof of this may well be the war in Afghanistan; so far the West (or Britain to be exact) has managed to collect two Soviet deserters (or what appear to be deserters) after a five-year war; one of these is apparently a drug addict, and the other has been sent to the army after some criminal offences in the Soviet Union. It may well be a serious mistake to assume that the privileged armed services, whose standard of living is kept purposely higher than that of the population, who are ideologically motivated, and proud of their achievements, would behave like the (mostly Ukrainian) deserters in the Second World War at the height of Stalinist terror.

Nor are the smaller national armies any more likely to desert their posts; the Czech army was not called out to defend the country against the invasion in 1968; there is a strong reason to think that their loyalty to the Dubcek regime could not be trusted; the Polish army stood by the government in its years of crisis; there is little reason to think that the East German army, the most disciplined of the lot, would desert en masse. The Hungarians and the Romanians may be doubtful, but the size of their armies makes little difference to the whole of the Pact. There may be mutual animosities between the national armies, reflecting animosities between the nations, but on the whole one must agree with Kolkowicz who stated that

> The Warsaw Pact has come full circle, from a minor organization of limited role and utility to one which has become very vital to the Soviet Union. Its main uses are political, rather than purely military, and it serves as an iron corset to hold together the communist bloc. In a larger sense, the Warsaw Pact serves as an alliance system through which the Soviet leaders seek to entangle their unwilling allies in the web of Soviet national interests.[11]

While Kolkowicz contradicts himself several times, because the Warsaw Pact is primarily a military tool, he is right in stating that it is a major force binding the Bloc together. There are more bilateral relations within the Pact than multilateral relations (indeed, the latter may be said to be almost non-existent), but this in itself is probably the main cohesive force. The divisions appear much more strongly in areas in which the relationships are fluid; this is in the region of economic relations of the Bloc.

3. CMEA's Economic Relations in the Light of Political Perspectives

In early 1979, a foreign correspondent of The Observer recalled what Kamenev is supposed to have said in the 1920s, before the signing of the first Anglo-Soviet trade agreement: 'With every additional shovel of coal, with every additional load of oil that we in Russia obtain through the help of foreign technique, capital will be digging its own grave.'[12] The correspondent asserted that at that stage there was no one in Eastern Europe or in the West, who believed in this dictum. Had he waited a year or two longer, he would have found the Reagan Administration's advisers (most particularly Richard Pipes, whose first book dealt with the early period of the Soviet Union) unearth Kamenev, Lenin, Marx and Stalin, to quote but a few Communist spokesmen, to prove that trade with the Soviet Union and the Eastern Bloc was A Bad Thing. Moreover, he would have witnessed the most self-wounding exercise performed by the Americans even before Reagan came to power: the grain embargo placed on the Soviet Union by the Carter Administration after the Afghanistan invasion.

Why has something which was a good thing in 1979 become A Bad Thing in 1980 and A Very Bad Thing in 1981-2? Is there logic in putting obstacles in the way of international trade by a government which believes in economic liberalism? Is there any logic when a government which believes in the 'building of socialism' is relying on its basic foodstuffs, like grain, from the world's most capitalist power? What good, or what bad effects can there be, on a global scale, in an activity which is as normal as taking food, drink and falling asleep? Trade has, admittedly, acquired a bad name in some religious circles in the Middle Ages, but this had more to do with usury than with the activity itself. Following the Christian medieval line of thought, Marx and his student, Lenin, decided that trade may be a good thing in itself; the people who carried it out - the 'middlemen' or 'meshochniki' of early revolutionary days, were decidedly bad. That was why private trade was abolished in the early Soviet years, though it was brought back in the NEP days, in order to stave off disaster in the cities. But foreign trade, and trade on a large scale have remained the prerogative of the state or state-founded organisations, despite the fact that the despised and hated middlemen behaved in the same manner in state organisations as they had done for centuries past: i.e. they drove the hardest bargain possible, which was consistent with obtaining what they wanted.

The USSR then, has an ideological blockage with regard to trade, and particularly trade with the USA which has withstood for almost two decades the temptation of starting up normal relations with the USSR. But the USA should not have such blockages. It has been founded on the basis of liberalism in trade, and despite relying on tariffs and other barriers over a long period of time (for protectionist purposes only), it has an ideological commitment to trading with everyone. While for many years, with the exception of transactions carried out by Armand Hammer, its trade with the USSR was non-existent, the war with Germany brought the USSR into the charmed circle of 'lend-lease' agreement and the barriers were broken; only to be renewed on the outset of the Cold War. The trade was renewed after de-Stalinisation, and strengthened during the period of detente. Therefore, it can be seen that the USA traded or did not trade with the Soviet Union for purely political reasons, which had little or nothing to do with economics.

The Soviet Union, on the other hand, traded with the USA and the capitalist countries on the basis of necessity or choice; i.e. for purely economic reasons. This curious reversal of roles has seldom been noticed, except by political scientists, critical of American politics. It has been obscured by a genuine sense of shame on the part of both governments about the jettisoning of ideological factors for the sake of performing what should be normal functions compatible with governmental responsibilities.

The beginning of the new era in trading is said to have occurred in 1966, when Lyndon Johnson requested the Congress to allow him to negotiate trade agreements with the Soviet Union and the Eastern European Bloc. He had already in 1966 expressed his wish 'to build new bridges to Eastern Europe - bridges of ideas, education, culture, trade, technical co-operation, and mutual understanding for world peace and prosperity'. Expansion of trade was approved the following year, with the recommendation that control of strategic goods be kept which could 'significantly enhance Communist military capabilities'.[13] The arguments which followed this recommendation are well-known: briefly, the Congress refused to pass the act for East-West trade relations, because of mainly Republican opposition, as long as the Soviet Union continued to aid North Vietnam.

Dean Rusk, then Secretary of State, argued that the growth in trade would reduce Eastern European dependence on the Soviet Union and would make the Eastern Bloc 'increasingly conscious of their stake in stability and improving peaceful relations with the outside world'. Walter Mondale, then a Democratic Senator, added 'that US restrictions on trade deprived American businessmen of access to markets which Western Europeans were happy to dominate.' The bill's opponents argued that the Soviet Union wanted to trade with the West to strengthen its economy and to obtain technology and machinery which it was unable to develop on its own. 'Trade with the Soviets was described as "an evil practice" and evidence of moral decay.' One senator even argued that the US should act on the assumption that 'all goods are strategic.'[14]

It was the Nixon Administration which finally prevailed in the wish to open up East-West trade. In 1972, US-Soviet trade agreements were negotiated, only to be almost stopped by the Jackson Amendment of 1974, which linked the extension of the most-favoured-nation status to emigration policies. Jackson also was instrumental in tightening restrictions on technology transfers, because he said that 'it is only the quality of our weapons, based on our more advanced technology and

know-how, which allows us to maintain an adequate
military deterrent.'[15] By the mid-1970s East-
West trade was no longer a fashionable subject for
liberal circles - perhaps because it had been taken
up by a Republican Administration - and even such
liberals as Adlai Stevenson objected to it on the
grounds that it increased Soviet military power.

Despite this, a five-year grain export
agreement and a maritime agreement were signed in
1975, but Congressional attitudes towards trade
hardened.

As late as 1979, President Carter expressed
the hope that most-favoured-nation status
would be granted both to China and the Soviet
Union. The stop-and-go emigration of Soviet
Jews, Moscow's treatment of domestic
dissidents, and various incidents involving
the arrests of Soviet spies in the United
States, and businessmen and US journalists in
the Soviet Union, served as irritants in the
American political process. The more serious
problem was Washington's displeasure with
Soviet actions in developing countries, its
relationship with Cuba, and what was perceived
as the growing Soviet military threat.[16]

It must be stressed at this point that while
the US-USSR trade was a separate matter from US-
Eastern European trade and non-US Western trade
with both, the matter is not easily separated. The
inter-linking of the blocs and the intertwined
interests have made it virtually impossible to draw
an exact line between one and the other. Perhaps
this can be best seen in the intrusion of the
Vietnam War into the trade agreements; the linking
of emigration with grain exports and the growing
Western European dependence on American high
technology within European industries. Another
problem was the status of Japan in the whole
equation; an American ally, it also began to
develop high technology well ahead of the US; it
was free to trade with the USSR, China and Taiwan
in many areas, and it has been asserted that this
is where the Soviet Union goes shopping for its
most advanced technological goods. It was only in
late 1983 that the Reagan Administration began to
press Japan to stop strategic exports, but one must
have doubts on how effective this pressure has

been. Another possible bridge between the East and
West for technology transfer is through the private
(and mostly secret) agreements between West and
East Germany. Like the US, they are supposed to be
linked to emigration; but unlike the US, trade is
constant, voluminous and moreover often includes
personnel trained in the use of machinery. So,
while in the period of the Reagan Administration,
the Western Europeans have been virtually forbidden
to trade with the Eastern Bloc, the West Germans
and the Japanese can do it, under the cover of
special agreements. Nor is this all. In July,
1984, British exporters have been stopped from
supplying a telephone system to Bulgaria, while the
Swedes are apparently going to be able to sell a
similar system, because they are not covered by the
American ban.[17] Other complications arise, which
are even more odd: Poland, which has allowed the
emigration of national minorities (mostly of Jewish
and German origin) almost freely since 1956, has
lost its most-favoured-nation status after the
introduction of martial law. She has nothing left
to bargain with to regain it; and the amnesty
announced in mid-July has proved insufficient to
move the Reagan Administration to restore it.

The deterioration of relations is usually
dated with the Soviet invasion of Afghanistan;
however, Kaufman points out that

> Long before the Soviet invasion of
> Afghanistan, Carter's decision to raise the
> rate of defence spending and his signing of
> Presidential Directive No. 18, indicated that
> a new policy was replacing the US-Soviet
> detente. The new policy placed trade
> relations somewhere between the denial
> approach of the Cold War and the more relaxed
> approach of the early 1970s. It was based on
> an assessment that relations between the two
> countries were becoming more competitive, that
> the Soviet Union had benefited more from East-
> West trade than had the United States, and
> that Washington needed to be more skilful in
> its use of economic leverage with Moscow. As
> one of Carter's key National Security Council
> advisors put it, the United States "must be
> able to open or close the economic door as our
> long-term security interests and political
> relations with the Soviet Union dictate".[18]

Yet, even in 1979, there was still hope and goodwill; if not in the United States, then certainly in Europe. Frankland stated that:

The evidence is that the East European countries are well on the way to developing a lasting economic relationship with the West which is far too important for them to be manipulated, as Kamenev hoped would be possible, for political purposes. A similar paradox has characterised the Western side of the relationship. Today no one is a more solicitous spectator of the Polish Government's now almost completed negotiations to obtain a massive $550 million loan from a consortium of Western bankers than the American State Department. Some American officials had even hoped the bankers would come up with a round $1,000 million, although Poland already owes Western banks and Governments $15,000 million and part of the new loan will have to go on the heavy interest payments on the earlier ones. It is an odd situation. The American and West European Governments are very anxious to help Poland out of a tight economic spot. But while they are encouraging their bankers to lend to the Poles, they are also paying their own soldiers to improve defences against a blitzkrieg thrust by the armies of the Warsaw Pact.[19]

There was no paradox in the above policy; only a dichotomy in the American attitudes towards the Eastern Bloc. This was clearly spelled out by Kaufman:

As a step towards centralizing decision-making about East-West economic relations, the National Security Council was given a role in the clearing of grain sales and in technology transfers. The decisions to deny export licences for certain computers in 1977 and 1978 and to slow down technology and equipment for the exploration and production of oil and gas were apparently taken as part of a strategy of identifying technology for which the Soviets have a critical need, and approving or disapproving licences for its export on foreign policy grounds. A key premise within the Defence Department and national security circles of the Administration was that <u>strategic technology was not being properly controlled by the Commerce Department</u>. Important members of the military committees in Congress shared this view and tried, in the 1979 renewal of the Export Administration Act, to give the Defence Department exclusive authority for identifying "critical" technologies and placing them on the controlled list. The law as finally enacted allowed the Defence Department to identify such technologies but restored the joint role of the Commerce and Defence Departments in deciding which items to place on the list. The disclosure in 1979 that a Soviet combat unit was present in Cuba contributed to sentiment favouring a tightening of trade restrictions. A more severe hardening of attitudes was provoked by the Soviet invasion of Afghanistan in December. The embargoes imposed by Carter in reaction to the invasion obviously ended what hopes were left for improved East-West economic relations during his term.[20]

By early 1980, the military were in the ascendant, aided and abetted by those members of Congress who had much to gain by increased defence contracts: 'The chairman of the Joint Chiefs of Staff, Air Force General, David Jones, warned yesterday that the chance of a US-Soviet military confrontation "will increase significantly" in the next five years.' This statement was made to a House Committee considering a rise in the defence budget by $15.7 billion to $142.7 billion, a rise of some 12-13 per cent. 'Earlier, the Defence Secretary, Mr Brown, had to defend Mr Carter's proposed increase in arms spending against hawks on the committee who believe that it is not enough.' Both Jim Wright on the Democratic side and Ted Stevens for the Republicans complained that the increase was not nearly enough, even though it provided for heavy spending on the MX mobile missile system, 1,700 new planes and 97 new ships over the next five years.[21]

The American pressure on NATO to boycott trade agreements with the Eastern Bloc spilt over into the EEC.

> On Tuesday, European foreign ministers will take the unprecedented step of using a routine Common Market meeting for a major foreign policy debate, to try to hammer out a common line on the Afghan crisis. Senior American officials will also fly to Brussels, for a special NATO meeting with the same objective,

said a correspondent from Brussels in January, 1980. The split was not only between the EEC and the US, but between countries within the EEC. Only Britain's Mrs Thatcher was ready to follow the Carter boycott without question; while Chancellor Schmidt for Germany and President Giscard d'Estaing for France regarded: 'the long-standing policy of <u>detente</u> in Europe - preserving good working relations with the east whatever the political disagreements - too valuable to be put at risk for far-off Afghanistan.' Despite personal telephone calls from President Carter, the two leaders decided that there was no question of matching the American boycott.

> Direct action to sabotage the US embargo is ruled out. But current trading links including even the controversial sale of cut-price butter to the Russians will continue. ... Germany (is) of all the countries the one with the most to fear from war and the most to gain from <u>detente</u> ...,

and it claimed that more, not fewer, links are needed to avoid a breakdown of relations. Dissent was also apparent in the Eastern Bloc: 'Romania had condemned the invasion, Poland had taken seven days and Hungary ten before giving it lukewarm support and only Bulgaria, Czechoslovakia and East Germany had shown official enthusiasm'.[22]
The above quotations will show that it is impossible not only to separate the issues of foreign policy from those of economic policy, but also the issues arising out of virtually <u>all</u> events which happen globally. Afghanistan, Cuba and Africa, to name but a few, have all played a part in what was essentially a normal exchange of goods between various countries or blocs. A complicated model could be built to show the inter-linking of issues but they should be plainly seen even without it. What is less clear, however, is

to what extent the fluctuations in East-West trade, due to political and military factors, improved or deteriorated the trade balances of both blocs. In addition, even the most sophisticated Congressional and security reports, commissioned with a view to finding out the 'profit and loss' balance on each side, were and still are unable to agree. Did the Soviet Union profit from the influx of foreign goods? Did they increase its military strength, or merely drain her gold reserves? Recent statements seem to show that the balance was negative: in July, 1984, Pravda carried an article charging that industrial equipment

> often imported at enormous expense from the West, was gathering rust waiting to be installed in factories which were in the event, not built. The implication was that billions of pounds worth of equipment was going to waste. ... The attack on industry concentrated, by way of example, on petrochemicals. Senior officials and other ministries involved, Pravda said, spent their time blaming each other for inexcusable shortcomings and gave evasive answers to official inquiries. At least as important was the attack on the State Planning Commission, Gosplan, which approves all imports of machinery and equipment. Pravda said that it was time Gosplan officials made sure that State money was being spent sensibly.[23]

The Soviet Union has found that the imports from the West, particularly those involving high technology, are often wasted because of inappropriate conditions or inability to adapt them to Soviet needs. Very similar charges are being made in Poland against the Gierek government; several top state officials stand indicted for wasting foreign loans on technology which was allowed to go to waste, because it was impossible to use it. Why has this state of affairs been allowed to go on for so long without a stop? And why is it being criticised now? The answer lies in the easy flow of money after the oil price rises. The Western banks, awash with Arab petro-currency were handing it out to all and sundry; Eastern Europeans as well as the Latin Americans, while at the same time raising interest rates to cover themselves in case the loans were not repaid. The Soviet and Eastern European planners are just as gullible about easy money as are their Western counterparts; having departed from a Marxist viewpoint, they saw no harm in taking what was so freely and cheaply offered. Moreover, every ministry or enterprise had its own axe to grind: delegations from each body would go out to the West, stay at the best hotels, be entertained in the most expensive fashion, and be talked into buying more and more equipment, most of it either superfluous or unsuitable for local conditions. All the countries of the Bloc, not only the Soviet Union, found it cheaper to import American cattlefood rather than grow their own; considering that these countries have an economy which is 50 per cent agricultural at the very least, this was the height of absurdity. The grain was used for cattle feed rather than for human consumption. The high technology was left to rot in the stores, or misapplied. The debt mounted, and the Western bankers began to worry. This worry about losing money had a strong, but perhaps desirable effect: in another, apparently paradoxical move, the USA began to reconsider its trading position with the East.

For apart from proving an expensive luxury to the CMEA, the American exports apparently had made a big difference to the American economy. The military interests and the armaments lobbies were unable to compensate a stagnant economy for the loss of the Eastern markets. In addition, whereas the Latin Americans were defaulting on the debt, the Eastern Bloc was at least servicing parts of its debt, and even introducing some of the stringent deflationary measures without being asked to do so by the IMF (only Romania and Hungary take part in the international monetary system through the membership of the World Bank and IMF).

The concern over the management of trade policy, so far as East-West trade is concerned, is rooted in an awareness that two successive Presidents have been unsuccessful in their attempts to use a strategy of selective trade denial in order to achieve political objectives. Both acted from high moral purposes in response to Soviet behaviour that was widely condemned, here and abroad.

The concern over the management of trade
policy, so far as East-West trade is
concerned, is rooted in an awareness that two
successive Presidents have been unsuccessful
in their attempts to use a strategy of
selective trade denial in order to achieve
political objectives. Both acted from high
moral purposes in response to Soviet behaviour
that was widely condemned, here and abroad.
Yet, both engendered domestic political
difficulties, dissensions from within their
own parties, and disagreements within the
Western alliance. Both are perceived to have
harmed US economic interests,

concludes Kaufman. In the case of Carter's grain
embargo, the sanction was imposed as a 'moral' one,
in - presumably - the full knowledge that the USSR
would be able to buy its grain from other
countries. It also hit one section of the American
public selectively: the grain farmers and grain
brokers, who

> complained that agriculture was being made a
> sacrificial lamb in Washington's political
> dispute with Moscow. The argument that
> farmers were being treated unfairly because
> non-agricultural trade was permitted during
> the embargo could not be answered
> satisfactorily, although some industrial
> products were restricted.

(It could be that had Jimmy Carter been a grain and
not a peanut farmer, the consequences would have
struck him more forcibly.) The additional damage
caused was that of the image of the US as an
unreliable supplier of goods, and 'that much of the
agricultural and non-agricultural business lost by
US firms would not be regained.'[24]

The Reagan Administration revoked the grain
embargo, while almost immediately afterwards, it
imposed the gas pipeline embargo, which hit not
only US interests, but even more painfully Western
European interests. The embargo was imposed,
without consultation with Western Europe, as a
sanction for the Soviet involvement in Poland. It
had no effect either on the Polish repression of
Solidarity or on the Soviet involvement in Polish
affairs. Moreover, the pipeline was completed

without American technology (or so it is said); thus proving that its uniqueness is in question. Unless, of course, American technology did go into the project, in a roundabout way, via Sweden or Japan, just as the telephone system will be sold to Bulgaria, though not by Reagan's faithful ally, Mrs Thatcher. Either way, the American embargo can be bypassed; whether by producing the same articles elsewhere, or buying them via a third party. In a Senate Committee hearing, most senators agreed that the embargo would be counter-productive, just as the grain embargo had proved to be.[25] Less than a year after their imposition, the Administration revoked the pipeline sanctions in an unpublicised manner, on 13 November 1982.

But the problem has not been shelved. Sanctions as such may be out, the hunt for technology-transfer transgressors is on and flourishing. Throughout 1983, the American press was full of examples of suppression of export licences for simple domestic computers; of arrests of foreign businessmen with export licences, for exporting forbidden goods; and of such absurd demands as that the Soviet consulate in San Francisco should be moved from its desirable residence on top of a hill to a house in a valley, because the high position gave it an advantage in spying on computer firms in the Santa Clara Valley. These and many other instances will be familiar to the readers of American newspapers, and are too numerous to quote here. In the meantime, President Reagan has justified the sale of grain to the USSR on the grounds that it has no technological value, while the exports of small British computers or German pipeline parts allow the Russians to improve their technology. Had he said that grain exports were needed for internal political reasons, and to increase the American gold reserves, he might have been sympathised with by Western Europeans; but the unfortunate statements he made merely exacerbated the already serious situation. To sum up: the Western exports to the CMEA may, or may not, have improved Eastern European technology. They certainly used up much needed hard-currency, and a large part of them was misused or under-utilised. They all but destroyed the Polish economy and seem well on the way to doing it to the Romanian and Hungarian economy. The countries which borrowed least: Czechoslovakia, East Germany and Bulgaria

are at the top of the economic league in the CMEA.
We cannot account for the amount of harm or good
they did the Soviet economy, partly because of lack
of realistic statistics, but partly also because
the Soviet economy is so large and so involved that
it takes a long time to make a proper balance.
However, we do know that the grain imports have
removed incentives to improve farming methods and
productivity in the USSR; that the machinery stands
idle; and that Soviet R & D, instead of being
developed, spends time and effort (not to speak of
hard-currency) on finding 'prototypes' abroad,
while Soviet universities turn out scientists with
a commitment to 'pure sciences', technology having
acquired a dirty, almost 'Stalinist' connotation,
and being regarded with a distaste which used to be
the prerogative of the British. On the other hand,
Pentagon experts still maintain that Soviet
military technology is ahead of the American
technology (though this is disputed by the CIA),
and that it will take some five years - in 1984 -
to catch up with it.

Volumes have been written about the last
point, but they cannot be discussed in this space.
We do know, however, that star wars schemes and
counter-missile missiles have been developed by the
Soviet Union simultaneously with the American
schemes. Many of them have been abandoned because
of their impracticability. Similarly, the USSR has
considered a 'space-shuttle' - whether borrowed
from the American design or not - and has rejected
it, while it took the shuttle disaster of June 1984
for the American air force establishment to
consider scrapping it for the more practical and
reliable single-use rockets. The Russians may not
pay much for technological development compared
with the American defence establishment, but if the
American taxpayer has to pay two thousand dollars
for a ten-cent part (examples of this have been
given recently), then much of the American research
funding is lost on the way. The profit motive may
be a desirable idea, but in practice - as the
Russians had discovered in 1914 - a fat armaments
contractor usually means that the soldier goes into
battle without boots and with an imitation wooden
gun. In the USSR, as a result of the Tsarist
experience, the 'profit motive' is called
'corruption', and if the lack of it inhibits
military technology development, it also makes it

easier to skip one step in the race. The Russians progressed from simple German prototypes of rockets to <u>Sputniks</u> within some ten years; they developed nuclear weapons within two years of the Americans, despite the ravages of war; they were ahead of the Americans with the heat-seeking missiles; and - if the Pentagon is to be believed - they are now ahead with short- to medium-range missiles and with the <u>Cruise</u> type of missile. They even appear to have the <u>Stealth</u> plane, or its equivalent; and that has been one of the most guarded American secret weapons. Recent disclosure that at least a third of the Latin American debt is in private bank accounts in the US and Switzerland makes one wonder - though of course it is unlikely in the case of the US contractors - if all the money spent on defence, if all the technological advances one is told about, are not wasted, not through corruption, but through sheer overkill and parallelism; exactly the same faults that the USSR finds within its own system.

If the CMEA does not profit much by trade with the West, and the West loses by its prohibition, who is the gainer and who is the loser? And would the sharing of technology not be a much simpler and more profitable undertaking than secreting it away and having it stolen from under one's nose? This question could well be behind the stand of some American senators, when they insist on the continuation of trade with the East; it is certainly always in the minds of the Western European governments.

4. The Significance and Volume of East-West Trade

In view of the political implications and rifts which the question of East-West trade generates, it would be useful to find out how big a proportion of global trade this involves for the CMEA as a whole. It is well known that Western Europe, and particularly Western Germany, which plays a larger part in the trade than the rest of the EEC, have only a very small proportion of their global trade tied up with the CMEA. This excludes special arrangements which West Germany has with East Germany, because on the face of it, they do not affect the Bloc as a whole.

It may surprise no one that the volume of trade even at the height of <u>detente</u> was very small in relation to: a) the size of the Eastern European market; and b) the trade within the CMEA. This will be seen from a brief summary of the trade's importance. In the heyday of good relations in 1971, the CMEA imported from Western Europe but a fraction of its global needs.

Bulgaria	2.8	per cent of GNP
Czechoslovakia	3.0	"
East Germany	3.2	"
Hungary	4.7	"
Poland	2.1	"
Romania	2.9	"
USSR	0.4	"

By 1972 the CMEA, with the addition of China, Cuba, Korea, Mongolia and Vietnam as well as Yugoslavia, increased this import by 23.5 per cent in current prices. No comparison can be made with 1972, because this inclusion of the additional areas, and the inflationary curve, vitiate any such comparisons. However, the West also increased its imports, in terms of prices, from all the above countries, by 21.1 per cent. Thus, it can be proved, as stated by one economist, that: 'In speed of growth ... East-West trade thus continued to be more dynamic than world trade as a whole', though while the market had an annual turnover of $26 billion,

> it would doubtless be significantly larger if the socialist countries chose to become more dependent on trade. As a group they must account for over a third of the world's manufactures, but their exports (including those to one another) are only about one-eighth of the world total.[26]

Kaser further states that, while the projections for the future growth of trade are much higher (they were in fact completely upset by the oil crisis and the debt problems) for the late 1970s, they would still be completely asymmetrical as they were in 1971 and 1972. 'Farm and mineral products predominate in Comecon exports to the West, whereas Western deliveries are concentrated in manufactures, particularly machinery. According to the major UN study of East-West trade, chemicals, machinery and transport equipment account (in 1967, the report's base year) for 82 per cent of exports from the EEC to Comecon, whereas food, raw materials and fuels accounted for 60 per cent of Comecon deliveries to the EEC.'[27]

However, protectionist measures by the EEC stop the development of this trade, and Kaser concludes, after discussing various schemes, that:

> All the above measures will not ... be adequate to enable Eastern Europe to finance an annual import bill of $20 billion from the West by 1980; this region is therefore faced with the need for very substantial credits. Provision of huge credits by the West is clearly the crucial factor in the Comecon members' efforts to import the equipment and know-how required in order to develop the production of exports needed to repay such credits and - as they hope - to yield incremental returns at home.[28]

It was on such dubious premises that the loans were made to the CMEA countries; the premises were dubious both on economic and on political grounds; the only certain thing was, as Kaser stated, that without credits there could be no further imports into the CMEA. But without exports from the CMEA to hard-currency areas, there could be no repayment of credits. A classical dilemma which had been tested many times; perhaps the most obvious one being the Latin American default on debt in 1930; but repeated many times since, most particularly since 1975. No one asks the economists and the bankers to become prophets; but one would expect them to remember their financial history: in this case, they were intent on forgetting it. American intervention and sanctions merely exacerbated what was already an impossible situation for the Eastern European countries, and it is possible that even without the oil crisis and the recession which followed it, the debt crisis would have mounted.

The result of such flawed reasoning or rejection of past experience has been witnessed in its extreme form in the Polish case. As an economist stated recently: 'It is necessary first to reject the notion that Poland's economic crisis was brought on simply by muddled policies, by the mistakes, incompetence, and corruption of the leadership and its planners and administrators.'

Having cited the usual simplistic reason that the nature of the system is to blame, - he then forwards the real reasons:

> After the riots of December 1970 ... Edward Gierek and his advisers tried to achieve economic modernization through a "new development strategy". Its key was large-scale import of capital and technology from the West. Its essence was that an increase in investment was necessary to restructure and modernize the economy but that a simultaneous increase in consumption was necessary to create incentives. ... Gierek and his planners had high expectations. They hoped to increase the export of some high quality manufactured goods, which would be produced in new or newly modernized plants with the help of Western machines and equipment and according to Western specifications. ... The result would soon be an excess of exports over imports, and the debt would be repaid quickly. ... There were many flaws in the implementation of this ambitious strategy. The rates of investment were too high, and the investment front was too wide. ... In industry, imports of investment goods and intermediate goods were excessive, and foreign licences were purchased in numbers too big to be absorbed by the economy within a short period of time. ... In foreign trade, <u>the way in which the planners tried to insulate the economy from the impact of the world-wide stagflation contributed to significant difficulties</u>, primarily by increasing price distortions and inefficiency throughout the economy.[29]

By 1981, Poland's industrial production declined by 12 per cent, because it depended on up to 23 per cent of imports from the West. Instead of tackling the economy in an administrative manner, this economist suggests that the question of foreign trade should have been tackled first. But how was this possible, since, owing to the American pressure, the West was virtually forbidden to grant Poland even the slightest breathing space? The Poles reverted to 'Neo-Stalinist' economy, according to the author, for which he chides them

soundly. Again, what other choices did they have?
Unless it was designed that they should be freed
from the constraints of the CMEA by means other
than those of strike and civil disobedience (and
that would involve external intervention), there
was absolutely nothing they were able to do. In
the late eighteenth century, Polish peasants
fighting with Kosciuszko against the Russians
threw themselves onto the barrels of Russian guns,
to stop their firing. Is this what the author
propagates? One hopes not, but one can never be
certain. This is one case where the economics of
sanity must be applied instead of the insanity of
politics.

CHAPTER EIGHT: FOOTNOTES

1   The Observer, 4 May 1980.
2   James Angleton, quoted in: CIA 'trained
    secret E. European armies', The Times,
    1 December 1976.
3   Robert Kaiser: The ring of American steel
    around Russia, The Guardian, 14 March
    1977.
4   The Times leader, 24 May 1977.
5   Has putting Salt on the shelf done anyone any
    good?, The Times, 15 January 1980.
6   Henry Brandon: Carter's Ultimatum, Sunday
    Times, 13 April 1980.
7   Roman Kolkowicz: The Warsaw Pact: The
    Entangling Alliance, Survey, Winter-
    Spring, 1969, p. 86.
8   Kolkowicz: The Warsaw Pact, pp. 86-87.
9   Kolkowicz: The Warsaw Pact, quoting General
    Prchlik, p. 95.
10 Kolkowicz: The Warsaw Pact, p. 100.
11 Kolkowicz: The Warsaw Pact, p. 101.
12 Mark Frankland: East and West forging strong
    economic links, The Observer, 8 April
    1979.
13 Quoted by Richard F. Kaufman: Changing US
    Attitudes Toward East-West Economic Relations
    NATO Colloquium 1983, p. 53.
14 Kaufman: Changing US Attitudes, p. 54.
15 Quoted by Kaufman: Changing US Attitudes,
    p. 55.
16 Kaufman: Changing US Attitudes, p. 56.
17 Financial Times, 17 July 1984.
18 Kaufman: Changing US Attitudes, p. 57.
19 East and West, The Observer, 8 April 1979.
20 Kaufman: Changing US Attitudes, p. 57,
    emphasis added.
21 Alex Brummer: US-Soviet War threat 'will
    grow', The Guardian, 30 January 1980.
22 Keith Richardson: Nato's split ranks,
    Sunday Times, 13 January 1980.
23 Pravda, 17 July 1984, quoted by Michael
    Simmons: Soviet managers get last warning
    about gross inefficiency, The Guardian, 18
    July 1984.
24 Kaufman: Changing US Attitudes, p. 58-59.
25 Senate Committee on Foreign Relations See:
    Kaufman - Changing US Attitudes, pp. 59-60.

26 Michael Kaser: Comecon's Trade, Problems
    of Communism, July-August, 1973, p. 3,
    figures extrapolated from Table 2, p. 3.
27 Kaser: Comecon's Trade, pp. 8-9.
28 Kaser: Comecon's Trade, p. 14.
29 Z. B. Fallenbuchl: Poland's Economic Crisis
    Problems of Communism, March-April, 1982,
    p. 2 and p. 5, emphasis added.

Chapter Nine

THE ROAD TO THE UNKNOWN

---

1. Perceptions of Eastern Europe in the West

The last chapter discussed at length the
consequences of the 'opening up to the West' in the
Warsaw Pact and CMEA strategies, and the subsequent
restrictions on the opening up coming from NATO and
the EEC. This, in itself, is something of a
novelty. It must be remembered that with a few
exceptions, the USSR and later the Eastern European
Bloc were autarkic, more by necessity than by
choice, and practised adversary politics with all
but the members of other socialist countries. This
state of affairs had existed since 1917; was
enhanced after 1945, and was barely breached after
1956. It was the period of detente which made
the greatest difference to the relations between
the East and the West. Though we have already
stated that the changes occurred over a longer
period of time, and were imperceptible to most
observers, the Nixon-Kissinger policy brought them
to the fore in the early 1970s. They were made for
various reasons, and it is difficult, at this
stage, to establish who the prime movers were. It
hinges on several issues, the most important being:
who was most tired of, or most frightened of, the
continuation of the policies of Cold War?; who had
the most to gain from a period of relaxation?;
whose economy or political system would benefit by
detente?; and various other issues, which still
await formulation. In any case, all these issues
were figurative, at the very least, for Cold War
had been dead since Stalin's death, but its
aftermath, be it 'disengagement' or 'coexistence',
was still in force in almost every respect. By

this, it is meant that if 'normal' relations between states or blocs mean: freedom of travel; freedom of information; freedom of association; freedom of trade and freedom of political beliefs, then these only existed on a very imperfect basis in the period of 1953-1970, even though the situation had been improving. In any case, perceptions of what is normal are only very relative. During the Polish-Tartar conflicts in the seventeenth century, it was considered the height of civilised behaviour if Polish ambassadors to the Great Khan were not put to death in some unpleasant fashion; but were actually allowed to discuss peace terms. By the same token, a relaxation which allows forty students to study in the other Bloc, in place of the previous twenty, must be considered an improvement. It is not 'normal' in the sense of open and unconditional scholarly relations. Similarly, if some forms of trade are allowed to exist, but other forms are forbidden on very spurious grounds, one cannot call this arrangement 'normal'.

One could go on discussing this matter in volumes, but it must suffice to say here that in the early 1970s 'normalisation' of relations took several steps forward. One of the main reasons was the prolonged Vietnam War, which made _detente_ desirable from the American point of view: _detente_, or

> relaxation of tensions with communist superpowers Russia and China allowed the US more latitude in Southeast Asia and was certainly a major - some would say principal - reason _detente_ was adopted by Nixon and Kissinger, each of whom prided himself on being a pragmatist and power realist in international politics. Such _realpolitik_ satisfied very few, however, and became a subject of bitter debate almost from the start. Conservatives, who supported the renewal of bombing and the Cambodian incursion made possible by _detente_, nevertheless held a visceral contempt for negotiated deals with the USSR and People's Republic of China. Liberals, who applauded the easing of Cold War tensions, were to the same degree appalled at the cynical application of _detente_ in

231

re-escalating the level of destruction in Southeast Asia.

However, the war in Vietnam proved disastrous despite (or perhaps because of?) the _detente_. As it neared the end,

> Conservatives, joined by disgruntled hawks ... from within the national security/foreign policy establishment, buried their differences on Vietnam and began to speak with one voice urging an end to _detente_ on grounds that the Cold War had not slackened but intensified. Liberals and Establishment doves like Warnke, on the other hand, attempted to rescue _detente_ from the Metternichian calculation of Kissinger, and in the process transform it into a contemporary version of the old Wilsonian dream of <u>a harmonious world order built upon unfettered trade</u>. This latter interpretation of _detente_ threatened to eclipse not only the militarism of containment, but the geopolitics of Kissinger as well.[1]

The fear of _detente_ was not the prerogative of right-wing Republicans and the military in the American establishment. The Coalition for A Democratic Majority (CDM), under the chairmanship of Eugene Rostow was set up in 1972; in 1974 it published a paper entitled The Quest for Detente, which

> argued that for the Soviet Union the policy of _detente_ was little more than Lenin's formula of "peaceful coexistence" where the USSR retains the right "to provide military assistance in wars it regards as just". Kissinger's response to the CDM Task Force's suggestion of a new ... Soviet Threat was equally adamant in tone. ... "We frankly see no evidence of a Soviet headlong drive for first-strike capability in both nuclear and conventional arms ...". Kissinger's assumption that the USSR would behave in a traditional balance-of-power manner, despite its ideological Marxist-Leninism, if handled properly, was the conclusion reached by Kennan and Bohlen in the early years of the Cold War.

To a containment enthusiast like Rostow, however, who had proclaimed for a quarter century that the Russians were driven by an insatiable expansionism, the revival of such a notion was heresy.[2]

Like the term 'Cold War', therefore, the term 'Detente' could mean different things to different people. And it turned out that it would be interpreted by each Bloc in its own way, depending on the needs of the hour, or the beliefs (rather than rational reasoning) of each party. But by the early 1970s there was a new participant in the game: the Europeans themselves. It took Europe about thirty years since the war and some twenty years of prosperity to wake up to the fact that the super-powers were playing over its body. Up to 1968 to maintain that the Soviet Union was in the wrong was heresy for Western European Communists; in 1968 several Communist Parties condemned the Warsaw Pact invasion of Czechoslovakia in very strong terms. Up to the scandal of Watergate, any condemnation of US policy by a European was equated with 'fellow-travelling' or worse. It took the revelations of corruption, vulgarity and putridity in the White House and the ruling caste in the US, coupled with the bombing of Kampuchea, which finally made the Western Europeans realise their own strength. A few brave students and academics stood up to the Gomulka regime in 1968 and almost won; the Czech party and intellectuals stood up to the Warsaw Pact and gained a moral victory; two young journalists (admittedly backed by a powerful newspaper) overthrew an American president - this put the Western Europeans in an invidious position. Sheltering under the American nuclear umbrella; secure in the knowledge that the MAD strategy would keep them safe and American prosperity would ensure theirs, the Europeans were happy to build up butter mountains and wine lakes, and contribute taxes to further, even more horrifying 'deterrents'. The invasion of Czechoslovakia made them aware of the vulnerability of the nuclear umbrella; the bombing of Kampuchea made them realise that in a MAD strategy, any area contiguous to the conflict is likely to be destroyed; the growing financial crisis and search for new markets made them responsive to the call for intra-European trade.

This was not a repetition of De Gaulle's dream of independent glory; it was a sober (and sobering) realisation of the consequences of their own passivity in relation to the intentions of the super-powers. The realisation took on various forms; it led to the new treaties between West Germany and the Warsaw Pact countries; it led to improved diplomatic and trade relations; it led to a greater flexibility in every field of exchange of information that was allowed under the restrictions of CoCom. It led to the granting of credits to Eastern Europe on a scale unheard of at any time in living memory. And, among the Soviet Union's most faithful allies, the Communist parties of Western Europe, it led to the phenomenon of Eurocommunism.

There are many theories about the birth of Eurocommunism; all of them credible. For the purposes of this book, all we need to know is that the Eurocommunist trend applied to many Western European and non-European Communist parties; that it originated in the early 1970s (though it had its roots in much earlier days; during the Yugoslav drive for independence in the 1950s and the Polish and Hungarian 'humanist socialism' era) and that it aimed at a twofold result: on the one hand, it was intended to separate the parties' decision-making processes from those of the CPSU; and, on the other – it wished to divest itself of the theology of a revolutionary take-over of power. The Euro-communist was a Communist; but one who, while admiring the CPSU for being the first party in power, was ready to condemn it for the Stalinist excesses, as much as for other infractions of legality. The Eurocommunist realised that the Bolshevik Revolution was inevitable, but that in his days, an evolutionary way would be better. The Eurocommunist, finally, acknowledged, that in a democracy a multi-party system is much preferable to a single-party system; and that parliamentary democracy, while not perfect, is perhaps better than a Soviet democracy.

Three Western European CPs: the Spanish, the Italian and the French, were the ones to invest most in the Eurocommunist ideology; by the mid-1970s one of them, the PCI, was passively engaged in the support of the Italian Christian Democratic government; a year or so later, the second one: the PCE, was legalised for the first time since the Spanish Civil War, and in the early 1980s the third one, the PCF, joined a coalition government with the French Socialists. Other parties, including the CPGB sympathised with the trend, and followed the Eurocommunists by dropping the insistence on the revolutionary way from their ideology.

The Eurocommunist ideology has been set out by the then First Secretary of the Spanish Communist Party, in a book first published in 1977[3] but his formulation was merely a re-assessment of the Italian Historic Compromise, which had been set out by Enrico Berlinguer, the First Secretary of the PCI in the early 1970s. Not that Carrillo lacked originality; on the contrary his strong views and objections to the Soviet system of socialism earned him severe strictures from Moscow; but he took up the question at a point at which Berlinguer left some vagueness. The resultant problems within the Communist movement were serious, but they paled by comparison with the problems which Eurocommunism provided for the West. Because of historical reasons, the PCI, PCF and PCE, were parties with very close links with Eastern European countries; the additional factor of the closeness of the PCI to the Yugoslav party made the links all the closer. And though the PCE did not command a large electorate in Spain, both the PCI and the PCF received a great many votes in each national and local election.[4] Additionally, whereas the French First Secretary, Georges Marchais, only commanded respect in his own circles, both Carrillo and Berlinguer became statesmen with international stature, generally admired and listened to.

The Western governments were in a quandary: to accede to the general concensus that the Eurocommunists were genuinely independent of Moscow (which was perceived though not proven), would mean to admit that Communists were 'legitimate' and could be trusted in government. The Italian government had few qualms about accepting the PCI's proposal for 'negative support' in the 1970s; in 1981, the new French Socialist president, Mitterand, had few doubts that Communist ministers were a necessity for his government; in Spain, the Communists did not provide the same challenge as their share of the vote was too small to matter; the British government, a Labour one, was too busy destroying itself in its fight against the radical left within the party, to notice the Eurocommunist

CPGB (miniscule by Continental standards in any case) much more to the right than the Militants, and apparently agreeable to some compromise with the Labour Party.

This left the one government which did matter: the US Administration. After some initial hesitation (one might even say 'fudging', to use the SDP terminology), both Henry Kissinger and Zbigniew Brzezinski, the Carter Administration's National Security Adviser, came down on the side of caution: a Communist is a Communist, and the fancy dress of Eurocommunism made little difference to the fact. Not even help from Moscow, in the shape of strong condemnation of Carrillo's book in June, 1977, convinced the successive American Administrations that Eurocommunists are anything but the proverbial Trojan Horse in Western democracies.

However, little could be done about the impact of Western Eurocommunists on the anti-Communist ideology of the extreme right. The very fact that some CPs condemned the invasion of Czechoslovakia; that most of them condemned the invasion of Afghanistan, and most of them protested about the outlawing of Solidarity in Poland, and that yet, all of them were received in Moscow; that all of them maintained former ties with Eastern Europe, and that some of them took up relations with the People's Republic of China (the acid test of the pro-Moscow parties), made the claims about a monolithic bloc or an exclusive ideology seem ridiculous. How seriously Eurocommunism was being viewed in the West can be seen from the spate of articles by various commentators devoted to it in the 1970s. Also seriously to be considered were their comments:

> Some analysts view Eurocommunism as a "new look" or sudden shift in the tactics of West European communist parties, designed primarily to reinforce domestic positions; others see it as the product of profound changes in several European communist parties, but principally as a historic reversal in the basic flow of influence, from an East-West to a West-East direction. In the opinion of this writer, Eurocommunism is a product of a long historical trend in the European communist movement and not a phenomenon limited solely

to Western Europe. On the contrary, it can best be depicted as an outgrowth of a constant two-way flow of ideas, influences, and experiences between the East European and West European communist parties, stated a writer in late 1970s.[5]

This assessment is probably the most correct one; and finds little favour either in Moscow or in Washington. Whether it can be stated with utmost certainty that the Eurocommunist parties are independent of Moscow or of Washington (if one considers that the 'Trojan Horse' theory could work both ways), has not been established. But the fact that Moscow has been - and still is - ready to condemn Eurocommunist independence, while on the other hand, Washington has decided that Euro-communism is dead, as has been stated very recently in yet another article skirting the subject gingerly:

The communist parties in Western Europe have been a prime instrument in Soviet attempts to transform the domestic systems and the foreign policy orientation of the countries concerned. However, in line with the declining attraction of Soviet ideology among Western intellectuals, the effectiveness of the communist parties in promoting Soviet influence has decreased. More often than not, the impact that can be made by various "peace" campaigns on domestic politics in Western Europe crucially depends on the ability of the organizers to refute the charge that they are acting on behalf of the Soviet Union. Furthermore, electoral support for communist parties has correlated nearly inversely with their pro-Moscow orientation. But more independent or even outright anti-Soviet positions do not help much either. Thus, "Eurocommunism", which thrived on the idea of a model of communism different from that of Soviet and East European Marxism-Leninism, and which to many observers seemed to become a major political force in the late 1970s, is today a dead issue,

seems to prove, beyond any doubt, that Eurocommunism is alive and well.[6]

237

For at the same time as these strictures were being issued from both Moscow and Washington, there were still four Communist ministers in the French government (they resigned later on in the summer of 1984), and the Italian party had already designed a new, post-Historic Compromise strategy: this is to strive for 'a Europe from the Atlantic to the Urals'. The term 'Eurocommunism' is not used very frequently nowadays; this has done little to stop the movement to united Europe; to eliminate the line dividing it into Eastern and Western spheres of influence; to introduce democratic government in all European countries, and to attempt to do it in a socialist manner; but should the people choose the capitalist way - the Eurocommunists would not oppose it in any other way than the ballot box.

This theory lay behind the Eurocommunist support for Polish <u>Solidarity</u>, and sustains the Romanian and Yugoslav parties in their attempts to carve out or retain 'the separate road' to socialism. Moreover, this theory had a very strong bearing on the whole history of the Polish struggle in the years 1980-1984, on the relaxation of tensions between the East and West German governments, on the improvement in Yugoslavia's relations with the USSR; and - outside of Europe, but not unrelated to it - to the renewed Sino-Soviet trade and diplomatic relations. For while the Reagan Administration may have put economic pressure on the Jaruzelski government after <u>Solidarity</u> was outlawed, the Polish regime could have withstood it. Economically, Poland could have got support from the USSR. It was the moral pressure put on the PUWP by the PCI, the PCE and to a lesser extent, the PCF and CPGB, which provided the release of prisoners, and the removal of martial law measures. The contacts between the Eurocommunists and the dissidents in all Eastern European countries have given the Eastern Europeans - not those committed to the abolition of socialism, but those who believe in a humanist socialism - a new hope and a new measure of support, not only moral, but often financial, to carry on their struggle against the state monopoly on what is allowed and what is not allowed.[7]

In these respects, at least, Eurocommunism is not only alive, but serves an important and serious purpose: its ramifications will only be assessed with time. In the meantime, it is clear that the

Eurocommunist link has not only changed the perceptions of Eastern Europe in the West; it has also changed the perceptions of the West in Eastern Europe; and even more importantly; it has changed the Soviet perceptions of its own role in Europe. For perhaps one tends to forget one important factor in Western Europe: that the greatest part of Soviet territory, if not the majority of the Soviet people, exists outside of Europe, beyond the Urals. Like Tsarist Russia before 1917, the USSR has to consider itself a European state, before it can be expected to behave in a European fashion. Alexander Blok's prophetic poem: The Scythians has as much relevance in 1984 as it did in 1918; it is almost as difficult for the USSR to understand the European point of view as it is for the American Administration, particularly one domiciled in California. And these factors make it all the more important for the Europeans to face the future with some idea of what Europe is to become; whether this is a Eurocommunist plan or not. Disengagement or 'de-coupling' in the modern jargon, from both super-powers may be a better choice than total destruction.

Naturally a disengagement would produce some economic problems. It has already been discussed in some detail how badly, or well, the Eastern European economies have fared in the period since the 1960s. It would be well now to summarise the balance.

2. Economic Balance in Eastern Europe

We have already discussed the economic problems of separate Eastern European countries and the problems associated with the CMEA and its attempts at integration and harmonisation. None of the discussion was conclusive; while some areas showed significant gains, others showed significant losses. This applied both across the board in all countries, and in bilateral relations. It has been pointed out that in the present state of knowledge and statistics-gathering, an objective balance is virtually impossible to draw up. What one analyst will consider a favourable phenomenon, another considers an economic disaster. To take but one example: the high level of employment in the Eastern European economies (which is guaranteed by constitutional means) has been described as 'uneconomic' by the monetarist school, and as 'beneficial' by the neo-Keynesians. Indeed, we have shown that some Eastern European economists have embraced the monetarist theory of high productivity and lower levels of employment as one way of grappling with deficits and labour unrest. However, such lapses from Marxism are still novel in the CMEA. By and large, the economy is geared to full employment and low productivity, with results which do not prove either of the main economic theories of the second half of the twentieth century. But then, none of the existing data on economic performance is easily assessed; or, to put it in a more partisan manner: it is assessed according to the political beliefs of the analysts.

Thus, one commentator describes the Soviet economic performance in the 1970s as an abysmal failure:

> Soviet GNP stabilized at around 55 per cent of US GNP in the 1970s. Economic growth rates have shown a long-term declining trend. (According to Soviet figures, they fell from around ten per cent in the 1940s to approximately eight per cent in the 1950s, six per cent in the 1960s and four per cent in the 1970s. Growth rates of two per cent are probable for the 1980s). The USSR did not achieve its aim of overcoming the perennial technological inferiority <u>vis-à-vis</u> the West. The structure of Soviet foreign trade is still very much that of a developing country - importing finished products in exchange for raw materials and energy supplies.

Other difficulties facing the Eastern Bloc are labour shortages, adverse demographic trends, low productivity and low competitiveness on world markets.

> All this casts doubts on the existence of a Soviet economic strategy designed, as Richard Pipes has argued, "to make the West Europeans maximally dependent on the Eastern bloc" by deliberately "promoting heavy indebtedness of the Comecon countries" and achieving "maximum control of West European energy supplies". ...

To put it more cautiously, even if there was such a strategy, it has not worked very well. The primary reason for the interest of the Soviet leadership in East-West economic exchanges, in the foreseeable future, will be due not to Soviet external political objectives but to domestic economic requirements.[8]

Adomeit's thesis is that, because of worsening US-Soviet relations, the CMEA has tried to shift its trade from the US to Japan and Western Europe, but that despite some changes, there is still a strong reason for the Bloc to desire more trade with the US, particularly since certain types of equipment can only be purchased in the USA, and because the large potential of the American industry is useful in developing the Siberian resources. In fact, he states that

the share of the CMEA countries in overall West European trade has been falling steadily since the mid-1970s. In the early 1980s, there has been a slight increase again in the USSR's share, but a further decline in the share of the other European CMEA countries. Credit relations conform to the same pattern. It is understandable that, for financial and economic reasons, the East European countries have increasingly come to be regarded by Western banks as credit risks. This should not apply to the Soviet Union, which possesses huge gold reserves and natural resources, and whose foreign indebtedness is quite low. Yet its creditworthiness, too, has significantly suffered. Net financing flows from Western banks to the Soviet Union have decreased to a trickle. The decrease cannot be explained solely on economic grounds. It is undoubtedly due to political reasons, i.e. to the general atmosphere of tension and uncertainty prevailing in East-West relations.[9]

An unambiguous judgement is clear here: the Soviet Union and its dependents, the CMEA economies, have problems which they cannot overcome without American aid, and which are bound to get worse, because they are structural. The demographic problems (which happen to be correctly

241

assessed), that is, low birth-rate and higher life-
expectancy in Western USSR (where most of the
industrial base lies), and which are said to be
connected with developing economy, are in fact,
classed by everyone as problems of an industrial
economy. Shortages of labour - the Western
European countries should wish to have them in the
1980s - were experienced by the developed Western
European countries, Germany, Britain and France in
the period of high growth. But when they happen in
the CMEA, they are classed as problems of an
underdeveloped economy. The growth rate in the
1970s - four per cent - is one which is considered
to be very good in a developed country - but in the
USSR and the rest of the CMEA it is said to prove
deterioration. Similarly, the high Soviet gold
reserves (about which later) and the natural
resources are useless as well: but presumably the
US inability to return to the gold-standard,
despite it having figured in the Republican
programme in 1979, because of its high deficits, is
proof of credit worthiness and growth. It is not
the purpose of this work to judge the value
judgements of other commentators, merely to put the
facts before the reader.

And to prove that the same facts can be given
a completely different political slant, we need
only consult another analyst. This author
maintains that the economies of the CMEA, not
counting the USSR, have been affected by two major
developments in their external financial situation:
a credit squeeze by the West and deteriorating
terms of trade with the USSR. In order to reduce
their hard-currency trade deficits and to earn
surpluses, the Eastern European economies were
forced to adopt deflationary economic policies. As
a result, the Eastern European economies began to
operate with significantly lower levels of hard-
currency imports and were able to export some
additional goods, which would otherwise have been
sold on the home markets. The position of the
economies was further aggravated by the significant
price rises of Soviet energy exports (already
discussed in this work) in the 1980s. In 1981, the
average Soviet rouble price of oil to Eastern
Europe increased by 25-28 per cent, and in 1982, by
21-27 per cent. At a rough estimate, the
corresponding increase of Eastern European exports

242

to the USSR was seven per cent in 1981 and an
additional five per cent in 1982. Further:

> It is virtually impossible to separate the
> impact of the Western credit squeeze on East
> European economies from the impact of the
> deterioration in the terms of trade with the
> Soviet Union. The need to curtail the growth
> of nominal ruble trade deficits with the
> Soviet Union had an effect on these economies
> similar to that of trying to increase hard-
> currency trade surpluses.

In fact, according to this analyst, the result was
a success story:

> With regard to the hard-currency trade balance
> adjustment ..., five East European countries -
> Bulgaria, Czechoslovakia, East Germany,
> Hungary and Poland - had an aggregate trade
> deficit of close to $1.6 billion in 1980, but
> in 1981 this was turned into a surplus of
> slightly under $200 million and, in 1982, the
> surplus grew to $3.6 billion. Thus, over a
> two-year period, these five countries
> succeeded in improving their trade balance by
> more than $5 billion. When Romania is
> included, the turnaround in the aggregate East
> European hard-currency trade balance is even
> more dramatic. Compared to a trade deficit of
> $3.1 billion in 1980, in 1981 a trade surplus
> of $400 million was achieved, which surged
> further to $5.1 billion in 1982.

Similar success was achieved in trade with the
USSR, which remained at a roughly constant 2.1
billion roubles.[10]

This seems to be a success story so far.
Naturally, such success cannot be achieved
painlessly. The author demonstrates that:

> the ratio of national income used to national
> income produced steadily declined in all
> countries except Bulgaria and the Soviet
> Union. ... In the initial stages of macro-
> economic adjustment, central planners
> generally attempted to protect consumption
> from cut-backs and forced most of the
> adjustment on investment. In 1981, the growth

243

of national income devoted to personal and collective consumption was still positive in all countries under study, except Poland. Even in Poland, which faced an economic crisis of extraordinary proportions, central planners maintained the level of consumption at the 1980 level. On the other hand, the amount of national income allocated for accumulation declined absolutely in five countries in 1981. ... Only Bulgaria enjoyed an investment boom with 14.8 per cent growth in national income used for accumulation.

However, during 1982, it was seen that cut-backs in consumption had to be achieved as well; and while in Poland and Romania the consumption declined absolutely, the other countries registered no growth in consumption. Two exceptions were noted: East Germany registered growth of about one per cent, and Bulgaria an estimated 4-4.5 per cent.[11]
The adjustments were made, but they required cut-backs in capital expenditure in the first place, and some cut-backs in personal consumption in the second place. However painful such cut-backs must have been (and in the case of Poland and Romania they were extremely damaging both to the consumers and to the economy), one must account for the 'slack' in Eastern European estimates; the 'slack' which operates in both ways: firstly, it overestimates production and consumption figures to obtain higher investment; and secondly, it underestimates the size of the 'grey' and 'black' economies, which make good some - though not all - of the shortages. Additionally, Vanous stresses the fact that the debt position of the CMEA countries was improving steadily, and had never been very serious, compared with the debts of other countries. Taking USSR alone, at the end of 1982, its debt to the West stood at $8 billion, that is, about 0.5 per cent of Soviet GNP and less than 20 per cent of annual Soviet hard-currency export earnings. In 1982, the Soviet debt-service ratio stood at seven per cent, and was projected to fall to four per cent in 1983. On these figures, the USSR (if taken alone) could well afford to raise its hard-currency debts to a much higher level. Further:

We anticipate that in the course of 1983 Western bankers and government lending officials will gradually come to realize the enormous external economic adjustment achieved by Eastern Europe over the past two years. In 1982, the aggregate East European hard-currency account deficit was eliminated and, if Poland is excluded, the remaining five East European countries earned a combined current account surplus of $2.7 billion. We expect that in recognition of this achievement and in response to higher profit margins in lending to Eastern Europe, Western banks and governments will resume lending to Eastern Europe.[12]

Finally, the author takes a look at comparative statistics. On the assumption that Soviet debt-service ratio will remain in the region of 6-7 per cent, and remembering that Soviet gold reserves were estimated at 1,900 metric tons, and were expected to rise to 2,500 metric tons by 1987, the value of Soviet reserves exceeded the size of the country's net debt by a factor of three. This article was published before the fall in the price of gold, but already anticipated the fall in oil prices. Even so, Soviet reserves are more than enough to compensate for its debts. However, critics might say that no one questions the USSR's wealth; but this does not ensure that the smaller CMEA countries will profit by it. This would be completely incorrect: all loans to Eastern European countries (possibly with the exception of recent loans to the GDR by West Germany) are made on the assumption that they are guaranteed by the USSR. And the USSR, as the 'Big Brother' of the CMEA may groan, and may at times force a reduction in the living standards of the smaller countries, if they have been disobedient, but it has never yet gone back on its obligation to support the debt repayment to the West. It has probably gone as far as the US in its problems with the Latin American debts, in so far as it has lent money to Poland in order to service its debt, though not quite so absurdly, because the debt was mostly to the West, not to the Soviet Union.

Which takes this analyst to his main conclusion:

The current financial crises in three Latin American countries - Mexico, Brazil and Argentina - have finally put the East European indebtedness into a new perspective. At the end of 1982, the net hard-currency debt of six East European countries was estimated at slightly over $53 billion - roughly two-thirds of the size of either the Brazilian or the Mexican debt. Viewed in aggregate, this debt represents about eight per cent of combined East European GNP and amounts to roughly $480 on a per capita basis. In contrast, Brazil's external debt of $84 billion probably exceeds 30 per cent of the country's GNP and Mexico's $80 billion debt represents certainly over 35 per cent of the country's GNP. On a per capita basis, the Brazilian debt is around $650 and the Mexican debt is over $1,100. Whereas Mexico and Brazil are only beginning to make the necessary external adjustments to avoid default on their debts, Eastern Europe has already made most of the necessary adjustments over the past two years. While Mexico, Brazil, Argentina and many other developing countries will require tens of billions of dollars in net new lending over the next few years ... Eastern Europe will require only rolling over the existing debts ... to insure its economic recovery. In spite of these facts, an attitude persists in world financial circles which is appropriately illustrated by a recent statement of a well known New York banker, Felix Rohatyn, that "... much of Eastern Europe is bankrupt; Mexico, Argentina and Brazil are staggering under huge debt; the Third World is largely a disaster". However, the facts are quite different. In comparison to the three Latin American countries and most of the Third World, the economies of Eastern Europe - with the exception of Poland - now appear to be in much better shape.[13]

With two such completely different assessments made almost simultaneously by two American commentators, it is little wonder that the matter is still shrouded in mystery. There is no doubt that the economies of the smaller CMEA countries have been under stress since 1973; but there is a great deal of evidence to show that they have, with the help of the USSR and various - often deflationary - policies, managed to square the circle of debt and hard-currency imports by the early 1980s, though this was done with some pain and at the expense of manufacturing industries. If there was no real economic crisis, only a temporary problem of hard-currency debt, then where did the difficulty lie? One can only conjecture that it lay in the sphere of politics, not economics.

3. Eastern European Problems in the Light of Soviet-US Relations

Perhaps it is appropriate that the previous section should have ended with a quote from Felix Rohatyn, 'a well known New York banker', because the problems of Eastern Europe were most intimately linked with the difficulties with Western banks, and the banks - as has been demonstrated - were themselves dependent on Western governments. Of these, the most important was the US Administration of the day. Thus, in an ironic fashion, the fate of the Socialist Bloc depended on the most capitalist institutions in the world: international bankers and the American government.

We cannot determine who it was that called the first shots; whether the USSR or the USA held the initiatives in international relations, partly because this differed in various periods, and partly - and perhaps more cogently - because global affairs had become so inter-linked that the initiatives were forced on the participants. But there are commentators who maintain that both super-powers did have a policy, and that they attempted to retain this policy in so far as possible. Thus, Aldomeit states that the Soviet view of detente was aimed at three main objectives: 'Europeanism', i.e. the encouragement of Europe towards neutralism; 'Atlanticism', i.e. a joint agreement with the US to solve European questions, and 'Pan-Europeanism', which was a combination of the two, and was intended at persuading all the parties concerned that a united Europe, without a large American and Soviet involvement, was the best solution for the future. To this end, the commentator maintains, the Brezhnev policy of detente, included new elements. These were:

247

(1) the unprecedentedly broad scope of East-West agreements ... (2) the unprecedentedly large scale of Western commitment envisaged for the expansion of East-West trade ... and (3) the inclusion of the West European countries as well as the United States in the overall approach, limiting the traditional attempts at playing off the "power centers" of imperialism and individual "capitalist" countries against one another.

However, the strategy was impaired by two factors; in the first place, the USSR, having ratified SALT I, strove for a higher level of armaments, the so-called 'parity-plus' level; and, secondly, the Americans were impatient with the slow pace of change in the Soviet Union. 'Vociferous Western demands regarding human rights are but one important example of this lack of awareness.'14

These two factors seem to have played a far more important role in the relations between the two blocs than has so far been acknowledged, and have contributed to a large extent to the demise of the detente. There is little need to go into the complicated matter of armament questions since that has been done by strategic experts at great length. We can only put it at its most simplistic level in this book: the main problem seems to be that military and space technology grows at a very quick pace, and that neither super-power wishes to be left behind in the race for 'better' weapons. The situation is not dissimilar to that in the late nineteenth century, when the great naval rearmament race between Britain and Germany was in progress. The growth of big, heavily armed warships constrained each power to build more: '... the British had at last taken the decisive step of strengthening their navy. The Naval Defence Act, passed in March 1889, revolutionized British naval policy; it looked forward to a time when the two-power standard would be a reality ...'. On their side, the German government had no choice but to go along with the race, though the new Chancellor, Caprivi, said on taking office: 'In naval policy I did not ask how big the navy should be, but how small. There must be a battle and the great war, which hangs over Germany's head, must be fought, before we can build as many ships as Germany and especially the Emperor, who is very keen on the

development of the navy, want.'[15] The simple
conclusion, then as now, is that super-powers never
have enough modernised armaments to fight the next
war, and yet they always manage to spend a sizeable
portion of their budgets on new armaments and a war
finally occurs. We hope that history will not
repeat itself in this case, but, perhaps
fortunately, we are not in the business of
prophecy.

The question of human rights, or to put it
more precisely of 'moral superiority' of each
super-power, is equally complicated, but plays a
different role from that of the armaments question.
Here the problem is that Marxism is perceived in
the Third World in particular, to be a 'third way'
towards development. It is also perceived in some
circles to be a humanistic ideology of helping the
weak to help themselves. We cannot go into the
practice of Marxist ideologies in the Socialist
Bloc to support or negate this; we are merely
concerned with <u>perceptions</u>. As the first
exponent of Marxism in practice, the USSR is seen
by the USA to have an ideological and moral
advantage over the ideology of capitalism, which,
in its crudest form, equates with the 'survival of
the fittest'. Hence, the US must find a way of
presenting the USSR as an oppressive power, rather
than one which supplies a liberating ideology. One
way of doing this, is through stressing the lack of
'human rights' in the Socialist Bloc.

This is very easy, for the Eastern (some might
say 'oriental') system has always been less
concerned with the rights of the individual and
more with the rights of the administration than the
Western system. As one recent commentator
suggested, there are many critics, both Marxist and
non-Marxist who argue that the Western concept of
human rights cannot be applicable in a state
socialist system, particularly with regard to the
Soviet Union:

> First, ... the doctrine of Marxism-Leninism is
> alien to the concept of human rights.
> Second, ... individual rights are not defended
> because of the monistic structure of society.
> Third, ... the Russian heritage of orthodoxy
> and absolutism has continued into the modern
> period and provides no political supports to
> Western concepts of rights.

This author disagrees with this, saying that: 'Marxism has a humanistic rights tradition as well as an authoritarian one'. However, Soviet infringements of legality, most obvious in the Stalinist period, but not lacking in other periods, support the non-humanistic theory.

> Contemporary dissenters in the Soviet Union are harassed by the police, independence of thought is denied and foreign travel, writing and residence is restricted ... fundamental freedoms of speech, communication, person, association and movement are curtailed. ... But condemnation of the USSR must be tempered by the realization that human rights in all societies are infringed. The United States has used civil rights as an agency of its foreign policy to condemn the Soviet Union.

He further states that the Western concept of human rights may well be an ethnocentric one, and that the Soviet Union compensates for the infringements of individual political rights by implementing social rights; '... socialist states seem to place greater emphasis on and have a better record with regard to economic rights than do Western democratic societies'.[16] Lane further points out that the concept of human rights and the rights of the individual versus the state in particular, have received considerable boosts from post-Stalinist leaders, and that the 1977 Constitution of the USSR extends the legal position of the individual.

The reason for this is the growing differentiation of society, which involves greater autonomy and 'rights-claims' of individuals and groups: 'The scientific and cultural intelligentsia (of whom Sakharov and Medvedev are 'dissident' representatives) are a major force in this movement'. But such relatively weak protests may not be enough in countries which have not experienced the Russian tradition of autocracy: 'In Poland, the rise of Solidarity movement epitomises Polish claims for rights'. Solidarity's demands were very wide-ranging and took in every aspect of social, economic and political life of the country.[17] This, claims Lane, means, that despite the outlawing of Solidarity, the rights of the individuals will have to be extended:

In Poland, the state has been unable to meet the economistic expectations of the population and has remained illegitimate; rights have been perceived to be claims on the state. The Solidarity movement in Poland, the Political Reform movement associated with Dubcek in Czechoslovakia in 1968, the emergence of "dissident" groups in the USSR, together with a tendency since Khrushchev towards greater legality by the political elites, and the claims of the 1977 Constitution, all point in different ways to the evolution of claims for civil rights under state socialism. ... The significance of these developments is that they are indicative of claims on the guardians of political power ... which the authorities ignore at the cost of political stability and social solidarity.[18]

The American insistence on human rights has other reasons apart from the claim for 'moral superiority'. Any American president, with an election looming ahead, is very conscious of the ethnic vote. The Eastern European voters in the US have always tended to vote on the Democratic ticket, but can be swayed by a Republican candidate, if he expresses their aspirations. President Carter's linkage of the human rights issue to the detente followed a time-honoured custom. His boycott of the Olympic Games in Moscow after the Soviet invasion of Afghanistan came, very fortuitously, just before the presidential elections. He was outbid in his human rights and rearmament policies by Ronald Reagan and his strongest supporters: The Committee on the Present Danger, and lost. Reagan, in his turn, returned to the 'human-rights' theme and elaborated on it, while simultaneously embarking on the largest American rearmament programme ever.[19]

By then, however, the global opinion had become somewhat weary of the American insistence on human rights, the more so, since the Reagan Administration's policy in Latin and Central America with regard to human rights had come under close scrutiny. The Catholic Church was the first to condemn the torture, assassinations and poverty in Latin and Central America. It was difficult for Reagan, probably himself a lapsed Catholic, to use the Catholic Church in condemning the USSR, without also condemning the death squads in El Salvador. Neither the American electorate, nor the European NATO countries, were very impressed by the trebling of the defence spending. The West Germans may have insisted on Cruise and Pershing missiles, but they did not expect to have to pay for them. In general, a new policy had to be found.

This lay at the bottom of Reagan's new line on the USSR: the Soviet Union, according to gospel as pronounced by Reagan was 'the focus of evil in the modern world'. On 2 January 1984, the Time magazine ran a main feature discussing the rift in US-Soviet relations. Across the page a large quote by Reagan read: 'They are the focus of evil in the modern world'. The commentator stated:

> In the beginning were the words ... Ronald Reagan denouncing the Soviet Union as an "evil empire" ... Yuri Andropov responding that the Reagan Administration had "finally dispelled" all "illusions" that it could be dealt with. ... After the words, the walkouts ... Now, in silence, come the missiles, no longer metaphorical but physical and nuclear.[20]

The commentator then continues:

> The US and the Soviet Union have not reached The Day Before the missiles fly. Indeed, Washington and Moscow share a keen apprehension not only of the terrible power of their nuclear weapons but also of the danger that any shooting at all between their forces could conceivably bring these weapons into use.

Having surveyed the events of the year, he comes to the conclusion that the US policy throughout that year was motivated by one factor alone: to impress on the world - not on the USSR - that it was determined to combat Marxism wherever it occurred; be it Grenada or Poland. The balance of victory was not clear; the US suffered a serious catastrophe in the Lebanon, and won a rather silly battle in Grenada. The USSR managed to quell the Polish revolt and maintained its base in Syria and the Lebanon. The Soviet air force shot down a

Korean airliner with 269 passengers, killing them all. The Americans responded by calling it cold-blooded murder. The concensus in the aftermath was that the airliner was almost certainly engaged in a spying mission - this view was expressed not only by the Soviet side, but by American researchers.

The _Time_ commentator, having first drawn our attention to the fact that all the events of 1983 were connected by the struggle for world opinion between the USA and the USSR, and not by a desire to start a nuclear war, then pins the blame firmly on Reagan's personality and his early experiences in Hollywood, when: 'He became convinced that the dispute had been fomented by Communists who were trying to take over the US movie industry on Moscow's direct orders. ... Thinking his life was in danger from Communists, he took to carrying a gun to ward off attackers.'[21] But there is a much deeper and more calculating reason for the policy:

The Reagan Administration, indeed, is remarkably cocky about US-Soviet relations. In its view, the US military build-up ... has the Soviets on the run. Says one official: "For a couple of decades the Soviets were sure that the economic and political balance ... was shifting their way. But the past few years the balance has been going the other way, and they have begun to realise that. They have lost ground in the Middle East compared with a few years ago. Their politics aren't selling in the Third World any more. Afghanistan is a problem for them. Their economy still suffers from terrible rigidity, and their foreign policy is in confusion." ... Sooner or later, and probably sooner, Moscow will conclude that it can get a better bargain from a President who is running for re-election than from one who has been returned to office for another four years.[22]

Two main objectives stand out in this assessment: the first one - and in this writer's opinion, the most valid one - is the search for a world-wide legitimacy in preaching the gospel of American capitalism; the second one is the electoral dilemma. Faced with the need to get re-elected, an American presidential candidate has to

face both ways: he has to try and satisfy the
electorate and he has to threaten the perceived
enemy. In this difficult task the Reagan
Administration has gone through various somer-
saults; the result of the election and subsequent
relations with the USSR will show how successful
they were. In the meantime, the main sufferers
from these difficulties are the smaller CMEA
countries, in particular, Poland and Romania.
While sanctions against Poland have been relaxed in
the run-up to the American elections (a sop to the
Polish-American voters), the most-favoured-nation
status has not been restored (to appease the
American Right). Poland had to reject
participation in the Olympic Games in Los Angeles,
in return for some financial help from the USSR;
Romania, on her side, participated in the Games,
and is being discriminated against by the CMEA.
According to one Polish official of senior rank,
the game was not worth the candle: Romania's
economic problems would not be solved by the
Olympic gold medals; Poland gained economically by
not participating.

Hence the other side of the coin is the Soviet
claim to global legitimacy: as the self-professed
centre of developed socialism, it feels constrained
to preach its virtues to the rest of the world,
most particularly to the Latin Americans. While at
the moment the focus of attention is on Eastern
Europe, the next step in the struggle will almost
certainly not be in Europe or in the Middle East,
but in the Western Hemisphere. To return to the
Time's analyst's view:

> Violence in the Caribbean Basin ... brought
> the superpower confrontation into still
> sharper focus. The invasion of Grenada,
> Reagan claimed, prevented Marxists from
> turning that island into a Soviet-Cuban
> colony. Elsewhere in the region, however, no
> such quick or decisive victory for
> Administration policy seemed in sight. US aid
> to the conservative government of El Salvador
> in its fight against a leftist insurrection,
> and to the contra rebels battling the
> Marxist-led government of Nicaragua, did
> little more than sustain grim guerrilla wars.
> Just as the US did after the 1979 Soviet
> invasion of Afghanistan and the imposition of

martial law in Poland in 1981, the Soviet Union volubly denounced the US moves but did not so much as hint at military action in retaliation. This underlined a rule of US-Soviet competition that neither side will ever acknowledge publicly: <u>each has a sphere of interest that the other respects.</u>[23]

Global legitimacy for one's own ideology has, then, to be offset by the theory of 'spheres of influence'. But the idea of spheres of influence has been denied by Reagan in his election campaign in August, 1984: 'Mr Reagan, calling for free and democratic elections in Eastern Europe, told Polish-American leaders on Friday that he did not accept that the wartime summit conference in the Crimea of the leaders of the United States, the Soviet Union and Britain implied US consent to a divided continent', reported a British newspaper.[24]

Soviet protests at this statement were coupled with indignation at the German <u>rapprochement</u> before the expected visit of First Secretary Honecker to West Germany in September, 1984. The West German government was being accused of trying to reunite the two Germanys under a capitalist government. This shows that the USSR has no more solutions to retaining its sphere of influence in Europe than the US has in Central and Latin America. Persuasion, bribery and show of force have worked for some forty years since the end of the Second World War. Neither super-power has spared its efforts in retaining what was - according to most historical sources - agreed in wartime conferences: both have failed in securing their final objective: that of gaining the hearts and minds of the population. It is this, rather than crude force or financial help, which will be the decisive factor. There is no need to quote the examples of Cuba, Nicaragua, Poland or Romania; they have been amply illustrated. But it is interesting to note that the desire for independent decisions has, by mid-1984, produced one of the most interesting developments in Europe: the <u>rapprochement</u> between the two Germanys.

4.   East-West German Rapprochement - The Index of
      Change

It has already been stressed in this chapter that
the problems of Eastern Europe must be seen in the
light of perceptions in Western Europe, but that
the primary set of rules is that decided by US-
Soviet relations.   It has been generally
acknowledged that each super-power has an implicit
right to impose its policy on its own sphere of
influence, and that the other super-power makes
obligatory responses of criticism and righteous
indignation, but little else happens.   However, as
indicated in the last section, the position of
smaller nations vis-à-vis their big protectors
has been changing over the last decade.   With
growing populations, increasing literacy and
increasing standards of living, the smaller
countries have built up a credible record of
resistance to super-power pressures.
     This work has analysed the resistance to
super-power pressure in Eastern Europe in some
detail. However, a similar record could be made
for the small countries in the US sphere of
influence; and a glance at the intermediate sphere
(i.e. areas where each super-power has acknowledged
interests but no exclusive rights of influence)
would also show examples of considerable
resistance. Such resistance was registered in Iran
through the overthrow of the Shah and the invasion
of the US Embassy in Teheran; and a parallel
situation exists in Afghanistan since the Soviet
interference in 1979. Hence, the claims to
success, whether made by the Soviet or the US
governments, do not ring true. Rather, the recent
deterioration of relations between the two super-
powers betokens an implicit fear not of each other,
but of the consequences of holding too large a
sphere of influence, and of such influence
crumbling either suddenly, or step-by-step. This
fear underlies much of the propaganda which has
been issuing from Moscow and Washington over the
period of 1980-84. And some events seem to prove
that the fear is justified.
     Judging by the comments made by serious
analysts over the last decade, only two scenarios
are possible in the future: the first, that there
is an all-out war (nuclear or conventional) between
USA and USSR and that one of the protagonists wins

it; the second, that there is a nuclear war between the two protagonists and that the world comes to an end. Naturally the two scenarios are not mutually self-exclusive; i.e. the second scenario could be the result of the former. The third scenario is only envisaged by the so-called 'doves' and has not been fashionable since 1979: this is the one in which a mutual accommodation is arrived at by the super-powers, and both rule happily in their respective spheres of influence.

However, the events of the last four years, and even more importantly, events in evidence at present (in the autumn of 1984) could give rise to a new scenario; one which is much more historically viable. This scenario presupposes that the two super-powers are sufficiently weakened by the mutual struggle to retain superiority, to loosen their grip on their spheres of influence. Such an event would be accompanied by a growth of dissension within the spheres of influence, and by the eventual overthrow of the super-power's dominance. Iran has proved that this could happen; Solidarity almost achieved it in Poland; in the future other countries could follow, and the snow-balling effect could be irreversible.

One such possible event was envisaged in Germany in the summer of 1984. Of all the American allies, West Germany has been the most loyal one; its two major political parties, the CDU and the SPD have supported US policies, including the militarisation of Germany without any reservations throughout almost four decades. It was the West German Social-Democratic Chancellor, Helmut Schmidt, who is said to have been instrumental in demanding further American nuclear missiles to be placed on German territory. (Despite evidence proving this, evidence recently released, seems to indicate that Schmidt's request was made at the request of the Pentagon; but this is outside the scope of this chapter). Yet just over two years later, after the CDU's electoral victory in March, 1983, the SPD has called for the withdrawal of American weapons from the German soil, and has begun pressing for US-Soviet disarmament talks. The right-wing Chancellor, Helmut Kohl, has not abandoned the former government's Ostpolitik; on the contrary, he continued it and even expanded it. Even more strangely, the scourge of the left, the Bavarian right-winger, Franz-Joseph Strauss, began

257

making visits to the Eastern Bloc and discussing the possibility of a new 'Thaw' and improved economic relations. While the CDU/CSU government has accepted American missiles on its soil - as part of its electoral programme - it has made few bones about its disquiet that the missiles could actually be used. Chancellor Kohl is said to have voiced his objections to the American Administration in private; other German politicians, both in government and in opposition, have voiced them publicly.

No doubt, the German protest stems mainly from the fact that the first short-range nuclear missiles would be used on German soil; and that 'mini-nukes' have ten times the explosive force of the Hiroshima bomb. No doubt, there is also an element of Soviet pressure to be taken into consideration. As one American commentator noted:-

> ... The concentration of Soviet effort on influencing West German deliberations suggests Moscow's greater concern to stop NATO missile deployments - by pressuring the Germans into refusing to accept the missiles - than to seek a compromise settlement with the United States. Gromyko began this effort in January 1983 during his visit to Bonn, warning that the Soviet Union, in assessing the consequences of new NATO missiles, could not ignore "the fact that the FRG is the only state where plans call for deploying Pershing II missiles capable of reaching in a few minutes strategic objectives deep inside the Soviet Union". He continued to apply pressure during his October meeting with West German Foreign Minister Hans-Dietrich Genscher in Vienna and in the East German-Soviet communique that followed Gromyko's stop in East Berlin on his way home. The latter document ominously warned that the appearance of new US missiles on West German soil would "contradict the spirit and letter" of the treaties normalizing Bonn's relations with Moscow and with East Berlin.[25]

But there seem to be other considerations as well; considerations which may be much more important. For the change in attitudes did not occur only on the West German side. A similar

change has occurred in East Germany. East Germany
has been the Soviet Union's most faithful ally
since its inception, and has supported it in almost
every undertaking. But in the years since the
decision to employ missiles on its soil has been
taken by the USSR - in answer to the American
deployment in West Germany - its policy has taken a
decided turn. It could be that the East German
government had taken to heart the words of the late
Soviet leader Yuri Andropov, on the occasion of
Helmut Kohl's visit to Moscow in July, 1983:

> Under the present state of affairs, the Soviet
> intermediate-range missiles in the European
> zone are merely a counterbalance to the
> intermediate-range nuclear systems of the NATO
> countries in that zone. They are not aimed
> against the West German armed forces. But if
> American missiles are deployed on West German
> soil, the situation will change. The military
> threat for West Germany will be multiplied
> many times over. Relations between our
> countries will also inevitably suffer certain
> complications. As for the Germans in the FRG
> and the GDR, they, as someone recently put
> it, would have to look at one another through
> thick palisades of missiles.[26]

The appeal to the East Germans, made possible
by a West German chancellor's visit to Moscow, may
have been a unique and highly controversial move by
Andropov. But, nevertheless, it appears to have
worked. It was also supported, indirectly, by the
then Mayor of West Berlin, and the present West
German President, Richard von Weizsacker; a man
uniquely qualified by the nature of his post to
build bridges between the East and the West.
Interviewed in early 1984, he maintained that

> Experience teaches that it is not disarmament
> that points the way to peace, but rather that
> peaceful relations open the door to
> disarmament ... where concrete fields of
> co-operation are exploited or created, arms
> problems present a smaller obstacle to peace.
> ... Peace is the consequence of practical
> co-operation.[27]

Appeals such as these had to be made to the East Germans through intermediaries because East Germany had made a strong point about its 'separateness' from West Germany. As one writer commented:

The principle of <u>Abgrenzung</u> became the primary guiding light for Ulbricht and his successor Erich Honecker; <u>Abgrenzung</u> connotes division from something else, in this case, the Federal Republic and its policy and culture, but it also indicates the existence of internal forces for cohesion, so that one knows what it is that the regime wants to protect <u>against</u>, as well as what must be preserved internally. For the East Germans, then, <u>Abgrenzung</u> also connoted the development of a separate nationality in the GDR.[28]

Despite its 'separateness', East Germany finally succumbed to the pressure exerted on her, both from the West Germans and from Moscow. In the summer of 1984, East Germany graciously agreed to accept yet another large West German loan (200 million pounds sterling) in return, ostensibly, for relaxations in travel between the two states. As a journalist noted, this was not a new arrangement: 'The concept of a trade-off between money and human rights is not new in German-German relations. For years West Germany has been discreetly buying the freedom of East Germans arrested for illegally trying to leave the country. The Kremlin itself has been ready to accept a similar trade-off', hence, the Kremlin's apparent annoyance at the new deal surprised the writer.

The Kremlin is worried that East Germany might conceivably go the way of Poland in becoming so heavily indebted to the West that it begins to lose any bargaining power. The Kremlin's main concern is indeed that this may be Western strategy, at least of the Reagan Administration. Moscow has always watched for any sign of Western wedges being driven into the Warsaw Pact, and it has often talked of the so-called weak link theory.

But is East Germany really a weak link? Apparently not:

> No rational calculation in Moscow or anywhere else could seriously suggest that the visit by Erich Honecker to West Germany - the first by an East German party leader - is going to bring about the reunification of the two Germanies, or even their withdrawal from their respective military alliances. Neither side wants the latter, nor would their partners in Moscow and Washington permit it, if they did. As for reunification, the East German party leadership did not fight for the international recognition of their state for 25 years ... in order to surrender it now.[29]

Another Western journalist saw the situation in similar light:

> The Soviet Union is worried that East European allies do not have the stomach for its hard line on missiles in Europe. This is what lies behind Moscow's warnings against rapprochement between East and West Germany.

But he made a deeper analysis as well:

> Bonn was overplaying its hand with East Germany and had exploited Russian patience because it knew Moscow wanted detente. That is the heart of the problem. The Soviet Government is on the one hand bombarding the Europeans with warnings of catastrophe and on the other looking for their support to put pressure on President Reagan. The result is neither stick nor carrot.[30]

We have no means of knowing, at least at this stage, whether the rapprochement between the two Germanys is disliked by Moscow, or whether - as seems to have been the case - was actually initiated by it. Alternatively, it may have been initiated by it, but was not intended to go so far. However, as a Continental power, the USSR has the least to lose by de-militarising Germany; East and West. It is the US which would be the loser. Such proposals were made by the East many years ago, in the Rapacki Plan, and were rejected by the

Americans almost immediately. And as Steele noted, the East German leadership fought for recognition for twenty-five years, and had to be almost literally pushed by the Soviet government into talks with West Germany. Having begun the talks, Honecker may have suddenly gone senile, as one commentator suggests:

> The revolt of Erich Honecker, if such it can be called, may be no more than an elderly man's desire to see his home ground in West Germany's Saarland once more. It may also be a tit-for-tat for not being allowed to send East Germany's uniquely talented team to the Olympic Games. Or, as seems most likely, it may be a determined adherence to perceived national interest.

Whatever the reasons: 'The resolutely pursued defrosting of relations between the two German states has set off alarm bells in both East and West'. Then noting the Soviet disapproval, the writer continues:

> Western concern over the apparent shift in inter-German relations has tended to be overlooked. The French have never been slow to express their fear of West Germany going neutral for the sake of reunification; the Americans discuss withdrawing or reducing their troops in Europe and have more recently renewed their dispute with Bonn about leakage of high technology to the Eastern bloc by means of ever-growing inter-German trade relationship. The German question seems to be back in fashion on both sides of the ideological divide. ... Meanwhile, the superpower mentors of each Germany station more and more rockets on German soil and the Berlin Wall stands.[31]

The writer then suggests that Soviet disapproval is fabricated and that the German rapprochement is intentional and carried out with Moscow's blessing:

> Mr Honecker is a survivor with an ear keenly attuned to Moscow's wishes. Moscow's wishes are far from clear, reflecting a paralysis of

leadership. If Mr Honecker is taking a risk, we can rest assured that it is a most carefully calculated one. He probably knows something we don't.[32]

5. Eastern Europe and the Unknown

Erich Honecker may know something we do not; on the other hand, it may be that the situation in late 1984 has sufficiently changed for new initiatives to be taken. For it was not only Honecker who displayed a resistance to Soviet opposition. In March, 1984, a senior Hungarian official gave an interview to a newspaper in which he argued that small countries have a role in promoting compromise between big powers, when the situation is dangerous for all of them. While the Soviet press was attacking East Germany, General Jaruzelski of Poland - who owes his post to Soviet support - sent a telegram to Erich Honecker saying that:

> both East Germany and Poland were actively working for international security and against the "forces of imperialism" whose current efforts were described as the "greatest danger to humanity". The Polish backing was prominently displayed on the first page of Neues Deutschland, the East German party newspaper. East European analysts in East Berlin said it meant the Polish leader felt the Soviet Union would "forgive" Herr Honecker if he agreed to cancel his planned visit in September to West Germany. ... Herr Heinrich Windelen, Minister for Inner German Relations, said the Soviet attacks on ties between East Berlin and Bonn were a warning to all of Eastern Europe on its future ties with the West. He suggests the visit by Herr Honecker could still take place, as it was difficult to imagine that it had not been co-ordinated between Moscow and East Berlin.[33]

Some three weeks later, during Romania's 40th anniversary celebrations of liberation, Erich Honecker was the only top Eastern European leader to attend.

Diplomats from Eastern Europe said Herr
Honecker's gesture towards President Nicolae
Ceausescu, in the absence of the other
Communist leaders, underscored his own
increasingly independent foreign policy, which
has come under criticism from Moscow.

The other top leader who attended was: 'China's
President ... Peking has long favoured
Mr Ceausescu because of his resistance to Moscow's
policies in the past'.[34]
There are, of course, analysts in the West who
consider the whole matter a result of lack of
leadership in the Kremlin, and suggest that:

More enlightened members of the leadership
must be horrified at the damage that has been
done. Soviet foreign policy once looked
calculating and effective; in the past year it
has looked as if the Russians are determined
to shoot themselves in the foot at every
opportunity.

It is further suggested that Chernenko has lost his
grip and that the younger and more effective
Gorbachev is not yet allowed to make decisions.[35]
This, of course, is possible. Yet few leaders
nowadays seem to take personal decisions.
President Reagan is said to be asleep during many
crises; Mrs Thatcher is said to have taken personal
decisions during the Falklands War, but the
suggestion to use a Polaris missile on Cordoba is
alleged to have been made by the Acting Chief of
Staff.[36] President Brezhnev was ill and out of
touch during the last four years of his rule.
Mr Andropov hardly entered his office. Going
further back, Winston Churchill spent most of his
wartime years dozing; and Franklin Roosevelt was
seriously ill in the last year of power.
Decisions, in this complicated technological
age, are not made by lay politicians; they are
made by groups of experts. It has been
demonstrated in this work that in the Eastern
European Bloc the most powerful decision-making
body is the command of the Warsaw Pact forces,
closely followed by the CMEA committee. While it
was also stated that the Soviet members of both
bodies have a major role in the decisions, the
other countries must be taken note of. Most

Eastern European countries have been on a new
economic and political track since the late 1960s;
they have departed from Stalinism, from centralised
planning and from state monopoly in the economic
field to a great extent. Most of them have
suffered during and after the oil crisis, though
some have suffered more than others. Most of them
have applied a dose of monetarism to improve their
economic performance.

Despite the successive crises, the countries
of Eastern Europe have made considerable progress
in the region of industrialisation, health care,
education, and even in the weakest field - that of
housing - their performance has improved. But in
the course of the last two decades, they have had
to depart from the 'socialist' model as much as
they departed fom the 'Stalinist' model in the late
1950s. They have generated a large class of
technocrats to fill the middle-management posts,
but the top posts are filled by the 'clique' or the
'family'. It may be that not all Eastern European
leaders are as nepotic as President Ceausescu, who,
at the last count, is said to have about fifty
relatives occupying senior positions in the
government and party machine; including his wife,
son and two brothers.[37] However justified this
situation may be on the grounds of trustworthiness,
it is not a model of socialist government. But in
practical terms, it works. In practical terms, the
CMEA, for all its faults, also works; though the
model of fraternal co-operation is hardly to be
seen. In some ways, the Eastern European Bloc,
excluding the USSR, is the re-creation of the
Small Entente, broadened by the inclusion of East
Germany, which was created by the Europeans between
the wars, as a buffer between the big powers.

The Soviet Union is a pragmatic state: it may
genuinely prefer an independent Eastern Europe and
a unified Germany to the threat of American
missiles six minutes away from Moscow. Or
alternatively, and more likely, the Eastern
Europeans may be working for greater independence
of the USSR, just as some Western European
countries are working for greater independence from
the US. While the example of Finland is always
quoted, there are also other models: Austria, and
of recent years, Greece. There is also a
'socialist' model: Yugoslavia. One must not expect
the great powers to crumble away, or to give away

their spheres of influence without a struggle. But from a historical viewpoint, it is just as likely that the great powers will weaken their grip, will become absorbed in their own problems, and will allow their satellites to go their own way; as it is likely that they will engage in a war to end all wars. It is to be hoped that the lethality of the weapons available will ensure that this last scenario does not happen. If war can be excluded, then Eastern Europe is on the road to the unknown, but not a road without hope. And the same applies to Western Europe: there may yet be a time when the distinction will no longer be made.

CHAPTER NINE: FOOTNOTES

1   Jerry W. Sanders: _Peddlers of Crisis_, pp. 160-161, emphasis added.
2   Sanders: _Peddlers of Crisis_, pp. 150-151.
3   Santiago Carrillo: _Eurocommunism and the State_.
4   There is a vast literature on Eurocommunism; for one of the best and up-to-date assessments, see: Lawrence L. Whetten: (ed.) _The Present State of Communist International-ism_.
5   Jiri Valenta: _Eurocommunism and Eastern Europe; Problems of Communism_, March-April, 1978, p. 42.
6   H. Adomeit: _Capitalist Contradictions and Soviet Policy; Problems of Communism_, May-June, 1984, p. 13.
7   For Eurocommunist opposition to the stifling of _Solidarity_, see: Kevin Devlin: _The Role of Nonruling Communist Parties in Reforming Internationalism_; Lawrence L. Whetten: _The Present State of Communist Internationalism_, pp. 21-74.
8   Adomeit: _Capitalist Contradictions_, p. 13.
9   Adomeit: _Capitalist Contradictions_, p. 14.
10 Jan Vanous: _Convertible Currency Indebtedness of the CMEA Countries, Its Implications, and Outlook for 1983-87, NATO Colloquium 1983_, pp. 243-244.
11 Vanous: _Convertible Currency Indebtedness_, pp. 251-252.
12 Vanous: _Convertible Currency Indebtedness_, p. 263 and p. 264, emphasis added.
13 Vanous: _Convertible Currency Indebtedness_, pp. 271-272.
14 Adomeit: _Capitalist Contradictions_, pp. 8-11.
15 A. J. P. Taylor: _The Struggle for Mastery in Europe, 1848-1918_, pp. 326-328.
16 David Lane: _Human Rights Under State Socialism; Political Studies_, No. 3, September, 1984, pp. 349-353.
17 Lane: _Human Rights_, pp. 364-365. In fact it has been pointed out recently that the demands for trade union rights, conceded by the Polish government, would be mostly illegal under British law, particularly the recent trade union legislation.

18 Lane: Human Rights, p. 368.
19 On the Carter policies and Reagan's dependence on the CPD, see: Sanders: Peddlers of Crisis, particularly Chapter 8.
20 Men of the Year; quotation by Reagan on 8 March 1983.
21 Men of the Year, p. 22; The dispute in question was between the Screen Actors Guild, of which Reagan was a board member and the Conference of Studio Unions.
22 Men of the Year, p. 33.
23 Men of the Year, p. 21, emphasis added.
24 No Right to Question Yalta, The Guardian, 20 August 1984.
25 Myron Hedlin: Moscow's Line on Arms Control, Problems of Communism, May-June 1984, p. 25.
26 Hedlin: Moscow's Line, p. 25, quoting Pravda, 6 July 1983, emphasis added.
27 Interview with the Time Magazine, 2 January 1984, p. 39.
28 Trond Gilberg: The Political Order; Fischer-Galati: Eastern Europe, p. 150.
29 Jonathan Steele: German thaw that leaves Moscow cold, The Guardian, 7 August 1984.
30 Mark Frankland: Russia frowns on smiling Germans, The Observer, 5 August 1984, emphasis added.
31 The Germanies tantalise their friends, leader in The Guardian, 20 August 1984.
32 The Guardian, 20 August 1984.
33 Leslie Colitt: Jaruzelski backs East Germany, Financial Times, 4 August 1984.
34 Leslie Colitt: Honecker makes lone stand over Romania, Financial Times, 24 August 1984.
35 David Hatton: Inside Moscow, The Sunday Times, 26 August 1984.
36 For this, see: The Belgrano Cover-up; New Statesman, 31 August 1984, p. 10.
37 Roger Boyes: Can Romania's family rule on?, The Sunday Times, 26 August 1984.

CDM	Coalition for a Democratic Majority
CDU	Christian Democratic Party
CIA	Central Intelligence Agency
CMEA	Council for Mutual Economic Assistance
COMECON	See CMEA
CPGB	Communist Party of Great Britain
CPSC	Communist Party of Czechoslovakia
CPSU	Communist Party of Soviet Union
CSCE	Conference on Security and Co-operation in Europe
CSSR	Czechoslovak Socialist Republic
CSU	Christian Socialist Party
CoCom	Co-ordinating Committee for Multilateral Export Controls
DDR	German Democratic Republic
ECE	Economic Commission for Europe
EEC	European Economic Community
EFTA	European Free Trade Area
FYP	Five-Year Plan
GDR	See DDR
GNP	Gross National Product
IMF	International Monetary Fund
IRA	Irish Republican Army
KOR	Committee for the Defence of Workers
LCY	League of Communists of Yugoslavia
MAD	Mutual Assured Destruction
NEM	New Economic Mechanism
NEP	New Economic Programme
PCE	Communist Party of Spain
PCF	Communist Party of France
PCI	Communist Party of Italy
PUWP	Polish United Workers' Party
PZPR	See PUWP
RCP	Romanian Communist Party
RFE	Radio Free Europe
SDP	Social-Democratic Party of Germany
SED	Socialist Unity Party of Germany
SKS	Students' Solidarity Committee
UNO	United Nations Organisation

Note on Currencies

$	Unless otherwise stated, this denotes US dollar
Billion	Unless otherwise stated, this denotes 'one thousand million'
Ruble/Rouble	Soviet unit of currency

269

Neal Ascherson: The Polish August. The Self-Limiting Revolution. Harmondworth, London, 1981.

J. F. N. Bradley: Politics in Czechoslovakia, 1945-1971. University Press of America, Washington, 1981.

Comecon: Comecon Foreign Trade Data 1980. Macmillan, London, 1981.

Jan Drewnowski (ed): Crisis in the East European Economy. Croom Helm, London, 1982.

Robert R. Farlow: Romanian Foreign Policy: A Case of Partial Alignment: Problems of Communism, November-December, 1971.

Francois Fejto: A History of the People's Democracies. Pelican Books, 2nd Edition, 1974.

Stephen Fischer-Galati (ed): Eastern Europe in the 1980s. Croom Helm, London, 1981.

Galia Golan: The Czechoslovak Reform Movement. Cambridge University Press, Cambridge, 1971.

Jack Hayward & Olga A. Narkiewicz (eds): Planning in Europe. Croom Helm, London, 1978.

Jerry Hough: The Soviet Prefects: The Local Party Organs in Industrial Decision-Making. Cambridge Mass., 1969.

Robert R. King: Bulgarian-Soviet Relations: 'Socialist Internationalism in Action'. RFE Research Background Report 89; May, 1975.

Werner Klatt: The Politics of Economic Reform. Survey, Winter-Spring, 1969.

Andrzej Korbonski: Politics of the Socialist Agriculture in Poland. Columbia University Press, New York, 1965.

Olga A, Narkiewicz: The Green Flag. Polish Populist Politics 1867-1970. Croom Helm, London, 1976.

Olga A, Narkiewicz: Marxism and the Reality of Power, 1919-1980. Croom Helm, London, 1981.

NATO: NATO Colloquia, 1973-83, Brussels.

RFE: Radio Free Europe Research Reports, 1968-1978, Munich

Jerry W. Sanders: Peddlers of Crisis. South End Press, Boston, Mass., 1983.

George Sandford: Polish Communism in Crisis. Croom Helm, London, 1981.

SELECT BIBLIOGRAPHY

Harry G. Schaffer: Progress in Hungary. Problems of Communism, January-February, 1970.

Ota Sik: Czechoslovakia. The Bureaucratic Economy. IASP, White Plains, 1971.

H. Gordon Skilling: Czechoslovakia's Interrupted Revolution. Princeton University Press, Princeton, 1976.

Alan H. Smith: The Planned Economies of Eastern Europe. Croom Helm, London, 1983.

John W. Strong (ed): The Soviet Union under Brezhnev and Kosygin. Van Nostrand Reinhold, New York, 1971.

Dennis Swann: The Economics of the Common Market. Penguin Books, 2nd Edition, 1972.

Edward Taborsky: Communism in Czechoslovakia, 1948-1960. Princeton University Press, Princeton, 1961.

Jurgen Tampke: The People's Republics of Eastern Europe. Croom Helm, London, 1983.

Rudolf L. Tokes (ed): Opposition in Eastern Europe. Macmillan, London, 1979.

Imre Vajda: The Role of Foreign Trade in a Socialist Economy. Corvina Press, Budapest, 1965.

Michael Vale (ed): Poland: The State of the Republic. Pluto Press, London, 1981.

Lech Walesa: The Book of Lech Walesa. Simon & Schuster, New York, 1982.

Lawrence L. Whetten (ed): The Present State of Communist Internationalism. Lexington Books, Lexington & Toronto, 1983.

Wspolnota Socjalistyczna RWPG (The Socialist Community CMEA) Ksiazka i Wiedza, Warsaw, 1975.

Daniel Yergin: Shattered Peace. Pelican Books, 1980.

Alfred Zauberman: The Eastern European Economies. Problems of Communism, March-April, 1978.

INDEX